LEGALLY DEAD

HOW ONE MAN'S LIVING WILL
BECAME HIS LIVING NIGHTMARE

REGINA ROGERS

To protect the privacy of certain individuals, the
names and identifying details have been changed.

Copyright © 2018 by Regina Rogers

All rights reserved. This book may not be reproduced or stored
in whole or in part by any means without the written permission
of the author except for brief quotations for the purpose of review.

ISBN: 978-1-943258-89-5

Warren publishing

Published by Warren Publishing
Charlotte, NC
www.warrenpublishing.net
Printed in the United States

Foreword

If you read nothing more than the foreword and afterword of this book, you will understand the urgent message I have tried to convey to all individuals who put their signature on a power of attorney document and a living will. That message is this: those two documents can wreak havoc on a person's life like no other legal documents can, especially when the trust conveyed in those documents is given to the wrong individual. *Legally Dead* is the story of one individual's misplaced trust and the devastating consequences that followed when he suffered a temporary loss of speech due to a medical crisis.

Power of attorney documents are common enough and certainly necessary in many instances. Members of our armed forces have them in place, many people approaching retirement use them as part of a back up plan, and they are commonly used by individuals who travel frequently. But few people are aware of the absolute and broad power they grant to another individual and most people are equally ignorant of how those documents, coupled with a living will, can interfere and, in fact, legally deter a person's recovery from a medical event that would not otherwise be fatal.

If you are over the age of forty, this is one book you must read! According to insurance company statistics at the time this book was written, 221 out of 1,000 people will suffer a disability lasting ninety days or longer by the age of forty; by age sixty the numbers grow to 635 people out of 1,000. Over the age of sixty, the odds again increase dramatically as seniors are more prone to suffering heart attacks, strokes, and other debilitating injuries and illnesses.

Attorneys will use those statistics to convince you that all adults should have two documents in their possession: a living will and a durable power of attorney. In the event you fall on the unlucky side of the statistics, both documents can be incredibly useful if not downright necessary, but there are also legal pitfalls. If you become incapacitated for a prolonged period of time, your designated agent (attorney in fact, in legalese) can, by way of the durable power of attorney document, manage your financial affairs to ensure that your monthly bills are paid so you do not lose your home or car while you are temporarily incapacitated. A living will can prevent you from languishing for months or even years in a vegetative state when there is no chance of a recovery.

But what happens when those powers, that trust, is placed in the wrong hands? The results can be devastating. At best, you might lose everything you have worked for: your car, your home, your savings, and find you must start all over again. At worst, you could lose your life prematurely. Are you reading this and thinking it could never happen to you? Do you believe your family members can be trusted to do the right thing on your behalf without being influenced by the greed factor? So did I.

The story you are about to read contains all of the elements of a television drama: dementia, kidnapping, attempted murder, and greed in its purest form. The difference is that this story is true. The names of the people involved and their locales have been changed to obscure the identity of the guilty—God will settle up with them in a way no human being ever could—and to protect the innocent victims and their allies who often risked their jobs to do the right thing.

What I learned through this misadventure is that life truly is stranger than fiction, that the human will to survive—even when all hope appears to be lost—is nothing less than remarkable, and that manifested prayer is often all we have left to sustain and guide us when medical and legal professionals are unwilling or unable to mend a breach of trust.

CHAPTER ONE

The Race Begins

Monday morning, April 5

"Fear and trembling have beset me; horror has overwhelmed me. Oh, that I had the wings of a dove! I would fly away and be at rest."

—Psalm 55:5

The race begins. My cousin, Ben, and I knew we had no time to lose as we made our way south through the eastern states to Norfolk, Virginia, where our elderly uncle lay helpless and perhaps even dying in a nursing home after he was forcibly taken there weeks earlier by his stepdaughter, Julie. We had been sent by our family to extricate him, not even knowing if we would get there in time. I did not know it then, but the race to rescue Uncle Pasquale would quickly evolve into a devious contest of daring, wit, tenacity, and audacious scheming played out in the courts and medical institutions in two different states hundreds of miles apart.

We were in for a wild ride, but on that day, at that hour of the morning, the only wild ride we were experiencing was the drive across the mile-long bridge spanning the Susquehanna River on Interstate 95. Menacing forty-five-mile-per-hour winds threatened to hurl us into the river below as I tightened my grip on the steering wheel, struggling to remain in control without losing too much speed. Ben and I got on the road that morning later than I had hoped. As soon as we had the two-lane country roads behind us and an open stretch of interstate highway ahead, I dropped my foot on the gas pedal and got down to business. We had to cross four state lines in record time, but the inclement weather was impeding our progress and I resented it. True to form, the roar of furious winds ushered out the month of March, scattering the last remnants of snow as it went. The previous week saw unending flurries that only ceased the day before our journey, but the gale-force winds continued unabated.

Midway across the bridge, an over-sized LED sign flashed a warning above us: *Extremely high winds next 5 miles.*

"Yeah, no kidding!" I said to Ben, indicating the sign with my chin. I did not dare remove a hand from the steering wheel while the wind pounded against the driver's side door and rocked the car. "I thought if we could barrel through the states at around seventy miles per hour, we might just make it there by five o'clock," I told him. "But with this blasted wind I'm having trouble maintaining fifty-five."

"Anytime you want me to drive, just let me know," Ben offered.

I acknowledged his offer with a nod and silently hoped we would simply make up the lost time as soon as we were well away from the open countryside of northern Maryland and nearer to the Capital Beltway. Ben occupied the passenger seat with a bag of snacks at his feet, a bottle of spring water in the beverage caddy, and his mobile phone in hand. Less than two hours before, we had hurried through a breakfast of coffee and blueberry muffins before embarking from my little cottage in the Pennsylvania countryside. We tossed haphazardly packed overnight cases into the back seat of my SUV, our maps at the ready. I had only been in residence at the cottage for two weeks and was far from what anyone would consider settled in when the call came that interrupted my unpacking plans. While I drove, I took a mental stroll through the four-room cottage, where several boxes waited patiently to be unpacked in the kitchen and guest bedroom. At least thirty more covered one half of the loft; the other half of that area had quickly taken shape as my office.

A magnetic notepad stuck to the refrigerator door stood as testimony to unfinished chores: buy caulking for the bathtub, hang spice racks and a towel bar in the kitchen, install curtain rods in the dining room, call the telephone company to connect the landline for my desktop computer, find someone to mow my newly acquired half acre—Lord knew I did not have the time to do it myself—and buy bottled water. The list went on and with each passing minute, I moved further away from getting any of it accomplished.

The house had been vacant for almost a year before I moved in, according to my nearest neighbor, which may have accounted for the metallic odor in the water and the turquoise tint it left in the bathtub. I remember thoroughly examining my skin in the bathroom mirror after my first shower to make sure I hadn't turned turquoise as well. *Were there lead pipes in the house?* I silently wondered. Perhaps the plumbing simply needed a good flushing, but I decided to take the cautious, albeit more inconvenient, route and began lugging home several gallons of bottled spring water from each trip to the grocery store. I wouldn't even allow my German Shepherd, Jette, to consume water from the kitchen tap. For the first two weeks of occupancy, that had been my only complaint of the little two-bedroom cottage with low ceilings and a second-story loft that otherwise seemed to have been built with someone petite like me in mind.

The setting was peaceful, with Currier & Ives scenery. Gently rolling slopes were dotted with grazing sheep and cattle with a few bison tossed into the mix. Ancient stone farmhouses surrounded by low fieldstone walls stood in clearings at the end of winding dirt driveways.

The cottage I occupied was nestled up against the edge of a farmer's fenced pasture. Each evening, as the setting sun bathed the field and trees in a reddish-orange glow, red fox and white-tailed deer tracked a path in the snow across my backyard and through the small grove of barren fruit trees on their way to foraging expeditions in the forest beyond.

The ten-minute commute to my office took me down the stream-lined country road, past eighteenth century stone houses, bank barns, fragments of ancient stone walls, grazing horses, and Herefords. During warmer weather in the following months, singing frogs would inhabit the stream while neon blue dragonflies flitted and glimmered in the morning sun near the banks.

My usual frenzied pace had slowed considerably after the move. Instead of barreling down a four-lane highway at breakneck pace to beat the tide of commuter vehicles, I actually took my time driving to my real estate office and enjoyed the scenery along the way. I found myself smiling as I braked for squirrels, pheasant, deer, and anything else that ambled across my path. Life was good.

As I sat in the driver's seat that Monday morning, my mind and heart raced in tandem with the speedometer while I mused over the irony of having just settled into a slower pace only to be torn abruptly away. My last conversation with my business partner, Grant, came to mind as I drove.

"Want to know how to make God laugh?" he asked after I had briefed him about the impromptu but necessary trip.

"I give up, Grant. How can I make God laugh?"

"Make a plan!"

"Here's my plan," I informed him in my best no-nonsense voice, with both hands planted on the edge of his desk. "I plan to get my uncle out of this predicament before Julie can finish him off and I'm bringing him back to Pennsylvania where he belongs. This time next week I'll be right back *here* where *I* belong. Meantime, you have two houses to get on the market, three buyers to find a home for, and a settlement to attend on Friday. Don't hesitate to call if you need me. I'll keep my cell phone on me."

That was indeed my plan and nothing, I determined, had better get in my way. I simply did not have the patience to contend with any of it longer than necessary.

Two hours into the drive, Ben was already phoning his wife to see how she was getting along. For the next few days, she would be managing pre-season opening preparations by herself for their roadside grill and ice cream stand.

"Annie, is everything under control? Did Kevin come in to help?" The look of concern on Ben's face matched the tone in his voice. We figured that our mission would take a few days, perhaps the better part of a week at most. Even so, Ben and his wife had worked past seven o'clock the evening before our departure to gain ground. They usually opened up the week after Easter, which was fast approaching. Steadily increasing demand in the months leading into summer usually kept them busy until they closed for the winter just before Halloween. I remembered Ben speculating at the family reunion the previous summer that small town businesses like theirs would eventually be nothing more than a memory as people took to the new six-lane highways and left rural roads behind.

Ironically, a new development under construction just a few miles up the road practically guaranteed a booming season for their business, so he and Annie were in the thick of preparing. They had placed orders with food supply vendors, pulled umbrella tables out of storage, and checked the ice cream machines, ovens, and grills just as events were unfolding that would pull him away to be my partner in the race to save Pasquale.

I have heard it said that while an angel watches at our right shoulder, the devil lurks at our left to thwart our good intentions. People who believe such things would say that the sudden potential for a banner season at Ben's Roadside Grill was the devil's brand of humor. My pragmatic cousin Mike would simply say no good deed goes unpunished! Oh yes, I'd had my fill of religion over the years. I was raised by a no-nonsense Catholic dad and eventually found my own way through the maze of various religious cults and camps, coming out on the other side believing in a higher power but no longer buying into any one brand of religion.

During my spiritual evolution, I pored over every sectarian tome I could find from the Bible to the Koran, from the Kabbala to the Tibetan Book of the Dead. The Bible refers to Satan as the master of fear and confusion, Mr. Chaos himself, but it also says that if we can stay focused on our goal long enough to side step the distraction we will go on to win the race. I wasn't sure I believed there was a devil, but I definitely bought into the "focus" part. The race that engaged us that Monday in April was a race unlike any that either of us had experienced before, but one thing was certain: we intended to win!

As we journeyed down the road together, Ben worried that Annie may not be able to meet the fast-approaching opening deadline without his help, no matter how many hours she worked. The emergency that took us far from our homes and lives could not have come at a more inopportune time for either of us. I left my real estate business in the hands of a new partner who was still learning the ropes; a scenario that can be a recipe for complete disaster. However, like Ben, I had no choice but to trust that my partner would handle all of the transaction details in my absence and make the right decisions while I continued to offer limited assistance via cell phone. Pasquale was family and he needed our help. At that moment in time, that's all we needed to know.

Ben and Annie's conversation drifted away as my mind centered again on the problem we were facing. We anticipated a battle with Julie, Uncle Pasquale's stepdaughter, and we had an attorney ready to meet us at our destination in Virginia. However, we didn't know what we would find when we arrived. In fact, for all we knew, Julie had already succeeded in convincing the nursing home staff to pull the plug on Pasquale's life support and let him die. If that were the case, we would be too late to reverse course and bring him safely home where his family could rally around him while he received the medical care he needed to recover.

As I drove, the warm air from the car's heating system released Jette's scent from my jacket. It was the fragrance of clean, well-groomed fur mingled with the earthy odor of pine bark mulch. At eight o'clock that morning, my four-legged best friend had greeted the day lazily nosing around in prematurely mulched flowerbeds, trampling a few winter pansies in the process. By nine, she had been delivered to the care of her veterinarian for safekeeping. It was the best place for her to be under the circumstances. My furry girl was aging, weak, and had a tumor growing near her spine. I didn't want to risk leaving her at the local kennel.

"I'll be home soon. Be a good girl," I whispered in her ear, choking back the anguish in my voice. I hated leaving her behind and for a brief moment I had considered tossing her food, toys, and blankets in the car so she could go with us, impractical as the notion was. The veterinarian's grim prognosis in January warned that I had precious little time left with her. Cancer invaded Jette's lymph nodes while the tumor had taken root on her spine. Her doctor thought she would last for no more than a few weeks before she would succumb. However, I stubbornly determined I was not ready to lose her, so I said a few prayers and plied her with extra vitamin and mineral supplements found at the natural pharmacy in town. To her doctor's amazement, Jette seemed to rebound. She actually regained a bit of her former spunkiness for two months, but her increasing weight loss and confused wandering reminded me it was only borrowed time. I fervently hoped she would be able to hang on until I returned. I did not want her to die in the arms of strangers.

Ben's voice brought me out of my reverie. "Annie says Kevin will be there to help her this afternoon; man, that's a load off my mind!" He snapped his cell phone shut and tucked it into the pocket of his jacket. "Annie can handle most of the set-ups and preparation, but she can't deal with computers and the vendors want all of their orders placed online these days." He shook his head and laughed, "My old-fashioned girl!"

Then, eyeing our surroundings from under the brim of his jeff cap, he changed the subject.

"Well, at least the wind died down. Let me know when you want to change places."

Ben was feeling antsy without a physical task to occupy the time. I knew the feeling but I was not yet ready to relinquish control, so I remained at the wheel while we skirted Baltimore.

"How many more hours until we get there, do you think?" Ben asked shortly after we crossed the state line into Old Dominion.

I pulled out the computer printout I had stashed between our seats, along with a Southeastern States map hurriedly snatched from a file cabinet drawer that morning, and handed them over. A GPS device would have been a blessing then, but like WiFi, it was years away.

"MapQuest said five hours total," I told him, "so we probably have just over two hours to go. I remember making this run a few times when my sister lived in Virginia and it is one long stretch of highway."

"Is Maxwell meeting us at the nursing home?" Ben asked.

"No. I thought we'd better head straight to his office. I'm sure he'll want the signed retainer agreement in hand before he takes any action on our behalf. Besides, who knows what we'll walk into when we get there. I don't think we should go in there without him."

Then I remembered my last telephone conversation with Jonas Maxwell. "He did say we should call when we get close to Norfolk so he can give us directions to his office."

I had a good feeling about Jonas Maxwell the first time I spoke with him. The attorney I recruited for the leg of the battle in Pennsylvania had found Jonas for me. When I first briefed him about my uncle's plight and what we wanted him to do for us, his voice resonated deep, deliberate and confident through the receiver. His was the kind of voice that comes with years of experience; a voice that surely came with a commanding physical presence as well, I imagined. During our first conversation, I conjured in my mind a mature man in his fifties, six feet tall, or perhaps five-eleven at the very least, broad-shouldered, probably weighing in at just below 200 pounds with a well-trained muscular build. I knew nothing about Max's professional credentials, having left that consideration to the Pennsylvania attorney who recommended him. I simply felt that I needed someone who could take control of the situation and deal sternly with

Julie. I was confident Jonas would take her down a few pegs and put a stop to her nonsense in short order.

That image was reinforced the afternoon before our departure as his voice resonated from the speaker phone while he addressed the small tribunal of Uncle Pasquale's siblings, nieces, and nephews. We listened in solemn silence, seated around my parent's dining room table, as Jonas Maxwell's voice came through the speaker. He insisted that everyone call him Max but the familiarity did nothing to diminish the authoritative tone in his voice.

I had related to Max the details of my uncle's situation, as I knew them, just a few days before the telephone conference. He already knew that my mother's brother, Pasquale, had suffered a brain hemorrhage that had kept him hospitalized since February. A family drama had played out in the ensuing weeks as his stepdaughter, Julie, fought with the doctors to remove Pasquale's feeding tube and let him die. As Pasquale lay in bed during that time, his demeanor changed from helpless sobbing to hopeless acceptance and finally to anger that he could only express in pantomime.

In answer to the family's questions about Pasquale's recovery, his speech therapist said, "When he gets mad enough, he'll talk." That is precisely what happened, and that event, one that should have been cause for celebration, was the event that imperiled Pasquale's life.

❏❏❏

In a small town, one rarely gets away with much without someone noticing. Pull a new car into your driveway and watch the neighbors drift out of their houses to gawk and gab. When someone else pulls that same car *out* of the driveway, someone other than the rightful owner, that news makes the gossip circuit as well. That was Julie's first mistake and the first indication that something underhanded was afoot. While Pasquale lay in a hospital bed, Julie's husband, Dan, took Pasquale's car to a local used car lot, convincing the owner of the lot that Pasquale would never be able to drive it again and that he, Dan, had the right to sell it. When Pasquale learned of the betrayal he got mad enough to try and read Julie the riot act. Unfortunately, his words got tangled on his tongue, sputtered, and failed to hit their mark.

A few days later, just as Pasquale began to recover the ability to speak a few intelligible words, Julie surprised him, surprised the entire family, in fact, by whisking him away via ambulance across state lines to a waiting bed in a nursing home hundreds of miles away. At the time, we were unaware of the other schemes Julie and her husband had in the works, but obviously, the fact that Pasquale might soon regain the ability to speak was a threat to their plans. It was a brazen move on Julie's part and there was reason to believe she meant him harm.

Ben and I meant to bring Pasquale back home where he belonged, but there were legal complications. At least a decade before, my uncle had signed a durable power of attorney document appointing both Julie and her mother, Pasquale's second wife, Nora, as his attorney-in-fact. Incapacitated by a stroke, Pasquale was at their mercy. Nora was suffering from medically documented dementia and that left Julie in charge. Julie had the legal right to do whatever she wanted with Pasquale and it quickly became obvious that she intended to allow no one to stand in her way, not our family and certainly not Pasquale himself, while she carried out her plan.

As the members of Pasquale's family arrived at my parent's home the Sunday before Ben and I left for Virginia, a cloud of hopeless despair hung over them. With Julie at the reins and legally in control of Pasquale's life, they doubted that anyone could do anything to take that power away from her. Huddled around the telephone that occupied the center of the dining room table that day, they voiced their fears to Max and asked for his legal opinion.

"Do you really think you can get Pasquale out of this mess?" Pasquale's brother asked.

Max seemed to weigh his words carefully, then spoke with a conviction that renewed their hope and a wit that interjected humor at just the right moments to ease their fears. Everyone present agreed that Max seemed to be the right man for the task. If we ran into strong opposition to our rescue plans, Max was definitely the attorney we wanted on our side. Pasquale's sister, Eleanor, wept as she pushed a sizable sum of cash across the table to me for Max's retainer fee. Ours is a close-knit family and everyone was prepared to do whatever it took to rescue one of our own.

Before the call with Max ended, he advised us that a representative of the family should make the trip to Virginia as soon as possible. Pasquale's brother and sisters were in their seventies. The stress of the situation had already taken its toll on them. They did not need the added strain of a long journey plus the hostility we were certain to encounter at the end of it. With that in mind, it had already been decided days before that the person making the trip would be me.

After confirming my appointment as the family delegate, Max cheerfully said in his genteel southern accent, "Well then, zip on down here and let's go see Uncle Pasquale!" At that, Pasquale's sisters clapped and cheered, with tears of relief streaming down their faces.

The events leading up to that point had me primed with anger and indignation over the selfish actions of Pasquale's stepdaughter. How dare she pull such a stunt! I felt I was ready to lead the charge, alone if necessary, to rescue him. However, I had no sooner been given the family's blessing when suddenly I felt very small and terribly inadequate.

I shot a worried glance at my brother.

"Are you sure you can't come with me?" I inquired.

He could not, nor could anyone else in the immediate family. Commitments at their jobs, declining health, or problems arranging childcare played a role for everyone but me. I was the only one in our family that was single and self-employed, which gave me more flexibility than those who had families and worked for a traditional employer. I had no choice but to accept the circumstances, take a deep breath and a leap of faith.

Minutes after ending the call with Max, the telephone rang again. It was my cousin, Ben, the son of Pasquale's youngest sister who had died years earlier. Ben knew of my efforts weeks beforehand to find an attorney for Uncle Pasquale but amidst all the turmoil, Ben had been overlooked when everyone else was called to the meeting at my parent's home. My mother apologized profusely before bringing him up to speed.

When Ben heard that I would be traveling to Virginia alone, he decided immediately to go with me. Ask and you shall receive! My traveling companion had been appointed. By eight o'clock that evening, Ben and I were on the Pennsylvania Turnpike making the four-hour drive across the state to the cottage, from which we would journey to Virginia the following morning. The race was on!

CHAPTER TWO

Adventures with Wine (Part One)

SUNDAY, FEBRUARY 22

Every Sunday morning my parents begin preparations for a decades-old tradition of gathering their children at their home in rural western Pennsylvania for Sunday dinner. I remember similar Sunday afternoons from my childhood when the gathering place was the home of my mother's Italian parents. All of my grandparents' children and their children's children were in attendance.

Amazingly enough, my senses still recall the aroma of my grandfather's spaghetti sauce as if I were somehow magically transported back to that time and into his kitchen. I can still see his short, balding figure standing at the gas stove wearing a crisp white apron tied around his substantial waist, stirring a deep pot of gently simmering sauce with a long wooden spoon. He made the sauce from scratch with hearty, vine-ripened tomatoes and seasoned it with fresh-cut herbs all grown in his garden. The finishing touch was a glassful of red wine made from the grapes that grew in the backyard. Ah, that wine! The taste first kissed my lips when I was all of eight years old.

My grandparents lived next door to us on the opposite side of a common wall. Our twin two-story homes were united by long front and rear porches. It was a very convenient arrangement for me and my siblings, but often the source of discontent for my mother as our grandparents doted on us. And we, in turn, reveled in their affection dashing out of our house and across the porch, hurling ourselves into their waiting arms to escape our parents' ire when a childish prank went wrong.

Silver-haired, hazel-eyed Grandma had a comfortably padded lap and a gracious smile. She was a source of constant encouragement and love in the midst of the frequent scoldings my brothers and I received as a result of our never-ending antics.

"My grandachillen canda do anyting," Grandma proudly proclaimed in broken English. Translation: we could do no wrong. It wasn't that my parents were any meaner than the average mom and dad; it's just that my siblings and I made up a small army of rowdy mischief-makers that often taxed their patience.

Grandma's patience, on the other hand, seemed limitless as she sat on her front porch glider telling stories to my brothers or attempting to teach me and my sister the fine art of crochet. That skill came easily to my sister. Grandma's legacy can still be seen today in the colorful seashell-stitched scarves, popcorn-stitched capes and hats, and the pineapple-patterned tablecloths my sister creates. I, however, was all thumbs and managed to make a mess of the simplest project so that it came out looking more like a ball of shapeless knots than an intentional work of art.

We all appreciated Grandma's kindness, warmth, and her loving spirit, so it was to our grandparents' home that my siblings and I ran when we were in trouble. When we cut ourselves playing where we weren't supposed to play, Grandma cleaned and bandaged the wound. Her comforting smile and consoling words dried our tears and lifted our hearts. Of course, she would have to answer to my mother later.

"Next time, send them home where they belong!" was my mother's usual reproof.

The warning did nothing to diminish Grandma's care. She simply loved us and continued to tend to our boo-boos and dry our tears. When we did not want to finish our chores, when we accidentally broke something—a dish, a lamp, a flowerpot—and knew we'd catch hell for it, when we needed to disappear long enough to avoid the next command from Mother ... in short, any time we wanted to trade our parents' discipline for the couldn't-do-anything-wrong adoration of our grandparents, we would simply scamper across the porch and share Grandma's glider or keep Grandpa company in his kitchen.

One day, while I was cleaning and reorganizing my bedroom closet at Mother's command, I discovered the loose wallboards in the corner that, when removed, enabled me to squeeze my little self through the common wall and into a bedroom closet in my grandparents' house. The words *disappearing act* took on a whole new dimension until Mother caught on and insisted that my father make the appropriate repairs.

Oftentimes, I would skip across the back porch at noon to share lunch with my grandparents. I particularly enjoyed the dense, crusty bread that accompanied each meal.

On occasion, one of their sons, usually Pasquale, would sail through the back door and greet us companionably.

"Ho-ho, look who's here!" he proclaimed upon seeing me there. Then Pasquale would take up a place at the table next to us.

One hazy summer afternoon, a wonderful aroma wafted from Grandpa's kitchen and came across the porch to find me. I followed the scent and the sound of clattering kitchen utensils to the screened door of his kitchen. With my hands cupped around my eyes, I peered through the screen. Grandpa waved me in with his free hand while he stood in front of the stove stirring and tasting.

"Come onah," he invited with a smile. Then, gesturing toward the table, "Sit. You eatah?"

I shook my head.

"You eatah wid me."

It was more of a pronouncement than a question.

I made my way into the kitchen and sat on a wooden chair whose seat had been rubbed smooth by so many fannies sliding on and off over the years. As I watched in silence, Grandpa clicked off the gas burner then began dishing out the aromatic contents of the cast iron skillet. On the table before me, he set down a white china serving platter edged in gold with tiny pink rosettes painted on the rim. The plate was laden with red peppers roasted with cloves of garlic and spritzed with olive oil. Another plate with wedges of a pungent, pale yellow cheese was placed on the crisp white tablecloth next to the peppers while Italian sausages coated with tomato sauce filled another dish. Atop a small wooden cutting board sat a loaf of crusty bread. The ever-present green glass jug filled with red wine occupied a prominent place in the center of it all. What a feast! Finally, Grandpa took a seat next to me and began to fill our plates.

Like many people from *the olla country*, Grandpa firmly believed that a glass of wine a day kept his rheumatism in check and his heart strong.

"Gooda for da blood," he proclaimed as he raised the glass to his lips.

Had he been able to foresee that medical research decades later would prove the benefits of grapeseed extract, as well as an occasional glass of red wine, I am certain he would have simply nodded in somber confirmation and said, "I tolla you."

Grandpa poured a glass of wine for himself then lifted the bottle toward me.

"Wan to taste?" he asked in heavily-accented English.

Without waiting for a reply, he poured some wine into a shot glass and set it before me. In my innocence, I nodded and smiled, feeling like a privileged grown-up attending a secret ritual.

I remember the sweet taste of crushed concord grapes mingled with something that warmed my tongue and sent a tingling sensation all the way down to my tummy.

Grandpa and I regularly shared a Coke or Nehi grape soda but this was different. In later years, I would come to learn that the name of that tingly something was alcohol. In the meantime, ignorance was bliss. Grandpa was a short, stocky man with a ring of snow-white hair around his balding crown. He had pale blue eyes, a slight arthritic limp, and he usually smelled of a combination of garlic and the minty ointment he rubbed into his aching joints. Before retiring he had been the village shoemaker and chef for hire, known and respected by all. Despite the arthritis that plagued him, he kept himself busy gardening, cooking, canning, making wine, and taking long walks. Sometimes he walked through the dense forest near our home to collect mushrooms. Other times he would walk two blocks to the center of our small hometown to enjoy the company of other Italian immigrants he counted among his many friends.

Before I was out of diapers, I had already accompanied him several times to the local beer garden, and Grandpa and I were regulars by the time I was five. With his gray felt hat on his head, a shiny ebony walking cane in one hand and holding my little hand with the other, he would set off down the tree-lined sidewalk with me skipping at his side. I liked the damp, yeasty smell of the beer garden in summer and the sound of cue sticks connecting with the colorful balls on the pool table. The dim, cool atmosphere, adoring smiles, and Italian greetings welcomed us as we made our way inside. Grandpa lifted me off the floor and set me down on one of the round, shiny, red vinyl-covered bar stools, then sat down on a stool beside me. He always ordered a shot of whiskey for himself and a cherry Coke for me.

In those days, the village tavern was not a rowdy arena for drunken brawls as too many of them appear to be today. Our little village tavern was simply a local gathering place where one went to learn the latest news from relatives and friends left behind in another country. For the immigrants who could not read or write (my grandparents were among them), it was a place where someone else could read aloud the letters received from across the ocean and pen a reply.

My visits to the beer garden with Grandpa were nothing more than the ritual showing off of the newest grandchild. I am certain that was the only reason my mother indulged Grandpa's whim and allowed me to go along. The practice was one that I witnessed decades later during a trip to Italy: families strolled down the piazza together in the evenings wearing their Sunday best with the latest arrival tucked into a baby stroller or held snuggly in the arms of an adult. It was a heart-warming scene.

My grandparents were a part of the generation that measured their wealth in the size of their family, their reputation in the kitchen, and the number of friends who graced their table. They were generous to a fault. All Italians seem to enjoy feeding their children and grandchildren; my grandpa was no exception. That afternoon in his kitchen, he looked on, smiling his approval after my first sip of his homemade wine.

"Es good, eh?"

I nodded energetically as I chewed bread and cheese then tentatively sipped more wine. I had just graduated from cherry Coke to the good stuff!

I left Grandpa's table that afternoon with a warm feeling in my tummy and a green glass pony-sized Coke bottle in my hand, a souvenir from Grandpa. But instead of a tin bottle cap, a cork sat wedged in the neck of the Coke bottle and instead of Coke, the bottle was half-filled with my grandfather's homemade wine. Stomach full, bottle in hand, I sauntered lazily across the back porch to my own back door, where my mother stood at her kitchen stove making preparations for our family's evening meal. Italians never seem to get out of the kitchen! As I entered, my mother turned slightly at the sound of the opening door, momentarily turned back to the stove, then spun around again with a look of fury spreading across her face. She dropped her cooking utensils on the stovetop, then snatched the bottle from my hand and held it up to the light, where the contents glowed a ruby red.

"What's this?" she demanded.

My mouth fell open but no words followed; I could not even manage to shrug my shoulders. As far as I knew, I hadn't done anything wrong, but the storm clouds gathering in my mother's eyes told a different story.

She hurriedly brushed past me, through the door, and across the porch in the direction from whence I had come with my prized bottle clutched tightly in her plump fingers. Immediately after the thwack of the wooden screened doors, first ours then Grandpa's, I heard her voice booming through the common wall over Grandpa's. I could not make out the words but I knew Grandpa and I were in for it so I did what most kids do when they are in trouble—I ran.

While mother was busy yelling out back, I tore through the house toward the front door as fast as my little legs could carry me, dashed across the front porch then threw myself, breathless, onto Grandma's glider. Grandma sat there calmly embroidering, seemingly oblivious to the pandemonium inside the house at her back. She looked up at the sound of my pounding footsteps, smiled, then moved her Bible and rolls of colored threads aside, inviting me to sit so she could show me what she was working on. I knew my mother would come to find me eventually but until her thunder died, I was safe at Grandma's side.

■■■

Later, I learned that my mother emptied the wine from my Coke bottle into the kitchen sink and tossed the bottle into the trashcan. I promptly retrieved it when she wasn't looking then hid it behind the dresser in my bedroom. Later that day, I spotted my grandfather across the back porch. He simply smiled and winked at me. Mother's wrath could never dampen his jovial spirit. That spirit seemed to be a family trademark among the male members of the clan but was most evident in Uncle Pasquale.

Grandpa died when I was barely in my teens. I have a habit of burying unpleasantness so deep inside of me that it just disappears altogether as if it never happened. I must have done that with the memory of my grandfather's passing because when I looked for it in my memory box it was gone. I couldn't tell you where he was, what he was doing, or what he was wearing when he died. He lived next door and I do not even know how he died. And I have no desire to ask the people who do know and risk disturbing an unpleasant memory that is safely tucked away somewhere. The memories that count, the ones I cherish, are all there in my mind in vivid living color.

Today, that little green glass pony bottle occupies a prominent spot on a shelf in my kitchen. Every so often I fill it half full with red wine and drink a toast to my grandfather.

That is how traditions are born, and so the traditional Sunday afternoon family dinner continues. My mother and father are now the grandparents. They bustle about the kitchen from early Sunday morning until just before noon, with the aroma of oven-baked chicken and homemade spaghetti sauce swirling around them.

My father's delicious garlic bread goes under the oven broiler just minutes before the vegetables and tossed greens salad are set on the dining room table. Daughters and daughters-in-law set out the plates and silverware then call the children in from play and their husbands away from the season's televised sporting event. During the meal, there are shared stories of the week's events, shared memories, the occasional squabble, and much laughter. My grandparents would have been proud to know that the tradition they began so long ago continues to this day.

Grandpa and Grandma had five children: two boys and three girls. The eldest daughter was born in Italy. She was just six years old when she waved good-bye to her father as he walked up the ramp of the ship that would carry him to America. The following year, after Grandpa had established a business and found a home, he sent for his wife and daughter. Their first son, Pasquale, was born in America a year later and other children followed in rapid succession.

The daughters were all pretty brunettes with hazel-green or blue eyes. The boys were tall, olive-skinned, handsome, and light-hearted. Both of the boys eventually defended our country in various wars from World War II forward, then came home to marry and raise families of their own.

Pasquale's brother, Salvatore, Uncle Sal to me, was the impish family prankster. For his brother, he was a source of constant amusement, but an annoying tease during their teenage years, according to his sisters. To this day, the memories he shares from his youth are some of the most humorous stories told at our family reunions.

Pasquale claims to have been a boisterous hellion in his youth. However, my memories of him as a young man are that he always seemed to wear a more serious countenance than his siblings. Perhaps, being the eldest son of immigrant parents, he felt that a greater responsibility rested on his shoulders to help support the family. After all, they had survived the Great Depression, which had to have had a profound impact in molding the personalities, characters, and the work ethics of every one of them. Maybe it was just that by the time I was old enough to take notice, he was already married and somewhat more settled. Perhaps it was because he was the first in the family to rise to the ranks of management at his job. In any event, Uncle Pasquale was *the boss* and no one in the family challenged that position.

During his early teens, he rode the public bus to attend a high school twenty miles away because our little rural town had only an elementary school. The construction of a local high school was finally completed by Pasquale's junior year and he graduated with honors in 1943. After graduation, he served in the US Army then married, moved to the big city, and worked his way up the ladder in the city's steel mill. He became one of the bosses there, liked and respected by everyone who knew him.

In those early years, I came to know the aspects of the personality behind the man who is Pasquale. During Sunday afternoon gatherings at my grandparent's house, my young cousins and I were usually busy playing a board game on the living room floor by the time Uncle Pasquale walked in with his wife, Angie.

He always set the tone by mischievously barking, "What are you doing!" as he entered.

It never failed. At least a few of us would be startled enough to twitch. If someone jumped, it was all the better for Uncle Pasquale's amusement and he would chuckle while walking through to the dining room to join the adults, satisfied that he had done his part in keeping us in check. My cousins and I feared and revered him, but as we grew older, we eventually caught the twinkle in his eye and the conspiratorial wink at another adult immediately after the barking session. Then the realization dawned that the lion's roar masked a teddy bear's spirit and that knowledge only served to endear him to us even more.

More than a decade later, when my cousins and I were in our teens, Angie died suddenly from an aneurysm no one suspected she had. Not long after her funeral, my mother began sending me to Uncle Pasquale's house on Saturday mornings to do housekeeping chores and iron his shirts. His marriage to Angie had produced no children so there was no one to look after him once she was gone.

During my youth, my mother frequently volunteered my services like that and it irritated me to no end. As a ten-year-old child, loaning me out to the neighbors meant extra pocket money and I did not mind so much. Except when I thought I had better things to do, like trailing along after my brothers through the woods, swinging on the thick vines that wound themselves around tall trees, walking single-file atop stone walls during army games, wading in streams to find crayfish and tadpoles.

It did not matter to my mother that I wanted no part of extra household chores; I was simply informed, "You're going and that's that."

As the eldest daughter in our family, it seemed that housekeeping chores, ironing clothes and linens, and the job of second chef always fell, rather unfairly, to me. When younger siblings arrived, I was appointed to the post of chief bottle-washer and babysitter as well.

I reluctantly admit that those disciplines probably helped to instill a sense of responsibility and a fierce independence in me, undoubtedly forging the close relationships my siblings and I enjoy to this day. At the time, however, I harbored typical childish resentment at being hired out at Mother's whim. On any given day, I might be sent to scrub floors for the elderly lady next door, who sat at her kitchen table smoking cigarettes and drinking beer while she watched me work. When the local church's cleaning lady took ill, I was sent to wax the pews or mop the floors. Clean, clean, clean! I felt that a huge chunk of my childhood had been stolen while I slaved away. Often, I took out my frustrations on the scrub brush and bucket, willing the brush to rub a hole in the stupid floor while I scrubbed, and I always clanged the aluminum bucket against the pews, creating as much noise as I could muster to disturb the sanctity in the quiet little church.

By the time Aunt Angie had died, it seemed that the business of playing housekeeper for Uncle Pasquale was simply one more of my mother's endless commands and I resented the unwelcome intrusion into my teenaged life. However, I relented and presented myself at Uncle Pasquale's door on Saturday mornings to commence with the vacuuming, ironing, dusting, and floor-scrubbing while I thought about all of the teenage activities I was missing such as driving around aimlessly with my friends while we engaged in important activities like comparing notes about our boyfriends or listening to the latest rock-and-roll records.

I cannot tell you exactly when or how it occurred, but shortly after I became Uncle Pasquale's part-time housekeeper something remarkable happened. The dreaded weekly chores evolved into comradely adventure. To my surprise, I found that I was hurrying to get the cleaning and ironing out of the way so I could stand next to Uncle Pasquale at the stove while he taught me to make spaghetti sauce like his father used to make. We even had cheese and wine lunches like the ones I enjoyed with Grandpa. Pasquale, in an attempt to look after my career as well, began to teach me about accounting as I helped him to balance the books for the local union.

From that day forward, Uncle Pasquale captured a corner of my heart and we enjoyed a special sort of father-daughter relationship. I took care of him the way a daughter would care for a widowed father and he seemed to take pleasure in counseling me on everything from my choice of career to the boys I dated.

"I understand you're going out with Tony Capelli," a stern-faced Uncle Pasquale announced to me one afternoon. I had recently met the young man at a party and had only been out with him once afterward but somehow, Uncle Pasquale already knew.

"How did you know that?" I asked.

"Never mind, just listen to me. I want you to stop seeing him, you hear me?"

The fatherly lecture that followed amounted to a crash course on the local mob. How was I to know I had been on a date with a boy whose father was a member of the mafia? I did think it was somewhat odd when he said he wanted to take me home to meet his father. Most young men want to introduce a girl to their mother, don't they? What did I know; I was young and naive and having too much fun being chased by the boys. Heck, I didn't even know our city *had* a mafia! But Uncle Pasquale knew, and suddenly I understood why he was always the serious one in the family. Pasquale had tangled with some of them in the past when they attempted to prey on elderly immigrants like my grandfather. Uncle Pasquale wanted to make certain I had nothing to do with their kind; he was watching my back. Reflecting on that time, I cannot help thinking what a shame it was that his marriage to Angie produced no children. I believe he would have been an exceptional father.

Uncle Pasquale seemed to have a gift for making money and he never hesitated to share. When his father was well beyond his prime and no longer able to ply his trade as a shoemaker, Pasquale saw to it that his parents had what they needed. In 1973, when my own father had a serious heart attack and was confined to six months of complete bed rest before the heart surgeon would even consider operating, my parents worried over the loss of his income and the possible loss of our home. Uncle Pasquale insisted on paying the monthly mortgage on our house until my father was able to return to work. Like his father before him, Uncle Pasquale was generous to a fault and he took care of his own.

As time passed and I grew out of those turbulent teenage years, blossoming into young adulthood, Uncle Pasquale moved beyond the pain of Angie's death and began dating. Mutual friends introduced him to Nora. She, too, had been widowed and seemed a likely match. Nora was good for Uncle Pasquale. She put the light back in his eyes, and within a few years she became his second wife. He no longer needed me to tend to household chores and iron his shirts, so I moved on too. I moved right out of the state, in fact, to begin my own climb up the corporate ladder.

◧◧◧

In later years, my visits to my hometown became less and less frequent until family communications were reduced to occasional greetings by mail, infrequent telephone calls, and my appearance at family gatherings during holidays. Too easily, it seems, we are caught up in demanding careers and the activities that constitute our daily lives.

The years seemed to fly by until one day I received a grim reminder that the people I love are aging, the time remaining with them was limited, and I had lost too many opportunities already not only to tell them how much they mean to me but also to be there physically to spend time in their presence.

It happened late on a Sunday afternoon in February 2004; I once again telephoned my presence to the family gathering from my own home several hours and many miles away from them. As soon as my mother answered the telephone, I heard the stress in her voice.

"What's the matter?" I instinctively asked.

Her sobbing reply wrenched my heart.

"Uncle Pasquale is in the hospital," she cried. "He's had a major stroke."

The story gushed out as she detailed the episode that sent the family rushing to the hospital emergency room two days before. His status: awake and breathing on his own, crying but unable to speak, limited movement of his left arm, but complete paralysis of the limbs on his right side. Then she delivered the bombshell: his wife and stepdaughter had requested the removal of all life support. I was stunned. That Nora would do that to Pasquale was completely inconceivable.

In spite of the fact that Pasquale was conscious and appeared to be stable, the attending physician had actually granted that request and removed the oxygen and intravenous feeding line. Fortunately, Pasquale was able to breath on his own or he would have simply suffocated to death.

"He's not even dead yet and they're talking about cremation and funeral arrangements," my mother sobbed.

"I'm coming home," I told her without hesitating. "I'll be on the road by noon."

I didn't know if my mother was simply being her usual overly emotional self, but I did know that if my childhood tutor, mentor, and protector was dying, I had to be there with him. I hung up the phone and looked at my German Shepherd, who had been lying placidly at my feet.

"Want to go for a ride?" I asked her.

Jette immediately scrambled to her feet. A few hours later, we were packed and on the road.

CHAPTER THREE

Blood vs. Ink (Round One)

TUESDAY MORNING, FEBRUARY 24

"Almost all of our relationships begin and most of them continue as forms of mutual exploitation, a mental or physical barter, to be terminated when one or both parties run out of goods."

—W.H. AUDEN

Pasquale's brother and sisters as well as several nieces and nephews were already standing in the corridor outside his hospital room in Smithton, Pennsylvania, when my parents and I arrived. The atmosphere in that corridor was thick with anger and hostility. I could read it in their furrowed brows, see it in their frustrated gestures and narrow-eyed, sideways glances at Pasquale's wife and stepdaughter. Pasquale's brother, Sal, stood silent against a wall, hands behind his back, wearing a look of utter disgust. Other members of the family either paced the floor with deep lines of worry etched across their foreheads or stood statue-like with arms folded defiantly across their chests.

When I arrived in town the previous evening, my mother brought me up to speed. Pasquale had been unconscious for almost forty-eight hours following the massive brain hemorrhage. His stepdaughter, Julie, quickly took charge upon her arrival from Virginia and gave the order to have Pasquale's oxygen and intravenous feeding lines removed. Fortunately, Pasquale was able to breathe on his own by then and quickly regained consciousness, although he was still unable to move or speak. What had upset his siblings most was that one of them had overheard Julie's whisper to a family friend.

"Don't tell anyone, but I'm having him cremated," she confided.

Unknown to Julie, her *friend* dutifully relayed those words to Pasquale's sister, who spread the alarm throughout the family. What did I say about not getting away with anything in a small town? Remarks from neither Pasquale's wife, Nora, nor the attending physicians indicated that Pasquale was dying. In fact, near as anyone could tell at that point, he was slowly emerging from the fog.

Adding to the confusion and my family's anxiousness was the fact that the doctors and nurses tending to Pasquale's care were not sharing any medical information regarding his condition with Pasquale's siblings. The medical staff spoke only to Nora and Julie. Although Nora remained cordial to Pasquale's siblings, as she had always been in the past, she revealed no specifics, leaving them to mutter their suspicions among themselves. As a result, the scene in the hospital had quickly deteriorated into *them versus us*, stepfamily against blood relations.

My mother was certain that Julie simply wanted my uncle to die, and from all appearances, Nora was going along with her for reasons that were not yet clear. Nothing galled Pasquale's siblings more than when Sal asked a nurse about his brother's prognosis and received her curt reply, "You'll have to ask the family."

"But, we *are* his family," Sal insisted.

"You need to speak with his daughter," the nurse demanded.

"He doesn't have a daughter," Sal informed her. "Julie is Nora's daughter."

"I'm sorry," was the only response the nurse could offer.

She truly appeared sympathetic but Julie had obviously given an order and the hospital staff was legally compelled to obey.

Feelings of compassion quickly turned to anger and resentment toward Pasquale's wife and her daughter, and my mother was in the thick of it. Still, I chose to reserve judgment until I could learn more.

Past experience with my mother has taught me that the first thing I need to do when I am presented with a family dilemma is listen closely, ask a few questions, step away and ponder, then go back and ask more questions before taking any action. This process has saved time, energy, and tears on more than one occasion. It isn't that my mother cannot be trusted to get the facts straight; she was simply created with more than an ample dose of human emotion. As quick as she is to laugh, she can be as easily incited to anger over a perceived slight. She can be quite the drama queen when circumstances are right. My mother has been known to giggle for hours over something that has tickled her or smolder for days in the ashes of a burning rage. Add a vivid imagination to the mix and sometimes the truth becomes a little murky.

With this in mind, I mulled over the information she had given me so far, considered a possibly over-zealous stepfamily, then adopted a wait-and-see attitude. If there were a plausible explanation, I would find it in due course. Besides, I simply could not fathom the concept that one human being could make an arbitrary decision to end another human being's life simply because that life was suddenly an inconvenience. An action such as that is nothing less than the epitome of evil and I did not believe Nora had a malignant bone in her body.

Was it Julie? If Julie was driving toward ending Pasquale's life, what was her motivation? Was she afraid she would be burdened with his care? Ours is and always has been a generous, caring family with no tolerance for such malevolence. Various family members had certainly nursed an aging Pasquale and his loving Nora through many minor illnesses over recent years. My parents drove them to doctor visits when Pasquale wasn't feeling up to it. Julie need not have worried about inconvenience. Pasquale's family would have continued to care for him and Nora long after Julie returned to Virginia.

"You don't want to go in there." Aunt Nan, Sal's wife, was the first to speak to me as my parents and I made our way into the family circle.

"Why not?" I asked.

"*They're* in there," was her short response. Then she added, "Nora and her daughter."

"So ... what does that mean?" I asked tentatively.

"They don't want us in there." Aunt Nan then elaborated with a hint of sarcasm in her voice, "Julie says it's too upsetting for her mother."

"This is upsetting for all of us," I countered, almost laughing at the absurdity of the remark. "But you are his family, too, and you should be in there with him."

"Hmph," was the grunted response from Uncle Sal as he shook his head and turned away, one hand wearily massaging the back of his neck. I glanced into the room where Uncle Pasquale lay.

"I don't see Julie in there," I informed my aunt.

"She just walked down the hall," Aunt Nan replied.

"Well, I drove for four hours to get here and I'm going to see my uncle."

Turning away from them, I walked purposefully toward Uncle Pasquale's room. His stepdaughter, Julie, suddenly appeared at my shoulder and spoke to me, matching my steps, as we entered the room together.

Without preamble or greeting she stated matter-of-factly, "*She* has power of attorney for *him* and *we* have power of attorney for *her*."

◼◼◼

It was obvious that the "she" being referred to was Nora. I later learned that "we" referred to Julie and her husband Dan. Not comprehending why Julie felt the need to offer that sudden insight into the legal affairs of their lives, I walked into Uncle Pasquale's room undeterred and greeted Nora with an apologetic smile and a hug. I had always liked Nora. As a matter of fact, I thought she and my uncle were good for each other, a feeling I believed Pasquale's siblings shared. For that reason, I was puzzled and somewhat disturbed by the comments in the corridor and the obvious hostility that had materialized seemingly overnight.

"How are you holding up?" I asked, gently taking Nora's hands in mine.

"Oh." Nora waived the question aside then offered, "He isn't getting any better."

"It's early yet, Nora. It's only been a few days," I encouraged. "It takes time to heal from something like this."

"I can't take care of him," she lamented.

For more than a year, prior to Pasquale's stroke, Nora had been under doctor's care for the treatment of a neurological condition known as dementia. Not only were Nora's memory and judgment compromised, but she also suffered with bouts of light-headedness and involuntary trembling. When I had visited Nora and Uncle Pasquale in their home the previous Thanksgiving, she could not even pour a cup of coffee. Uncle Pasquale had to keep an eye on her at all times. In light of her fragile physical state and precarious mental condition, I could sympathize with her concerns. Nora could not even take care of herself, let alone a convalescing husband.

"You don't have to," I assured her. "The doctors will take good care of him. You just worry about keeping up your own strength. Are you eating? Getting enough rest?"

※※※

Julie took that opportunity to launch herself into the conversation, brashly, from the sentry-like position she had taken up in a chair near the foot of my uncle's bed.

"She can't eat or sleep," Julie declared. "This is taking too much out of her."

Brushing off her biting remarks, I made no reply but proceeded to my uncle's bedside, where he lay with his eyes closed, breathing steadily. I sat in the chair next to the bed and lightly touched his arm as I leaned toward his ear.

"Uncle Pasquale," I said softly, "it's Gina. I've come to see how you're doing."

Pasquale's eyelids flew open and he suddenly reached over with his left hand to grab my arm with a strength that surprised me. Pulling me toward him, he began to cry into my shoulder. "You're going to be all right, Uncle Pasquale. Please don't cry; you'll be fine."

I kissed his forehead and rubbed his arm while I tried to reassure him. I had been told that his right side was paralyzed as a result of the stroke. Prior to the episode, his doctors frequently commented about his vigorous health and the strength that belied his seventy-plus years. Uncle Pasquale's right side may have been immobile, but the strength in his left arm was testimony to his resilience. It was that indomitable spirit that reached out to me physically but had no voice except for his anguished sobs.

"All he does is cry," Nora shook her head. "The doctor said it's normal for people who have had a stroke. They claim it's the only way they can express themselves."

I turned my gaze back to Pasquale.

"You're going to be all right," I told him again as I held onto his hand. "Do you remember what you used to tell me when I was down? " I smoothed away his tears as I continued. "Do you remember? You always said 'You're tough, don't you let this beat you.' Now it's your turn to be tough. And I know you can beat this. Don't you give up; we're all here for you."

He sent a worried glance in Nora's direction as she stroked his hair. I considered what he might be thinking then reassured him saying, "You don't need to worry about Nora, either. Julie is here to take care of her and you know your family will help her too. You just concentrate on getting better. I love you, Uncle Pasquale." I gently kissed his forehead, patted his arm and rose from the chair.

Nora had always been a slender, somewhat fragile-looking woman, but she seemed even more frail than I remembered. I addressed her as I turned from the doorway.

"Nora, let me know if you need anything. I'll be in town for a few days."

Back out in the corridor, the dour mood had not lifted. As I walked toward my family, I could hear Uncle Sal's agitated complaint.

"I just want to know what's going on," he said.

"What do you mean?" I asked as I approached.

"I want to know what the doctor said about his prognosis. And those two," he said, gesturing with his chin toward the room I had just exited, "won't tell us anything."

The solution seemed logical enough to me so I offered it up.

"Why don't you simply ask the doctor yourself?"

"When he was here yesterday, he and Julie were huddled over there," he gestured with his shoulder to a corner near the stairwell, "so we couldn't hear what was being said."

"Did you ask to be included?"

"Well, no," Uncle Sal admitted. "But, darn it, that was just plain ignorant. She could have included us. What's the big secret; that's what I want to know!"

"Well, you are his blood relations; she's only a stepdaughter. Surely a blood relative carries more weight than stepfamily."

"You would think so," he agreed. "But she says her mother has power of attorney over Pasquale. I think Nora just wants him dead so she can take his money then move South with her daughter."

There it was again. The same sentiments expressed by my mother the previous evening. Was one simply feeding off the other's suspicions? Or, horrific as it seemed, could they be right? Near as I could tell, Nora loved my uncle dearly, even clinging to him prior to this and refusing so much as a week's vacation in a southern climate without him. Now, according to Pasquale's siblings, Nora had suddenly decided to leave him for dead. How could that be?

"But isn't Nora being treated for dementia?" I asked.

"Yes," my mother, Natalie, confirmed. "I drive her to her doctor appointments."

"Well then, she doesn't have the legal capacity to make decisions for herself, let alone life and death decisions for someone else," I told them. "No court of law would uphold a power of attorney document with her name on it at this point."

"That's probably true," Uncle Sal acknowledged, "but Julie claims she has power of attorney for her mother."

Summoning up decades of corporate experience and my knowledge of these kinds of documents, I informed them, "Well, I've got news for all of you. One power of attorney does not piggyback off another. Any lawyer will tell you that. Unless Julie is specifically named as Uncle Pasquale's attorney-in-fact, she does not have the power to call the shots here. Has anyone asked her to produce those documents?"

"I asked the nurse but she won't show them to us," Uncle Sal countered. "And Julie won't give us any information either. All the nurses keep saying we have to ask Nora or Julie. And those two aren't budging."

"That's a lot of bull," I declared. "Telephone the doctor yourself and tell him you want to know about your brother's condition."

Just at that moment, a nurse appeared at the edge of our group.

"I understand there's a little dissension here," she said.

Her voice was calm, even somewhat pleasant, as she eased herself into our circle wearing a placating smile.

"This is perfectly normal under the circumstances," she continued in an obvious attempt to pacify everyone. "Family relations can often become strained at a time like this, so I have put the Ethics Committee on standby to resolve any issues." Then, to everyone's surprise, she added, "I also telephoned Dr. Simon, Mr. DiAngeli's neurosurgeon, and asked him to come and meet with the family today." We were stunned. Someone in the circle had managed to find their voice long enough to ask the nurse what time Dr. Simon would arrive, but she was not able to say. Regardless, it was the opportunity the family sought, and we were prepared to wait there, en masse, all day if necessary for the chance to get concrete answers to our many questions.

We were dumbfounded, standing there with our jaws open while the nurse slipped away as quietly as she had come. Pasquale's brother, Sal, was the first to react.

"Who asked for the Ethics Committee? I never called anyone. Did you?" he asked as he shot a glance at his sister, Eleanor, who simply shook her head in mild surprise.

"Don't look a gift horse in the mouth," I cautioned. "Someone is obviously looking out for us and, more importantly, for Uncle Pasquale. Let's just call it an answer to a prayer and see how it plays out."

Before anyone else could speak, Julie stormed out of Uncle Pasquale's room and into the hallway. Apparently, she had been eavesdropping. She invaded our little circle and demanded to know what our conversation with the nurse was about and who called on the Ethics Committee.

A heated exchange followed, culminating in Julie declaring, "Pasquale has a living will. He has told us many times that he would not want to live in a vegetative state. *We* are his family and we are simply attempting to carry out his wishes!"

There it was. Finally, the motivation for their secrecy had been unveiled. Julie and her mother were prepared to let my uncle die, supposedly at Pasquale's own request, and they did not want his family to know it. They did not want to risk the interference, the resistance they knew they would encounter.

The question that lingered was whether Pasquale had actually reached that point, the point of no return, or not. I had just witnessed the strength his body still possessed, and it certainly did not seem to me that he was near death. Then again, I am not a doctor. Only the physician who had been treating him would be able to shed some light on the matter and we would see him soon enough. Perhaps more importantly, we needed to find out if Pasquale had actually created such a document and then entrusted it to Julie.

Most everyone in the family was aware that Pasquale and Julie had been bickering in recent months. Over what, I had no clue. However, the general consensus was that his relationship with her had certainly seen better days. It stretched the imagination to believe he would entrust her with such a vital document. Until we could sort it all out, I knew someone had to keep a lid on the boiler before it exploded. With that in mind, I decided to jump into the middle of the fray and try to bring the two factions together. Admittedly, I am not always the one to play arbitrator, but the way things were heating up in that hospital corridor I figured it was worth a try. So, with a silent prayer to summon the right words, I dove in, vowing to be the peacemaker. Someone had to take on that role, I thought, and no one else was stepping forward.

Julie and I had had limited contact with each other over the years. What I knew of her, I knew from family gossip: a failed first marriage, a failed business that my uncle financed, part-time jobs that never seemed to stick, feigned illnesses, and a husband who was rarely seen with her. We could not have had less in common. Our conversations at family gatherings were only tentative and polite, covering safe topics like the weather in China. What in the world would I say to her now at such a crucial moment? Gently but firmly taking hold of Julie's arm, I steered her away from everyone.

"Julie, come and talk to me," I suggested. "Let's just give everyone a little breathing room and let them cool off."

As we walked slowly down the corridor together, away from the others, she held out her hands in a gesture of frustration.

"I don't understand what this is all about," she proclaimed. "I'm just doing what Pasquale wanted. And he always said he didn't want to live like a vegetable. He used to shudder when he and mom saw someone in a wheelchair. He always told her, 'Don't you ever let me live like that.'"

Somehow, I could definitely imagine Pasquale making a remark like that. However, even I, untrained in the medical field, could see that my uncle's condition was far from what could be considered a vegetative state. He had lost his capacity for speech, he had lost mobility in his right side, which was typical for a stroke victim but probably not a permanent condition, and he would be confined to bed for a time, but certainly not for the remainder of his life. How long Pasquale would remain that way would be anyone's guess, but to have his life support removed at that early stage simply because a piece of paper he signed years before gave his permission to do so was, I felt, premature at best and downright murderous under the worst of intentions.

It was yet unknown to me whether or not my uncle had actually signed a legal power of attorney document giving Julie control over his life, or if she had simply manufactured the document in her mind to keep the rest of the family at bay while she followed her own course. Nora made no secret of recent troubles and she had confided in Pasquale's sisters on more than one occasion that Pasquale was at odds with Julie over her constant pleas for cash.

Pasquale could not understand how two adults like Julie and her husband could fail to find enough work to support themselves. In fact, the evening Pasquale suffered the stroke, my mother informed me that Nora had voiced regret over an argument she had with Pasquale earlier that very day.

"It's all my fault," Nora confessed to Pasquale's sister. "We were fighting about Julie again. I wanted him to send money to her and he refused. He said he's given her enough."

While Julie and I made our way down the corridor, those thoughts ran through my mind. Could it be that Julie was making up the story about a power of attorney document? Surely she would not be that wicked just to get back at him, would she?

Julie and I had corresponded briefly by e-mail after seeing each other during the previous Thanksgiving holiday at Pasquale and Nora's home.

She had even asked for my assistance in locating an apartment, telling me that she was considering moving back to Pennsylvania so she could help Pasquale care for her mother. If she'd had a sudden change of heart, again, the question was, *why?* I was certain there was more to it than had yet been revealed. Naively, I still could not bring myself to believe anyone could have sinister motives toward my uncle. He had always been a kind, considerate, and generous individual. If he had, in fact, refused Nora's request to send money to her daughter then he did so with good reason. I knew my uncle too well to believe anything to the contrary.

Julie and I continued down the long hospital corridor together, side-stepping nurses pushing carts, while I attempted to reason with her amidst the clanging of bed pans and the sound of bedside buzzers.

"Julie, you are obviously looking after your mother's best interest," I told her. "And that's understandable under the circumstances."

I proceeded cautiously, attempting to smooth her ruffled feathers.

"But you need to understand that this is a very close-knit family. We always look after our own and Uncle Pasquale's brother and sisters are going to look after *his* best interest …"

She cut me off mid-sentence to defend her own actions.

"They aren't looking out for his interest if they aren't willing to abide by the wishes he expressed in his living will!" she spluttered.

"Surely, Julie, you can see …" I began, but once again, I was cut off, this time by my mother's frantic waving to us from the other end of the hallway. The moment everyone was waiting for had come: Pasquale's doctor had arrived. With white coattails flying, he strode down the hallway, deliberately and wordlessly, past the waiting family members, into Pasquale's room, and slammed the door shut. But not before ushering everyone else out, including Nora.

We listened from the corridor as Dr. Simon's deep voice boomed through the closed door, giving one command after another to Pasquale.

"Move your left arm," he demanded of Uncle Pasquale. "Now move your right arm. Lift your left leg. Now lift your right leg. Squeeze my hand. Again."

The door flew open as he exited the room in the same brusque manner in which he had entered. He was a tall, handsome man with sandy brown hair and green eyes that peered out from behind gold wire-rimmed glasses.

Under better circumstances, he was probably a congenial, compassionate physician with a wonderful bedside manner. Not so on that day. His entire demeanor conveyed a no-nonsense attitude.

Dr. Simon strode toward the waiting family, then came to a sudden halt directly in front of Nora. Addressing her with his arms folded across his chest, he made no attempt to soften his words.

"You are the wife," he sternly announced. "As the wife, it is your responsibility to make decisions regarding your husband's care and it's up to you how much information you share with other members of the family. These people," he made a sweeping gesture with his arm to include us all, "would like to know Mr. DiAngeli's condition."

He paused briefly before continuing. "I would like to have a conference in *that* room," he pointed off to his right. "But *you* have to say who is allowed to be there and who isn't. Do you want to include everyone?"

Again, he crossed his arms over his chest, chin resting on a fist, and peered down at Nora with narrowed eyes awaiting a response.

"I ... I don't know," Nora began, almost stammering. "I can't think."

Before she could utter another word, Julie stepped between her and the doctor.

Turning to face her mother with a placating smile, Julie cupped her hands around her mother's face, as one would do with a child.

"My mother wants ..." she began, but that time she was the one cut short as I snapped a warning to her.

"Let your mother speak for herself, Julie," I said.

So much for the peacemaker. I was not certain whether this particular doctor knew Nora's mental health history or not and I wanted to make sure that every opportunity was afforded Nora to speak, thereby making it known to anyone who might have any doubt about her decision-making abilities—or lack thereof! Surprisingly, Julie obediently stepped away from her mother. Nora looked down at the floor then shifted her glance down the corridor as if the answer might come from that direction.

Then without looking directly at the doctor she offered lamely, "Well, I guess it's all right."

"Good," Dr. Simon responded curtly. "Good! Let's all go in here."

As Dr. Simon led the way, ten people followed, with Julie and Nora at the head of the procession.

The room he led us into was not a conference room but just another convalescent room for patients complete with a bed, a few chairs, and various medical equipment. It would have to do. As we filed in, everyone attempted to find a spot near enough to clearly see and hear the doctor but at a discreet distance from Julie. Aunt Eleanor took a spot in one of the wooden chairs next to the bed. Nora seated herself on the edge of the bed with Julie on one side of her and my mother on the other.

My mother had been a good friend to Nora over the years and they had become especially close in the preceding months, as my mother was called into service as her chauffeur, delivering Nora and Pasquale to their many doctor appointments while Pasquale healed from first cataract surgery, then a case of gout. Nora's macular degeneration and Pasquale's recent back problems prevented them from driving themselves, though they refused to give up their own cars, both of which sat idle in the garage, polished, vacuumed, gas tanks full, awaiting their owners' next excursion.

As Nora sat perched at the edge of the bed, I couldn't help noticing that she was still a pretty woman despite her age. She was fair-haired and petite with fine facial features and smooth skin that belied her age. Her appearance was only marred by thick eyeglasses that bulged out of frames much too big for her delicate face. The resulting effect was one of comical sadness.

Her daughter, larger, and somewhat overweight, bore only slight traces of former beauty by comparison. Two inches of silver-white roots disturbed a head of otherwise caramel-colored hair. She wore a rumpled blue windbreaker over a coffee-stained T-shirt, bearing testimony to either a general lack of care in her appearance, or a hurried departure from her home state.

After everyone had found a place to sit or stand, Dr. Simon asked Uncle Sal to close the door. The doctor towered over all of us both literally and figuratively. He was a man with a commanding physical presence whose tone of voice and mannerisms made it clear he would not put up with any foolishness. He launched directly into his speech.

"Mr. DiAngeli has had a serious stroke. His brain hemorrhaged in three places but we were able to get the bleeding stopped. The loss of speech and paralysis of his right side are a result of the swelling of the brain.

There is still a lot of blood floating around in there that will be absorbed over time. It is still too early to tell what the extent of permanent damage may be. We will be able to make a more definitive assessment after the swelling goes down and excess fluid reduction takes place. If you have any questions, I will try to answer them at this time."

Uncle Sal spoke in earnest. "What are his chances of coming out of this?" he asked.

"With the progress he has shown so far, which is slight but evident nonetheless, there is, as of now, no reason to believe he won't recover. The next ten days will be critical as the swelling continues to reduce and we are able to assess the damage."

The doctor's words sent an almost audible relief through the small crowd. Pasquale's siblings relaxed visibly at the news.

"But will he ever be the same?" Nora's question had the tone of a whining child.

"Exactly as he was, probably not," the doctor responded. "But he could regain as much as ninety percent of physical and mental capacity. Again, it's way too soon to tell."

Julie stepped forward next. She clasped her hands and carefully chose her words.

"I love Pasquale ..."

Her words were met with groans and unkind muttering from Pasquale's disbelieving siblings.

"But he has a living will," Julie continued meekly.

"We aren't at the point yet," the doctor quickly interjected with an angry tone, "where that comes into play." That shut her up, for the time being.

After a moment of silence, Nora spoke up again.

"Well, what do you think we should do?" she asked the doctor. "Is he going to get better?"

"*Yes*," the doctor stated impatiently. "I *said* he is *recovering*. And as long as that's the case, I think we should help him. But as his wife, the decision is up to you."

That was the crux of the issue. It did not matter that Pasquale had, to that point, put forth a valiant effort toward recovery in the face of massive internal injury. Nor did it matter that his comprehensive ability remained intact as evidenced by the doctor's testing moments before. Pasquale's fate, unfair as it seemed, lay in the hands of his wife.

That day, all of us received a shocking lesson in the fundamentals of spousal rights, living wills, durable power of attorney documents, and their collective potential to wreak havoc to the utter detriment of the very people such documents were meant to protect.

Dr. Simon continued to glare at Nora. His facial expression practically dared her to oppose him as he awaited her response. She had to have felt the weight of the tension in the room; had to have felt ten pairs of eyes boring into her with the attending physician himself challenging her.

Again, she cast her eyes to the floor as if the answer had fallen there and if she stared long enough she might be able to find it. The family silently stared at her in turn, occasionally sneaking sideways glances at each other. Finally, Nora broke the spell as she voiced her decision.

"You're the doctor," she said with resignation. "We'll do whatever you think is best."

◻◻◻

While Pasquale's family breathed a collective sigh of relief, a look of angry defeat spread across Julie's face. She tightened her jaw muscles and silently stared at nothing across the room. In contrast, the doctor's expression visibly relaxed.

"Good!" he said enthusiastically. "That's the right thing to do! We'll reconnect his intravenous line and give him all the help we can."

With the matter finally put-to-bed, the doctor strode across the room toward the door, stopping momentarily in response to Uncle Sal's parting words.

"He's going to make it!" Uncle Sal proclaimed. "You watch and see. He's tough!"

For the first time, the faint glimmer of a smile lit the doctor's face as he replied, "I know he is. I *know* him."

The doctor resumed his hurried pace, shouting orders to the nurses as he marched the short distance down the corridor to Pasquale's room. A flurry of activity occurred as nurses rushed into his room behind the doctor to reconnect Pasquale's lifeline and record his vital signs.

At the sound of the proverbial bell signaling the end of round one, the stepfamily had been defeated, but Julie was not finished yet. Before everyone had managed to file out of the room, she opened her mouth once more. The sound of her monotone voice brought everyone to a standstill. Uncle Sal turned away from the doorway, crossed his arms, and glared at her. Julie remained seated on the bed next to her mother.

"You may not like this ..." she announced as she looked off toward the window, avoiding the accusing eyes of Pasquale's siblings. She clasped her hands together prayer-like, and then bounced her fingertips against her lips.

"But," she continued, "as soon as he's able to be moved I'm taking him to Virginia."

The dropping of a pin would have echoed like a cannonball in the silence that followed. Panic-stricken glances were exchanged by Pasquale's sisters as Sal stared at Julie with narrowing eyes.

While I observed the supplicant motion of Julie's hands, I recalled the steeple theory lesson taught to me by a mentor in the corporate world. During my climb up the corporate ladder a decade prior, I did a two-year stint as a traveling auditor for a bank holding company. Our audit team was fortunate to have an accomplished public auditor, Stan Larsen, as our superior. Stan believed in giving his staff the edge using a training program that was considered somewhat avant-garde for the 1980s. We were taught not only traditional audit functions, such as how to look for discrepancies that might indicate theft, but we were also required to take a short course on interrogation technique and body language. Lessons in the relatively new art of interpreting handwriting were thrown in for good measure.

During one of Stan's field trips to Pennsylvania, he and I enjoyed a relaxing dinner together after some rather intense auditing of the books at one of the company's branch offices. We talked shop and got into a lively discussion about yet another training session Stan was putting together for the team. During his discourse, we had done away with salads and entrees and as the waiter replaced our dinner plates with dessert, Stan leaned forward, conspiratorially, across the table from me.

"Have you ever heard of the steeple theory?" he asked.

I hadn't, I admitted, and encouraged him to tell me more.

"I'm sure you've seen someone do this at some time or other," he said as he laid down his spoon then clasped his hands together in supplication, temporarily ignoring the melting chocolate ice cream in front of him.

"Sure!" I enthusiastically responded.

Laying my fork aside, I imitated him with my own hands while reciting an old nursery rhyme.

"Here's the church and there's the steeple."

Then, lacing my fingers together and turning my palms outward I wriggled my fingers and finished the rhyme, "Open the door and there's the people!"

"Cute." Stan shook his head smiling gratuitously. "But, no. The steeple theory basically says that when someone places their hands together like this during conversation, they are attempting to convey their superiority to you. Or, at least, they would like you to *think* that they are superior, which will hopefully cause you to back down from whatever stance you are taking."

"Really?" I interjected with raised eyebrows.

"Yeah, but the interesting part is that it's just a cover ... a facade to mask their insecurity." The cheesecake laden fork stopped midway to my mouth. I gazed at him intently, willing him to go on; I was hooked.

"That kind of knowledge can come in handy if you're interviewing an employee suspected of stealing," he told me. "You see, if someone is feeling insecure, then we have to ask ourselves, why? The why could be because that person is simply nervous by nature, but more often than not, they're hiding something. The insecurity stems from fear of discovery; the steeple is erected in an attempt to pull the interrogator off track."

That was my introduction to the fine art of people watching, and that knowledge, given to me years before, gave me insight that day in the hospital. What else was up Julie's sleeve? If we continued to peel away the layers of deception, what else would we find?

Game on, Julie baby, I silently declared as I watched her that afternoon in the hospital room. But Uncle Sal wasn't through with her yet.

"How are you going to take him to Virginia, Julie?" Uncle Sal demanded. "In a box?"

Uncle Sal, incredulous at her latest insult, lashed out in anger. Up to that point, he had been content to grumble to his siblings about Julie's treatment of Pasquale but he would not confront her or her mother directly. Nora's dressing down by Dr. Simon minutes before gave Uncle Sal a newfound courage and he wasn't about to waste any more time dancing around Julie and her mother.

Upon hearing Uncle Sal's challenge, Julie's steeple collapsed into her lap.

I continued to watch her, looking for additional clues in her body language.

Then, in a desperate, emotional plea, my mother suddenly exclaimed, "We don't care! All we are asking is that you give him a chance to live!" she cried.

That is all she really wanted. It was all any of them wanted, for that matter. As the youngest of Pasquale's siblings, my mother was not emotionally prepared to lose any of them and she simply wanted her big brother alive and well.

However, once again, wisdom moved aside and gave way to her volatile emotions. She failed to realize that attempts to gain ground by pacifying the enemy are always futile and often counter-productive. One does not accept the enemy's terms without imposing a few terms of one's own or there will be hell to pay later. As the tension in Julie's shoulders relaxed, it became clear to me that she viewed my mother's words as nothing less than concurrence. None of us knew then that we would come to regret my mother's rash outburst much too soon.

Within minutes of our conference with the doctor, the nurses had finished the task of reconnecting intravenous lines and getting life-sustaining fluids coursing back into Pasquale's body. Afterward, his brother and sisters boldly filed into Pasquale's room, surrounded his bed, and smiled down at him in relief.

"You're going to be okay now," Uncle Sal told him.

Then, as he bent over the bed and leaned closer to Pasquale's face, he shook his finger at him, admonishing Pasquale like a child.

"You did a dumb thing putting them in charge," Sal told his brother. "But we got you hooked up again. You hear me? You're going to be all right."

Nora had hung back in the doorway while the others gathered around Pasquale's bed. Upon hearing Sal's remark, blotches of a deep rose color began to bloom on her cheeks. Visibly upset over the family's victory and Sal's condemnation, she stormed out of Pasquale's room. I followed her.

"Nora, what's the matter?" I gently queried.

To my surprise, she blurted out in fury, "All I want is to bury my husband the Catholic way then get the hell out of this damn town!"

I was stunned. The woman standing before me was not the placid, loving wife I remembered. Was dementia to blame for her sudden transformation or had she been brainwashed by Julie into thinking Pasquale would never recover?

Nora's outburst chilled my blood. Goosebumps coursed up my arms as her words registered in my brain. I simply could not allow myself to believe that this woman, a woman who had loved and lived with my uncle for almost twenty years, truly wanted to see him lying cold in a grave. It was unthinkable. Unfortunately, we would witness Nora's Jekyll-to-Hyde transformations many more times in the days that followed.

Had Nora and her daughter been successful in keeping my uncle from receiving life-sustaining fluids another few days, he most certainly would have died an unkind death of simple starvation. Still, I was convinced that we were dealing with a sick woman who had the mind of a frightened child and was, therefore, not responsible for her words or actions. I bit my lip, took her arm and attempted to reason with her.

"Nora," I said softly, "he isn't ready to be buried yet. You heard the doctor, he's getting better. Don't you *want* him well again? He just needs more time."

Her hands flew to her cheeks to catch the tears and as I dropped my hand from her arm, she turned and walked away.

Nora's hasty departure did not go unnoticed by Uncle Sal, who looked on anxiously as Nora walked away in tears. He returned to Pasquale's room and turned to the nurse standing next to Pasquale's bed recording his vital signs.

"Do you think we're doing the right thing?" Uncle Sal asked her.

"Absolutely!" was her unhesitating reply.

Pasquale was safely back on the road to recovery. That ended round one in the bout between Pasquale's siblings and the stepfamily. The only person missing from the scene that day was Julie's husband, Dan. As soon as his absence registered in my brain, I couldn't help wondering why. The answer would be known soon enough and would lead swiftly to round two.

CHAPTER FOUR

Blood vs. Ink (Round Two)
Monday afternoon, April 5

As soon as we crossed into Virginia, I took the exit ramp for the first rest area. After refueling my SUV and getting coffee and burgers to eat on the road, Ben and I resumed the chase south on the interstate. Ben took the wheel, steering us cautiously through multiple lanes of heavy traffic. He was a competent driver and I felt secure with him at the wheel but I was growing impatient with our slow progress. I am the type of person who feels the need to be in control of the situation or at least actively participating. I'm just plain rotten at being the passenger, but my arms needed a rest after fighting the wheel through the wind and I knew I needed to exhale and calm my nerves.

I turned on the radio for the first time since we left Pennsylvania and tuned into a station playing soft rock as I tried to tune out the voice in my brain that kept yelling, *time—we're running out of time!* Two hours later Ben exited at what would be our last rest stop. While I headed for the restroom, Ben called Jonas Maxwell for directions to his office. I took the wheel again for the final leg of the journey while Ben took charge of the map and kept an eye on the exit numbers.

As I drove, Ben took in the sights and kept up a running commentary that was interspersed with the type of comedic remarks I remembered hearing from him while playing games in grandpa's backyard decades earlier. It was fun traveling with him and his antics served to alleviate some of my stress.

The trip had given us the opportunity to become reacquainted after years of being immersed in our separate lives in different cities hundreds of miles apart.

"You have a little trouble sitting still, too, don't you?" I asked him with a grin.

"Yeah, I guess I take after my dad. He could never sit still either," Ben laughed. "Even when he got too old to do much, I'd go looking for him and he'd be out in the garage putzing around, lifting things he shouldn't have been lifting, doing things he wasn't supposed to do. But, you couldn't keep him down. I'd yell at him and he'd just laugh."

Most of the children in our family had remained relatively close to our hometown as adults, but eventually, some of us scattered across the state then into other states to pursue college and careers or to follow a spouse. Ben's sister was the first to move away, venturing to upstate New York to attend college. My brother was next, taking his wife and child to Florida in search of better job opportunities. Then another cousin moved across the state to attend a school for the arts in southeastern Pennsylvania. I was next since my climb up the corporate ladder required a transfer to another state. Younger cousins followed suit as they grew up over the years.

We were a happy, carefree bunch of kids when we were growing up and I know that all of us cherish our memories of Sunday afternoons spent having dinner at our grandparents' home and playing games in the backyard afterward. I had just turned thirty-four the month prior to our journey; Ben was only six years older. Memories of our childhood came rushing back as I watched Ben out of the corner of my eye while I drove. It was uncanny, but every time he smiled, I could still see the twelve-year-old boy who frolicked across the screen on the old reel-to-reel silent movies my father recorded during our childhood years. Ben's walking stride was exactly like his father's, and he even wore a jeff cap like the one his father used to wear.

◘◘◘

I was the third of five children, coming in behind two boys, to bless my parents' household. Between the brothers I emulated and a host of mostly male cousins who played rough, energetic, outdoor games as children then turned their time and energy to stock car racing and demolition derbies as young adults, what else could I be but a tomboy? On my hands and knees in the dirt alongside my brothers, I preferred their toy tanks and army figurines to my plastic dolls. Like an eager puppy, I followed them on daily adventures through the forest near our home. We strolled down wooded trails and swung on the thick vines that hung from tall, sturdy oak trees yelling *Tarzaaaaan!* We marched single file atop weathered stone walls and stood barefoot in a shallow, slow-moving stream to catch crayfish and salamanders.

Such were the experiences that molded me. Mother's influence made certain I was cleaned up and stuffed into frilly dresses for church on Sunday but scuffed knees, a bandaged elbow and, periodically, stitches often ruined the effect.

No one should have been surprised that when it came time to purchase my first car I wanted nothing to do with the modest, more practical sedans befitting a young lady. I wanted a muscle car, the Ford Mustang. One look at the little red coupe with a white vinyl roof, chrome wheels, chrome ponies on the sides and a 302 engine and I was hooked. That little car became my pride and joy and it took me everywhere (and in near record time!).

I quickly became a confident driver. Perhaps a little overconfident, as I sometimes ended up with the wheels stuck in a snowdrift in the dead of winter or in several inches of mud during the rainy season. Luck was usually on my side, however, when it came to avoiding traffic citations. I could often sense a radar trap ahead in sufficient time to avoid being ticketed.

As I grew older, my taste in cars steadily progressed toward larger, more practical four-wheel drive models but the natural inclination toward speed, driving not only for pleasure but to get there, remained. It was that part of my nature that prompted my younger brother's warning before Ben and I left Pennsylvania,

"Be careful," he warned. "And no speeding!"

"Don't worry, little brother," I laughingly assured him. "If God thinks I'm going too fast he'll stop me."

Stop me he did in the guise of a Virginia State Trooper. I batted my green eyes and started in on the family emergency story, but the cop didn't seem to be interested so I finally stopped and simply said, "May I please have the ticket? There's somewhere I need to be by five o'clock."

The man glared at me from under the brim of his official-looking hat, snapped the ticket off the pad, and handed it to me.

"No sense of humor," I complained to Ben after the man walked away.

While I rolled up the window, Ben cautioned, "Better take it easy. Those things aren't cheap."

"Yeah, yeah, I'll take it easy. No more than seventy-five for the rest of the trip!"

I tossed the citation on the small shelf on the dashboard while easing the car off the berm and back into traffic. Ben promptly retrieved the citation and read it front to back.

"It doesn't say how much the fine is. I'll bet it's going to be expensive," he surmised.

"It doesn't matter," I replied. "Whatever it is, Uncle Pasquale is worth it."

Ben put the citation back on the shelf, turned on the radio, and eventually found an oldies station. The familiar tunes helped to lighten our mood and put smiles on our faces as we sang the verses we knew. The radio and childhood memories would keep us company the rest of the way to Norfolk; however, it was not long before my thoughts drifted back over the events that had brought us to that point.

After the family's initial confrontation with Nora and Julie back in February, I remained in town for several days, spending hours each day at Uncle Pasquale's bedside along with my parents, aunts, uncles, and cousins. There never seemed to be less than half a dozen of us in his room at any given time. Uncle Pasquale was unable to communicate verbally, but he was well aware of the comings and goings in his hospital room and he responded with tears and pleading eyes when a family member entered or exited. We did our best to reassure him that he was making progress and that he just needed to try to remain calm while his body healed from the trauma.

Pasquale's general physician, Dr. Barton, was on vacation at the time Pasquale was taken to the emergency room. When he returned to his practice the following Monday, he received word from the hospital that Pasquale had been admitted. On Tuesday morning, he walked into the hospital room.

Uncle Sal sat in a chair on one side of Pasquale's bed. Nora was seated on the opposite side of the bed, her attitude one that indicated a half-contrived truce. Julie and her husband were nowhere in sight. Dr. Barton nodded to everyone as he entered, then removed the medical charts hanging at the foot of Pasquale's bed and looked them over. He already knew that Julie had attempted to enforce Pasquale's living will once and he did not hesitate to exert his authority and express his displeasure over her actions.

"Pasquale is my patient," he said to Nora dryly. "And I do not believe in euthanasia."

That was one more point scored for Pasquale's recovery. His siblings grinned.

The more time we spent at Pasquale's bedside, the more impatient we became with Nora's whining and negative comments and, ironically enough, her daughter's sudden lack of verbal communication when she showed up at all. It was a waiting game and neither Nora nor Julie was playing it very well. I had to keep reminding myself that Nora too was ill, both physically and mentally, and therefore deserved to be treated gently.

Julie, however, was another matter altogether. At times, she took up a sentry-like position in Pasquale's room, rarely making eye contact or speaking with members of our family as they came and went. Her countenance fluctuated between indifference and disgust as she silently challenged any of us to be cheerful in her presence. Much to her chagrin, we remained undeterred and maintained a steadfast, happy-faced presence, chatting amiably all the while, in an effort to rally Pasquale's spirits.

Knowing that my uncle was making progress, I decided mid-week that it was time to head back across the state to tend to my own business and the unfinished job of settling into my new home. The evening before my departure, I felt the urge to visit Uncle Pasquale one more time. Though I had already seen him that morning, I found myself once again driving toward the city and I arrived at the hospital shortly before 6 p.m. As I navigated the hospital corridors, the relative peace and quiet impressed me. It was a change from the hustle and bustle of a small army of nurses, doctors, and visitors that seemed to overwhelm the place earlier in the day. The floors gleamed in the absence of foot traffic; soft lights cast a warm glow down the corridors.

As I neared Uncle Pasquale's room, I noticed the lights near his bed had been dimmed for the evening and he was alone for a change. *Good*, I thought as I pulled a chair to the side of his bed and touched his arm. I smiled down at his questioning gaze, determined to fill his ears with positive reinforcement. He was calm and appeared to listen attentively, which made me happy that I had followed the urge to drive back to the hospital.

It was not long, however, before I saw, from my vantage point facing the door, Nora and her daughter as they walked toward Pasquale's room from the opposite end of the hallway. As soon as they saw me, Julie took her mother's arm and quickened her pace as if she were afraid they might be missing something important. Much as I hated to admit it, Nora and her daughter were fast becoming the enemy, a role they themselves seemed to have chosen when they made the almost fatal error of attempting to accelerate my uncle's demise instead of rallying for his recovery alongside the rest of his family.

From the day Dr. Simon briefed the family then ordered the IV tubes be reconnected, Julie had grown oddly silent. Her demeanor took on that of a rear guard and she rarely left my uncle's room when another family member was present, especially if Nora was not present. When we attempted, out of politeness, to include her in our conversations, her responses were curt and vague if she responded at all. More often than not, she simply sat there at her self-appointed post with her dark, beady eyes darting here, there, and nowhere.

Years ago, I remember reading a bit of rather humorous advice regarding one's behavior in the presence of an enemy. *Smile, for a smile makes an enemy wonder what you are up to.* I was still attempting to determine if Julie or Nora (or both of them) wanted my uncle dead and if so, why. Until I discovered the answers—all of the answers—I wanted to be sure to remain outwardly congenial to keep them off balance as much as possible.

That evening, as Nora and Julie entered Pasquale's room, I greeted them with a disarming smile and cheerful tone that rankled Julie to no end judging from her body language and surly facial expression.

"Hi! Did you go out for dinner?" I asked them cheerfully.

"We just went home for a bit," Nora wearily replied.

No response from Julie. I rose from my chair and offered it to Nora. She declined saying that she had been sitting all day and preferred to stand.

"He can't understand you, you know," she glumly advised me. "He isn't getting any better."

She was whining again and I had decided I'd heard enough of it. Vowing to be more firm with her I immediately countered her negativity.

"Yes, he is," I told her, gritting my teeth to keep from screaming the words.

"And *yes*, he *does* understand what is being said. He needs our reassurance, Nora. He doesn't need to hear that he isn't getting well."

Then I bravely ventured forward to challenge her.

"Don't you *want* him to get well?" I asked.

A look of mild shock co-mingled with guilt stole over her face.

"Well, of course I do," she defended. "But I don't see how he can."

"He *can* because he's *strong*," I confidently told her. "You *know* he's always been a strong man and that strength will pull him through. You just hold on to that thought."

Finally, it appeared my words had reached deep inside her troubled mind and perhaps given her a glimmer of hope. It was a battle, and I had no doubt that Julie took every opportunity to counter any optimism as soon as she had her mother alone. After that, Nora settled onto a chair on the opposite side of Pasquale's bed and combed his hair while we engaged in small talk. The Nora I remembered seemed to be tentatively peeking out from the haze and it gave me hope that she would rally to the cause yet, in spite of her daughter.

Pasquale had closed his eyes after they walked in and appeared to be sleeping.

An hour ticked away until, shortly after 7 p.m., Nora announced that she was tired and wanted to go home. Julie spoke for the first time that evening.

"No, I think we'll stay for a while yet," she said.

Whether it was the sideways glance Julie sent in my direction, the tone in her voice, or the stone cold expression on her face, I was certain that she did not want to leave until I did. Why? Why would she insist that her mother, frail and tired as she was, remain there when the unfortunate woman clearly needed rest? I decided to play it out to see if my hunch was correct so I stayed put and amiably rambled on about anything and nothing.

At 7:30 p.m., Nora again pleaded with her daughter.

"Come *on*. Let's go!" Nora insisted.

Julie again glanced at me, wordless, but made no move to rise from her chair. Finally, my own sense of compassion for Nora won out and I calmly addressed Julie.

"Your mom needs her rest too," I quietly conceded.

I rose from my seat, collected my jacket then took Nora's arm.

"Come, I'll walk out with you."

Those appeared to be the magic words as Julie wasted no time rising from her own chair. It seemed odd then that she was not in step with us as Nora and I had exited the room and started down the corridor. Sensing her absence not far from Pasquale's room, Nora was the first to stop and turn around.

"*Now* where is she?" Nora's irritability was evident in her tone.

We turned to look back in time to see Julie standing at Uncle Pasquale's bedside, her large frame blocking the upper half of him as he lay there. Julie's back was toward us as she stood there saying something inaudible to Pasquale. Her hands were not visible from our viewpoint but her arms moved with sporadic jerks indicating ... what? Animated speech? Was she attempting to smother him? What was she doing? Again, the red flag went up and a chill ran through me.

I wanted to run back in there and see what she was doing, see if those hands of hers were attempting to cut off his life support and hear the lies I was certain she was telling him. Instead, I stood there, frozen, forcing myself not to react to the alarm that was going off inside my head.

"*Come on*, Julie. I want to go *home*!" Nora again pleaded.

Finally, Julie turned and walked hurriedly out of Uncle Pasquale's room. That one was beginning to give me the creeps.

As the three of us exited to street level, I sent up another silent prayer humbly asking a higher power to send a small squadron of angels to protect my uncle. This was becoming a habit. I sure hoped someone up there was listening!

I drove back to my parent's home that evening with an uneasy feeling. That night, during supper, as I related the events to my parents, my mother reiterated her opinion that Nora and her daughter simply wanted to bury my uncle, collect his fortune, and head South. Part of me still didn't want to believe anyone could be so cold. How could anyone do that to someone they'd been happily married to for almost twenty years? And after all that Pasquale had done for Julie? He treated her like his own daughter.

"Surely, Uncle Pasquale isn't *that* wealthy," I reasoned aloud.

"He has enough," was mother's cryptic reply. "Enough to tempt the likes of them."

For years before he retired, Uncle Pasquale held a coveted position as a white-hat (a boss) in the city steel mill's management ranks. In those days, the steel industry was booming and the money flowed like lava spilling over the slopes of Mount St. Helens. Even young, unskilled laborers, some of whom were my friends, seemed to earn more money than they could reasonably spend. There is little doubt that Uncle Pasquale and his first wife, Angie, could have lived well with just his income, but Aunt Angie wanted a new house in a better part of town. Neither she nor Pasquale believed in buying things on credit, so Aunt Angie held a full-time job as a seamstress in a local clothing factory to help earn her new house. Later, since they had no children to support, no one to send through college, Uncle Pasquale regularly invested a portion of their earnings. I knew this from my conversations with him while I played housekeeper after Aunt Angie's death.

I also knew he was a wise investor, depositing his money in several different types of investment accounts and dabbling in real estate along the way. Like most savvy businessmen, he did not put all of his eggs in one basket. Just how well that wisdom paid off was anyone's guess. Uncle Pasquale was a private man. He never felt the need to boast about his success and good fortune. Besides, it wasn't anyone else's business. At least, not until he had a stroke and we found ourselves fighting against his stepdaughter's death wish.

"Those two aren't aware of just how much I know," my mother informed me in a no-nonsense tone. "Your uncle hasn't been able to drive for quite some time now so I've been driving him to his doctor appointments, to the shopping center, the bank. He's shared a lot with me, including the fact that the widow's pension Nora receives from her first husband's employer is endorsed and mailed directly to Julie every month. If Julie's husband knew he'd probably have a fit that he's been kept in the dark all these years."

I raised my eyebrows at that revelation.

"How nice to be supported by her mother at her age," I declared. "I always wondered how she was able to support herself and a daughter with only a part-time job and a wayward husband."

"Julie claims there's something wrong with her daughter," mother continued. "To hear Julie tell it, her daughter can't be around people and that's why she can't get a job. Yet she went to college, your uncle paid the tuition, and she drives a car and takes herself to the beach every day. Lazy, that's what she is."

"No, I wouldn't call that lazy," I told her. "I'd call that opportunistic. Why work when someone else is perfectly willing to hand you a check every month just for being alive?"

"Smart, that's what Nora thinks her daughter is," Mother harrumphed.

"I don't know how smart that is," I laughed. "Sooner or later the gravy train is going to dry up. Who will support her when her mother is dead?"

Then I remembered the failed pottery shop. Uncle Pasquale had invested his own money to set up the business for Julie years before in an attempt to help her become self-supporting after her divorce from her first husband. Julie set up shop in the wrong part of town, had no marketing skills, and no foot traffic. She promptly went out of business. After that, she tried a career in real estate. That didn't stick either in spite of Uncle Pasquale's efforts to get her off the ground by purchasing a vacation condo in Norfolk. I smiled as I remembered my conversation with him the previous Thanksgiving.

"How's the real estate business?" He asked me amiably.

I told him the market was good and I was doing well, to which he replied, with a tinge of playful sarcasm, "Julie couldn't make a go of it. She tried but just couldn't do it. Well, let me know if you get hungry." Then laughing he added, "I'll mail you a loaf of bread!"

Uncle Pasquale always had a great sense of humor and I missed that inimitable wit and the laughter that followed. The truth is Uncle Pasquale would give a person more than a loaf of bread, much more. Unfair as it seems, it was probably his giving nature that invited the sharks in for the final kill.

My conversation with my mother culminated in words of advice to her.

"If I were you," I cautioned, "I would find a way to see a copy of the power of attorney documents and the living will those two claim to have. Perhaps if you call Uncle Pasquale's attorney and explain the circumstances he'll be able to help."

"I'm just going to wait and see what happens," she replied stubbornly. "As long as they take care of him I'm not going to do anything."

That was my mother's position and when she has set herself firm, it takes an earthquake to move her. Two days later, the earth moved. The waiting-and-seeing part was over. The news came to me in the form of a frantic telephone call from my mother the Friday after I had returned to my own home on the other side of the state.

"You're not going to believe this," she announced, "but they tried to kill him again!" *They*, of course, referred to Nora and Julie. After the first incident when they ordered his feeding tube disconnected, Pasquale's siblings, not trusting Nora and Julie to keep their word, kept a daily vigil taking turns at Uncle Pasquale's bedside. It was Pasquale's sister who arrived at the hospital one morning and discovered that the intravenous line was no longer connected to him. She asked one of the nurses why, in light of the fact that Pasquale was making visible improvement, the IV had once again been removed.

"Because the family requested it," was the nurse's flat response.

The alarm was immediately raised among Pasquale's siblings, who promptly demanded an audience with hospital administration. Late that Friday afternoon, Pasquale's wife and stepdaughter, his brother and his sisters gathered in one of the hospital's conference rooms along with Dr. Simon and two members of the hospital's directorial staff. Dr. Barton, who, we later learned, had reversed his earlier anti-euthanasia stance and apparently had given in to Julie's demands was, oddly enough, absent.

Pasquale's siblings demanded and were shown copies of not one, but two power of attorney documents plus Pasquale's living will.

The first document, dated ten years prior, named not only Nora but also Julie as Pasquale's attorneys-in-fact in the event he became incapacitated. The second document gave Julie and her husband Dan the power to act on Nora's behalf under similar circumstances. It was now obvious that the fact Nora was legally incapacitated by virtue of the dementia that plagued her was a moot point. Julie was named as Pasquale's agent in addition to Nora. Unfortunately, that meant that either of them could act alone.

The living will, also executed by Pasquale the same year as the power of attorney, went to extremes in stating that absolutely no life-sustaining measures were to be given. Not even the administering of antibiotics was permitted, a fact that his siblings thought was just plain foolhardy. Would Pasquale really want to die from an infection that might be eradicated with a course of antibiotics? What had he been thinking? Sal had never heard of anything so ridiculous and he said so to the medical staff.

In any event, the doctors once again sided with Pasquale's brother and sisters, reminding Nora and Julie that the living will could be exercised only under certain circumstances and those circumstances were not yet in evidence. The odds were stacking up, once again, against Nora and Julie. Hospital representatives were clearly in favor of continuing the healing therapy and a heated exchange followed.

It became obvious during the meeting that Julie was the driving force behind the decisions that continued to put my uncle's life in jeopardy, actions that could only be described at that point as malicious. As reported to me afterward by my mother and Uncle Sal, Nora attempted to speak only once during the meeting, but was rudely silenced by Julie.

"Shut up, Mother, and let me handle this!" Julie told her.

After that incident, Nora sat passively throughout the remainder of the proceeding.

In spite of Julie's protests, the administrative staff determined that it was appropriate to continue with Pasquale's life-sustaining IV and, once again, the nurses were ordered to reconnect it. Though it was another victory for Pasquale and his siblings, they felt nothing but the mind-numbing effects of emotional exhaustion as they filed wearily out of the conference room. How much longer would they have to keep doing this? How many more times?

In light of Julie's continued attempts to pull the plug and let Pasquale drift off into oblivion, his neurologist decided that several tests were in order. Over the next few days, Pasquale underwent a brain scan and a noninvasive procedure that would assess the damage, if any, to his digestive organs. Almost two weeks after the stroke Pasquale showed near normal brain activity, all of his vital signs were good, and it was determined that he had sustained no permanent damage to his esophagus. He would, his doctor announced, eventually be able to eat solid food again to sustain his own life. Because the test results were favorable and it appeared Pasquale would recover after all, Dr. Simon was in favor of implanting a PEG tube into Pasquale's navel so that more substantial sustenance than that he was receiving through the intravenous line could be pumped directly into his stomach. Again, Julie refused to allow the procedure and again, Pasquale's siblings went to bat on his behalf.

Uncle Sal flew into action, demanding an audience with the hospital's Ethics Committee. The following afternoon, Pasquale's brother, Sal, his son, Sandy, and my mother, Natalie, faced off against Nora and Julie under the watchful eyes of the committee. Of Pasquale's attending physicians, only Dr. Simon, the neurologist, was present. The committee, consisting of the hospital's senior resident physician, the director of nursing, and a Catholic priest, would review the living will and Pasquale's medical charts, and recommend a course of action.

The course they ultimately recommended was to continue all methods of therapy: forced feeding through the stomach tube, physical therapy, and speech therapy. Julie held her ground, insisting that Pasquale's living will be honored and that he simply be kept pain-free while being permitted to die.

"Starvation is an ugly way to kill someone," Sandy informed Julie. "And hardly painless!"

The members of the Ethics Committee agreed that to discontinue the feeding tube at that point in his recovery would cause him quite simply to starve to death. It would be an unpleasant and unnecessary end in light of the progress he had made to that point. Unbelievably enough, the ultimate decision yet remained, legally, in Julie's hands by virtue of that blasted power of attorney document Pasquale had signed simultaneously with the living will.

What kind of perverse laws would give someone that kind of power over another's life? I determined that once Uncle Pasquale was out of the woods, I would have to look into it more thoroughly. Could the law truly be such a profound and complete ass, as Charles Dickens had written more than a hundred years earlier? And could we somehow wrest that power away from Julie legally?

The senior resident physician advised Julie, "We need a decision and it needs to be made quickly. In another twenty-four hours, he may suffer irreversible muscle damage without vital fluids and nutrients getting into his body." Julie said she would think about it and give her answer the next day, to which the doctor curtly replied, "Tomorrow will be too late."

The doctor then appealed to Nora. "Do you want your husband to live?" he asked her.

"Well, of course I do!" Nora immediately replied.

"Just shut up, Mother," Julie threatened. "You don't know what you're saying!"

Heart-rending pleas from Pasquale's brothers and sisters fell on deaf ears. At one point, according to my mother, Uncle Sal actually got down on one knee, folded his hands in supplication and pleaded.

"Julie, *please*, take your mother, take everything. But *please*, let my brother live!"

"I'll give you an answer tomorrow," was her cold reply.

Pasquale's brothers and sisters were not about to wait until tomorrow. Immediately after the meeting, they flew into frantic, misguided action like frightened mice trying to find their way through a maze. Completely bewildered and not knowing where to turn, they first called Uncle Pasquale's general attorney asking for his assistance. That turned out to be a mistake, as the attorney was then acting as advisor to Nora and her daughter. He gave Uncle Sal some advice all right, but it was the kind of advice meant to deter him from interfering with his current client's wishes. The gist of his advice was that they could take Nora and Julie to court for abuse of a power of attorney but, *in his professional opinion*, that action would be extremely costly and, in the end, unsuccessful.

Once more, fate stepped in. When Sal phoned his sister to tell her what was happening at the hospital, she told him that her son had a friend who was a lawyer. The lawyer was contacted and he agreed to try and help the family. His first action was to telephone the hospital's administrator and Dr. Barton, Pasquale's attending physician, who seemed to have disappeared from the scene.

For a modest fee, the attorney voiced the appropriate threats, managed to coerce hospital personnel into performing the stomach tube procedure, sans Julie's approval, then pronounced his job complete saying regretfully, "There's nothing more I can do."

I, on the other hand, was absolutely certain that something else could and should be done, legally, to put an end to the insanity once and for all. It was not as if Uncle Pasquale was in a coma. He was able to signal yes or no, he responded to the doctor's commands to move the various parts of his body. In fact, when asked to move his right arm, Pasquale reached over with his functioning left arm and picked up the right arm that refused to budge on its own. So why, I wondered, could those signals not be used to allow him to express his own wishes and revoke the current power of attorney?

There were no immediate answers and with yet another life-threatening crisis averted, Pasquale's siblings fell into a state of unsettled acceptance once more. By that time, Pasquale had regained movement in his right leg but his right hand and arm remained paralyzed. A physical therapist came into the picture at that point and placed a brace on Pasquale's right arm for support. Julie promptly removed it and informed the therapist that there would be no physical therapy.

"He is only to be kept comfortable," she ordered.

Pasquale had no patience for infirmity and his frustration over his physical circumstances had taken a toll emotionally. Though he tried desperately to communicate, the most he could manage was a series of garbled grunts and groans. He was yet unable to form words clearly and so he had settled into a mode of dismal acceptance whereby he would sometimes use hand signals to communicate yes and no, but mostly he simply waved away a question or remark in disgust knowing that he could not communicate his response.

Pasquale's speech therapist assured his family that he would indeed speak again as soon as he got mad enough to do so. With that encouraging prognosis, Pasquale's brothers and sisters waited hopefully.

After Pasquale's lifeline was back in place for the second time, it appeared, on the surface at least, that Pasquale's physicians were back in the driver's seat and doing everything medically possible to aid in his recovery.

In the days that followed, much to everyone's surprise, Nora even apologized to Pasquale's brothers and sisters. They graciously accepted though a hint of mistrust lingered. Pasquale's siblings continued their daily hospital vigils, in telephone-coordinated shifts, so that any further threats by the stepfamily could be immediately dealt with. The once dire need to find another attorney to represent the family for Pasquale's sake was all but forgotten by his siblings. As the days then weeks wore on, family and stepfamily maneuvered around each other under a symbolic truce so that neither side had to spend more than a few polite moments in the other's company.

Finally, Pasquale's paralyzed arm was beginning to show signs of movement. He attempted to speak but his tongue appeared to be frozen so that the resulting sounds were a sort of gibberish that would not be recognized as human speech anywhere on the planet. In his frustration, he either cried or became angry and sullen when he could not make himself understood. It was probably a good thing his right arm was still useless at that point as I am certain he would have used it to hurl bedpans, bottles, and anything within reach across the room. Uncle Pasquale was a proud, self-sufficient man. To his way of thinking, dependence and incapacitation were the ultimate insult.

Nevertheless, in the days that followed, Pasquale was making remarkable progress. He had earned a downgrade from his former critical status, resulting in his being moved out of the critical care ward and into a semi-private room where physical therapists and speech therapists began more intense sessions with him. The turn of events was greeted with yet another sigh of relief and congratulatory pats on his back from his siblings.

Coincidently, on the morning of Pasquale's first scheduled physical therapy session, Natalie and Sal arrived at the door to Pasquale's room while the session was in progress. Nora sat sullenly in a chair near the window; Julie was visibly absent. In stark contrast to her recent attempts at reconciliation, Nora did not return familial greetings. Observing the change in Nora's behavior and thinking it meant bad news from the doctors, Natalie addressed her with concern.

"Nora, is anything wrong? Are you all right?" she asked anxiously.

Nora stormed out of the room without a word while Pasquale's siblings exchanged confused glances. As my mother told me by phone later that evening, she followed Nora out into the hallway and demanded to know what the matter was.

"Why did you come now?" Nora challenged her. Red-faced with anger she continued her accusing tirade. "You only came because the physical therapy started today. You're just checking up on us!" Nora accused.

"Don't be silly." My mother attempted to defuse the situation. "We didn't know they were starting today." Then, becoming indignant at the insinuation, she let Nora have it.

"And anyway, how *would* we know, Nora? None of the nurses are allowed to talk to us because your daughter told them not to!"

Gesturing toward the therapist, Nora continued, "Well, I don't want them doing that to him. They were just supposed to keep him comfortable and now all of this is going on."

My mother narrowed her eyes, took a threatening step toward Nora and waived an accusing finger in her face.

"You really *don't* want him to get better, do you?" my mother was incensed. Fire blazed in her eyes as she decided she'd heard enough. "After the way he always took care of you this is how you repay him? I can't believe my ears!"

But Nora had already been distracted from the confrontation by the clanging of dishes coming from down the hall.

"Look!" she exclaimed. Then, taking my mother's arm amiably she announced, "They're serving lunch! Let's go get a bite to eat."

Good-bye Mrs. Hyde, hello Dr. Jekyll.

Such was the way with Nora's mind in those days. One minute she was raving mad, leveling unfounded accusations at everyone in sight and in the blink of an eye, the docile, congenial woman who loved my uncle, the Nora we all knew was in there somewhere, suddenly reemerged.

My mother had relayed all of this to me by telephone that evening. After mulling it over for a couple of days I decided it was time for another visit. I telephoned my mother and told her I would drive across the state on the coming Friday morning and spend another long weekend.

Friday had finally arrived after a hectic week at my real estate office. When one is engaged in the real estate business, one's time is rarely one's own. The general public never sees the behind-the-scenes details—countless telephone calls, an overwhelming amount of research, and endless paperwork. I know the general consensus is that real estate agents have the life of Riley—getting paid the big bucks to show someone through a few houses. If it were only that simple!

Between showings, listings, creating marketing ads, making phone calls, research, and paperwork, a realtor's work day often equates to ten-hour weekdays plus weekends. And this is after logging many miles and hours with a client to find exactly the right home for them, then negotiating exactly the right terms, helping them through the mortgage process, making sure they do not miss their contract deadlines for home inspections, delivering their insurance and mortgage commitment on time to the title company handling the settlement. Many of us have no personal life as a result, but we continue to do what we do simply because we love the business.

Though the ongoing crisis had created additional stress that no one in the family needed, including me, I relished the idea of having an excuse to get away from job pressures for a few days, so I set myself to the task of packing. As I made one trip from the house to the car, arms laden, then another, I marveled at the fact that it always seemed to take more time to pack necessities for my German Shepherd, Jette, than to pack my own overnight case. We never went on a trip together without her bedding, doggy first-aid kit, doggy toys, towels, brush, vitamins, treats, food, food and water dishes. While I checked each item off the list, Jette danced at my feet, eager to get out the door and on our way.

Finally satisfied that nothing important was being left behind, I opened the car door, inviting her to hop in, and we headed off down the road toward the turnpike with her beautiful head poking out of the rear window to catch the scents on the breeze. In spite of her illness, she still traveled well and always looked forward to a ride in the car. Hours later, in my parent's driveway, the process was repeated in reverse as first Jette's creature comforts, then mine, went from car to house.

During dinner that evening, my mother brought me up to date on the most recent antics of Pasquale's stepfamily. My cousin, Seth, happened to see Pasquale's car parked at a small used car lot in town that week, sans license plate. The Cadillac sedan was unmistakably Pasquale's as it bore a digital combination lock on the driver's door, next to which his initials were prominently displayed in gold and black letters. The conclusion was that the car had been taken there by Julie's husband to be sold. The mystery of what Dan was doing when he didn't show up at the hospital was solved.

Pasquale was not frivolous with cash and he did not take such high-ticket purchases lightly. He bought the best he could afford, paid cash, was meticulous in caring for his possessions, and he held on to them for many years. By the time he landed in the hospital, the car was already nine years old but still in pristine condition with less than fifty thousand miles on it. And the title, of course, was free and clear of any financial encumbrances. In other words, it was ripe for Julie's cherry-picking expedition. It riled Pasquale's siblings to no end that Julie would have the audacity to dispose of one of Pasquale's favorite possessions without seeking his approval.

When the opportunity presented itself during her next visit to the hospital, Aunt Eleanor mentioned to Julie that Seth had seen Pasquale's car on the used car lot. Julie explained it away by saying that the car was in the shop for minor repairs and state inspection.

Suspecting that was a lie, Aunt Eleanor conveyed the information to Seth, who promptly paid another visit to the car lot to speak to the dealer himself. Seth learned not only that the car had been taken there with the intention of selling it, but also that it had been promised to a buyer just the day before. The dealer also told Seth that Nora's son-in-law, Dan, had handled the transaction. Seth enlightened the dealer about the circumstances that resulted in the car being brought to his lot and the fact that Dan had no legal authority to act on Pasquale's behalf. The dealer, Seth told his mother, appeared disturbed by the tale.

The information raised eyebrows among Pasquale's siblings as well. By that time they had seen the power of attorney documents for themselves and knew that Dan had no business posing as Pasquale's agent. At that point, Pasquale's family couldn't help wondering what else was being "liquidated" at home while Pasquale lay in the hospital.

I tried to smooth my mother's ruffled feathers and reasoned with her that Uncle Pasquale had not been able to drive the car himself for months prior to his stroke. He would probably never drive it again so if his stepfamily decided to sell it rather than pay for the upkeep, so what? It was, after all, just a car.

However, she insisted that Julie and her cohorts were up to something more and she was afraid that other possessions would soon begin to disappear.

"I don't care if Nora sells her own stuff," she huffed. "As a matter of fact, I wouldn't care if she took everything that belonged to her and went down South with her daughter. Just as long as she leaves my brother alone; that's all I care about."

It was a small consolation to anyone that the used car dealer, upon hearing the details of Pasquale's circumstances from Seth, promptly drove the car back to Pasquale's house, turned over the keys and title to Julie and Dan, and demanded his money back. Months later, we would learn that Dan simply *purchased* the car himself and Julie, acting as Pasquale's agent under the power of attorney, transferred the title into Dan's name. It was the first in a string of Pasquale and Nora's assets that would be liquidated or otherwise disappear in the weeks to come.

However unfortunate, the fact was that as long as Pasquale lay in a hospital bed unable to give voice to his own wishes, Julie could pretty much do whatever she wanted under the guise of his attorney-in-fact. And unless his brothers and sisters found a lawyer willing and able to find a way to upset that power, there wasn't anything the family could do but stand aside and watch it happen.

The morning after I arrived back in town, I arose early. I was anxious to see Uncle Pasquale's progress for myself. Aunt Eleanor, her husband, two of her sons, and Uncle Sal were already seated near Pasquale's bed when my parents and I walked into the room. Nora and Julie had not yet arrived and without their gloomy presence hanging over us, we were able to enjoy a light-hearted conversation.

I leaned over Uncle Pasquale's bed and greeted him with a smile and a kiss but received only a shrug in return. That was a good sign, however, as it meant that his lovable, grumpy facade was returning; Pasquale was definitely on the mend.

"He's trying to talk," Aunt Eleanor reported, "but we still can't make out what he's trying to say and it just makes him mad. Maybe you can understand him, Gina."

As I stood beside his bed, he did try to tell me something, quite earnestly, but in vain, as I was no more successful in grasping the words than his sister was and Uncle Pasquale knew he was not getting through to us. While he angrily waved me aside, I looked down at him apologetically, shaking my head in regret and explained to him that his words simply were not coming out coherently even though I was sure he thought they were.

Since he was right-handed, we knew it would be useless to attempt written communication. His right hand, still swollen and immobile, was not yet able to grasp a pen. And, thanks to Julie, that hand was not receiving the attention it needed from a physical therapist.

As I sat there, trying to think of other methods of communication to employ, I suddenly remembered the magnetic alphabet boards my nephews played with when they were toddlers. If I could find one of those at a toy store, I thought, perhaps Uncle Pasquale would be able to manipulate the letters with his left hand and spell out words to get his point across. Later that evening, I found such an apparatus at the local shopping mall and, like a giddy child on Christmas Eve, I could not wait to show it to Uncle Pasquale the next day.

Sunday morning arrived with sunny skies and a slight chill in the air. Winter had not completely released our region of the state from its grasp. I attended a church service with my sister and her children, helped with dinner preparations and the subsequent clean up with anticipation building all the while toward the afternoon drive into the city. After what seemed like an interminable amount of time, we finally made our way to the hospital.

Pasquale was in good humor upon our arrival; he greeted everyone with a smile. Once again, aunts, uncles, and cousins gathered around his bed. And, again, we were miraculously spared the stepfamily's presence. That suited us just fine.

Pulling a chair up to the edge of Pasquale's bed, while his brothers and sisters anxiously looked on, I told him I had something for him. He watched me with a somewhat amused expression as I opened the bag and showed him the magnetic board and box of alphabet letters. But when I began explaining how to use the board and why I brought it to him, his smile quickly turned into a frown. Lines of indignation furrowed his brow as he pursed his lips in a bah-humbug attitude and waved the board aside, taking the wind out of my sails in the process. Pasquale was a proud man and this, this toy, was an insult. I should have foreseen it.

Though I was terribly disappointed, as were the others, I graciously tucked it all back inside the bag, telling on-looking family members, "Well, perhaps he just isn't ready for this yet. Maybe we're rushing him."

Then addressing Uncle Pasquale I offered, "I'll just leave it here and maybe we can try again in a few days."

"Maybe he'll talk on his own pretty soon," Aunt Eleanor said, trying to be consoling. "The speech therapist said he'd talk as soon as he got mad enough." Then, looking to my mother for confirmation she added, "Didn't she, Natalie?"

Natalie nodded in agreement, then Seth added wryly, "Well, then he ought to be getting mad enough pretty soon. They already sold his car and who knows what's next."

Just then, a light bulb went off inside my head.

"Does Uncle Pasquale know that?" I asked, glancing from one to the other. "Did anyone tell him?"

"No, we didn't want to upset him," my mother replied.

"He's a grown man, Mother!" I declared in exasperation. "He has a right to know what's going on. Maybe if we all made more of an effort to talk *to* him instead of *about* him he would respond to us."

Uncle Pasquale, seeing the change in my expression, nudged me with a questioning look on his face, obviously wanting to know what was going on but unable to hear clearly enough without his hearing aid. In response to his inquisitive gaze, Mother leaned over Pasquale and began to address him in a child-like tone.

"Come on, honey," she cooed. "Talk to us!"

I rolled my eyes. My mother meant well but that was not exactly what I had in mind and apparently, not what Uncle Pasquale wanted to hear either. He turned his head sideways and gave her a lopsided glare as if she had just sprouted wings and flown across the room.

"Oh for heaven's sake, Mother, he isn't a child!" I admonished her. "We need to talk to him like an adult, not as if he were a baby!"

Growing impatient and even more anxious for Pasquale to speak, I simply hit him with it.

"Uncle Pasquale," I touched his arm to turn his attention back toward me. "Did you know that Julie sold your car?"

Deep lines creased his forehead again as he gestured *huh?* with his chin then cupped his left hand around his ear to signal that he did not hear the question. I repeated it louder and more slowly as I enunciated each word.

"JULIE. SOLD. YOUR. CAR!"

That time it sank in. Pasquale's eyes widened, his mouth fell open, and words immediately tumbled out.

"Ah, damn it!" He cried, pounding his left fist on the bed. "Damn it, *damn* it!"

Tears spilled from Aunt Eleanor's eyes and as her hands flew to her cheeks she exclaimed, "You did it! The therapist said he just had to get mad enough and he did!"

I didn't know whether to laugh or cry. Pasquale's siblings dabbed tears from their eyes while my cousins stood by with grins blossoming on their faces. That was the turning point we had all hoped for and although it was achieved at Pasquale's expense with the delivery of bad news, we were, nonetheless, ecstatic.

"Wait 'til Julie hears this," I told them. "Won't she be surprised!"

Uncle Pasquale tried desperately to say more but the only intelligible words were swear words.

"Nothing like a little soul-cleansing cussing session," I whispered to Seth as he stood there with a satisfied grin on his face. No matter how it came about, and at whose expense, we saw the incident as just one more milestone on the long highway toward recovery.

Our family has a deep abiding faith in a higher power. We may worship in different churches and although some of us, like me, prefer not to report to a church building on Sundays at all, collectively we believe there must be a God that is somehow accessible and, in some inconceivable way, does indeed hear and answer prayers. What else could be responsible for Julie's continual, punishing defeat? Since Pasquale's stroke, family and friends had sent many prayers skyward. That afternoon, we felt we had seen evidence that those prayers were being answered and we held every hope that Pasquale would, eventually, experience a full recovery and banish Julie from his life forever.

In contrast to our unrelenting petitions for healing, Nora had called in a Catholic priest, twice, in the preceding month to give Pasquale the sacrament of Last Rites, a ritual typically performed for those who are visibly dying. It was as if she were just waiting for him to die, even willing it to be so.

We chuckled amongst ourselves as my cousin Seth stated wistfully, "Wouldn't it be great if it backfired and he was completely healed?"

However, it was not a matter of backfiring. No, not at all. According to the Christian religion, the biblical principle of anointing the sick is actually a healing ritual: *Is any one of you sick? He should call the elders of the church to pray over him and anoint him with oil in the name of the Lord. And the prayer offered in faith will make the sick person well; the Lord will raise him up!*

On that afternoon, it appeared to us that Pasquale was indeed rising and we knew Julie would be sorely displeased.

CHAPTER FIVE

Premonition

Monday, March 29

*"For God does speak ... when deep sleep
falls on men as they slumber in their beds ...
and terrify them with warnings."*

–Job 33:14

Startled awake in the dead of night, I fought my way up and out of the depths of sleep to defend myself. I could feel the hands of my attacker pressing into the pillow on either side of my head as they held the edge of my blanket taut across my nose and mouth. Terrified, I lay there struggling against leaden eyelids, gasping for breath. Suddenly, I could see the slender arms and feminine hands of the perpetrator. Why was a woman trying to strangle me and who was this person who dared to invade my home? Her hands were wrinkled and spotted with age and as I turned my head to the side in an effort to find air, I caught the glint of a gold wedding band reflecting the glow from a nightlight plugged into the wall socket several feet from my bed. The shock of the situation brought me to full consciousness. My eyelids flew open and one final physical effort freed me from the suffocating blanket as I thrust my body up into a sitting position. My attacker was gone.

As I sat there panting, heart racing, I anxiously searched the shadows around my bed. When my gaze fell on Jette, she responded with a questioning whimper from her prone position on the floor. My attacker evaporated like the dream in which she had arrived. I was completely alone except for Jette. As old as she was, Jette would never have allowed an intruder to get that close to me. I should have realized that. There was no blanket over my face after all and no stranger in my bedroom. It was my vivid imagination running wild, I thought, and nothing more. Or was it? According to the illuminated digits on my bedside clock, it was 4:07 a.m.

◼◼◼

The dream was so lucid that it completely rattled my psyche. I knew that any further attempt at sleep would be useless. Slipping off the edge of the high four-poster bed, I rubbed my arms against the early morning chill while my feet found my slippers. Carefully stepping over Jette, I pulled a thick sweater off the bedroom chair and slipped it over my nightshirt then made my way down the short hallway and into the kitchen. Nothing for it but to put the teakettle on and wait for sunrise.

It was a tiny kitchen, no room for furniture, and I could not summon the strength to walk a few more steps to reach a dining room chair. Physically drained from fighting my phantom attacker, I simply allowed my body to slide down the wall in the corner of the kitchen and sat on the floor shivering. Within minutes, I heard the gentle click of Jette's toenails on the hardwood floor as she traced my path. She slumped down next to me and dropped her head into my lap so she could watch me worry. When I laughed, Jette danced. When fear plagued me, Jette followed me around the house periodically pressing against me until she could feel my body release the tension, signaling that the trouble had passed.

I began running my fingers through her lush black fur, gently massaging her neck while I closed my eyes to find the dream again and figure out from whence it came. The details were still vivid. I could still feel the soft, heavy blanket on my face; still see the details of the hands that held it there. When I realized I could still feel the pressure of those hands against my shoulders, my body gave off a slight shudder that caused Jette to lift her head from my lap and raise her eyebrows in question. Just then, the whistling teakettle brought us both to our feet.

I had experienced similar troubling visions many times before, dating back to my childhood, when midnight screams would bring my father rushing to my side. My parents chalked it up to growing pains and the influence of my prankster older brother, who enjoyed locking me in the basement any time the opportunity arose.

Although my nightmares were fewer and less threatening in my teens and early twenties, they were still there nevertheless. I dreamt of airplane accidents and earthquakes that eventually made the newspaper. I saw friends and family members involved in events that came to pass, sometimes days later and sometimes months or years later.

Frighteningly real nighttime visions either had me moaning in my sleep or caused me to sit bolt upright in bed at the sight of what appeared to be a spectral visitor looming over me in the middle of the night.

My Christian friends claim these manifestations are one of the "gifts" mentioned in the Bible. If that's the case, I'd like to return mine, please. I never wanted any part of this so-called gift. By the time I entered adulthood, however, what I came to realize is that most people have this radar-like capability to some degree.

Think of the man who suddenly decides not to board an airplane that later crashes; the woman who had a nagging feeling that something happened to her child who should have been safe at school but instead had been killed or severely injured in an accident on the way. Call it a gift, sixth sense, or ESP if you will. I believe we all possess it but because some people pay more attention to it, their senses become more acute while others shrug it off as meaningless until something catastrophic occurs to alter their opinion.

Years into our adulthood, I learned that my younger sister, Carla, also had strange dreams. Events might come to pass just as she had dreamed; other times the dreams appeared to be symbolic and, like me, she puzzled over their meaning sometimes for days until the uneasy feelings wore off. Our sibling relationship had been a bit shaky through our childhood years as we fought over closet space, drawer space, and space in general in a tiny shared bedroom. We developed a tighter bond when we lived in Pittsburgh together, me at my first management job while she attended college a few blocks away.

After graduation, Carla decided to give Florida a try and moved in with our brother in Fort Lauderdale. Though we did not see each other for a few years, we remained in touch with holiday cards and phone calls, continuing to share laughs and life. So it was my sister who came to my mind in the wee hours of the morning as I slumped back down on the kitchen floor next to Jette and sipped the steaming tea.

As I mulled over the dream and what it could possibly mean, my eyes drifted from the telephone affixed to the wall above my shoulder to the kitchen clock near the stove. It was barely 5 a.m. and it would be at least another hour and a half before I could telephone Carla without waking her, two hours if I waited until after she roused her children and packed them off to school.

I took my tea into the living room with Jette trailing behind me like a second shadow, then settled into an over-stuffed chair to wait for morning's light to sneak up over the treetops and come peeking through the lace curtains. In the meantime, there was no one to talk to but God.

Several years before, I had become a member of a nondenominational Christian church. The experience was quite a departure from the rigors of the ritualistic Catholic church of my upbringing. It was the first time in seven years of Sundays that I had walked through the doors of a church except for a wedding or funeral. I actually enjoyed the joyful singing and close, nonjudgmental fellowship.

At the urging of the pastor, I set aside time each evening to read the Bible. Over the course of nine months I had read it cover to cover. During that time, a whole new world had opened to me as I pored over the words and engaged my mind in the details and footnotes, sometimes until the wee hours of the morning.

True to my nature, I doggedly researched every story and parable in that book looking for factual supporting evidence, or human prefabrication, in the writings of historians and archaeologists. If there appeared to be adequate evidence to support what I read, I took it to heart. If the story was more metaphorical, I considered the lesson valuable or discarded it based purely on gut instinct.

But I trusted the pastor of that church and eventually shared with him my nocturnal dream experiences. With his guidance I learned to accept the dreams as a fact of my life and disciplined myself to record them and wait for the meaning to reveal itself. As I sat curled up in the living room chair early that morning, I did just that. I already knew that the dream involved Uncle Pasquale. That was my first impression when I rose from my bed and I have learned from past experience that the first impression is usually the correct one.

As is often the case with dreams of that nature, my body seemingly takes the place of the person for whom the action is intended so that I see what that person would see and I can feel what they would feel. As I pondered the other details, I found that I instinctively knew that the hands that attempted to smother me, smother Uncle Pasquale, belonged to his wife, Nora. What I needed next was confirmation of my interpretation. I trusted God to fill in that part then provide a game plan if I was to do something about it. Both would follow soon enough.

In the preceding weeks, Uncle Pasquale's doctors seemed to be pleased with the progress he was making toward recovery. Then his health insurance company, with the infinite financial wisdom those folks possess, stepped in and announced that he had reached the limit of his allotted hospital stay and would have to be moved to a convalescent facility for continuing care. So Pasquale was moved across town, by ambulance, to a nursing care facility.

The move pleased Nora and Julie since it resulted in a halt, at least temporarily, to the physical therapy sessions to which they had both objected. In addition, they no longer lived in the shadow of the hospital's Ethics Committee. It should have come as no surprise then, that they would make a bold move to regain absolute control in a short time.

With Uncle Pasquale safely ensconced in full-time nursing care, I did not feel the need to make the four-hour trip across the state quite as often to check in on him. Family members kept me up to date on the latest developments in his recovery by telephone. A few weeks had elapsed before I managed to make that trip for another visit with Uncle Pasquale and, as fate would have it, before Julie could make good on a forgotten promise.

During my visit, I once again tried to coax Uncle Pasquale into making a more conscious effort to enunciate his words by speaking more slowly. I informed him that his house had been listed for sale, the latest of Julie's efforts to dismantle his former life, and that he needed to tell me if he wanted me to hire a lawyer to stop them before it was too late. Pasquale's incoherence was frustrating for both of us and my heart ached to see this man who had always been in complete command of his life suddenly lying there totally helpless. Tears welled up in my eyes when I left him that day.

The following morning, I again visited with him before starting the return trip to my home in eastern Pennsylvania. Uncle Pasquale was alone in his room, sitting propped up against several pillows, and he greeted me with an anxious nod as I pulled a chair close to his bed. Taking my hands firmly in his and with a look of utter seriousness, he tried in earnest to speak. Unfortunately, the words were still as garbled as they had been the day before. It was as if he held half a dozen marbles inside his cheeks and could not spit them out. I could make neither head nor tails out of what he was attempting to tell me and shook my head in apology and regret over our inability to communicate.

Just then, Nora and Julie walked in. Nora spoke first, asking in an amiable tone if I had been there long. I wanted to tell her I had been there for hours just to get Julie's goat but I did not. I am not a malicious person by nature and I had no desire to upset Pasquale further. Nora walked to the opposite side of Pasquale's bed. Stroking his hair, she calmly announced to him that she had just given Julie two hundred thousand dollars from her joint savings with Pasquale and put their house on the market for sale. It was the house Pasquale had built for his first wife, Angie, decades before. With some reluctance, he had added Nora's name to the deed several years after he and Nora were married.

"Do you want to sell the house?" She quietly cooed as if she were talking to a baby. Pasquale turned his head away from her. His eyes momentarily met mine in silent anguish before he shut his eyelids tight. A single tear escaped from the corner of his eye.

"I think he's mad at me," Nora stated matter of factly as she stepped away from his bed. "He won't even look at me anymore when I come in."

I wanted to scream at her, grab her by the shoulders and shake some sense into her. At that moment, Nora's illness evaporated from my memory and all I saw was a cold, calculating woman who was destroying my uncle. He was a kind, respectful gentleman who had never harmed a soul, a man who could not bring himself to even consider placing Nora in a nursing home when her dementia was diagnosed, no matter how difficult it had been for him to care for her, and that man was being repaid with greed and torment.

I sat there holding Pasquale's hand and seething in silence along with him. After a few minutes, I made the excuse that I needed to get on the road when I really just wanted to get out of there to avoid adding to Pasquale's grief by crying in his presence. I kissed Uncle Pasquale's forehead and said good-bye. I could not bear to be in the same room with Nora and Julie any longer; could not bear to watch Nora rip the very heart and soul out of Pasquale while Julie sat smirking from across the room, arms folded triumphantly across her chest.

Why in the world would Nora do that? I couldn't help wondering as I walked out of there. It was not that long before that she complained about Julie's constant requests for money and now she was simply handing it all over to her. It made no sense. As I made my way out of the hospital I wore sadness like a half-ton weight on my shoulders. There did not appear to be anything I could do to intervene for Pasquale.

Back in my own home forty-eight hours later, I once again answered my phone and heard my mother sobbing at the other end. She was barely able to get the words out. Without warning that morning while Pasquale's brothers and sisters were visiting, ambulance attendants came into Pasquale's room with a gurney and strapped him onto it. Julie had finally acted on her threat to transport him to Virginia. Pasquale had not been warned of the impending move so it came as a nasty surprise.

When he realized what was happening, Pasquale thrashed about in an attempt to protest being taken away. Minutes later, a nurse injected Pasquale with a sedative as he grabbed at his brother's arm and held on fiercely in a futile attempt to prevent being torn away from his home and family, his eyes pleading for someone to stop the insanity. It was a pitiful scene that my mother described, with Pasquale thrashing about, cursing at Nora and Julie, but there was nothing his siblings could do. Pasquale's attending physician had given permission for Pasquale to be transported and Julie, wielding her power of attorney document, was determined to take him away from there.

In what had become a rare showing of concern for her husband, Nora actually cried along with the rest of the family and told my mother that she was taking Pasquale to a nursing home in Virginia.

"You weren't supposed to tell them that!" Julie spat furiously at Nora.

Whether from fear of reprisal or an attempt to mend fences with her in-laws, a flushed Nora began to cover her blunder by saying that she and Pasquale might return some day if Pasquale ever got better. She claimed there were more qualified doctors where she was taking him and that he would receive better care. In the meantime, she was sure Pasquale would like Virginia once he got there. Everyone knew that was a lie.

If Nora had intended for the move to be a temporary measure why had she listed Pasquale's house for sale? What was more, everyone knew that she and Pasquale had argued for months prior to his stroke over plans for their retirement. Pasquale wanted to sell the house and move to a smaller home in a nearby retirement village. Nora wanted to move to a retirement home in Virginia so she could be near her daughter, but Pasquale stood firm. He told Nora that he was born and raised in Smithton, Pennsylvania, and he planned to die there as well.

Though he did not relish the idea of spending his remaining years alone, Pasquale attempted to pacify Nora and had offered to provide the financial means for her to join her daughter and move South if she really wanted to go there. However, Nora refused to leave without him so it remained a bone of contention between them. Then fate stepped in and it appeared that Pasquale's stroke had provided the perfect opportunity for Nora to have her way. Pasquale's still fragile state of health and the potential for the long journey to inflict additional damage was apparently secondary to Nora's, and Julie's, wishes.

Recovering adequately from the shock to take charge again, Sal demanded to know exactly where in Virginia they were taking his brother. Julie claimed that she had left the name, address, and telephone number of the nursing home on the kitchen counter at Pasquale's house and would return to give the information to Uncle Sal as soon as Pasquale was en route. Forty-five minutes later, Uncle Sal still sat, waiting alone in what had been Pasquale's room, but there was no sign of Julie.

He telephoned Pasquale's house; Julie answered the phone and gave him a lame excuse: her mother was not feeling well and she did not want to leave her side. Never mind the fact that Julie's husband had also been there and could certainly have watched over Nora for the twenty minutes it would have taken Julie to deliver the information to Uncle Sal. For that matter, why didn't she just give Sal the information by telephone? Sal had had enough and told Julie he was driving to Pasquale's house to meet her.

Hearing that, Julie quickly conceded and agreed to drive back into the city but not before she had kept Sal waiting for another hour. When she finally arrived and handed over the information, Sal was steaming. As far as he was concerned, Julie had just declared war.

Before Nora's departure from the nursing home earlier that day, my mother made her promise to call with regular reports of Pasquale's progress.

"If you don't call me, I'll be calling you," Mother firmly stated, pointing a finger at Nora.

My mother fully intended to see to it, as best she could from a distance, that Pasquale continued to receive the medical care he needed to ensure a full recovery. And for a few days after Pasquale's departure, much to everyone's surprise, Nora actually complied with my mother's demand and called her with daily reports.

It was not long, however, before the daily reports faded to weekly updates and began to alarm my mother. Nora's mental state had reached a level of such confusion that she actually believed Pasquale had been flown to Virginia by helicopter instead of having been driven there by ambulance. What was more, her reports about his health fluctuated daily from *recovering nicely* to *near death*. One day she would tell my mother that Pasquale was eating solid foods and the next day that a priest had been called in to administer the sacrament of Extreme Unction, or Last Rites, as it is more commonly known, again.

In the innocence of her addled mind, she related every detail, at least as she saw it, including her claim that Pasquale had asked his attending physician to remove his feeding tube so he could simply die. Had Pasquale become that desperate or was it just another convenient lie? At times during their conversations, my mother said she could hear Julie coaching Nora from the background and that only served to deepen her suspicions.

"I'll bet Julie could have choked her mother when she heard her telling me that Pasquale wanted to die," Mother stated when she related the incident to me. "That's the last thing Julie would want us to know."

□□□

"Have you called the nursing home yourself to confirm any of this?" I asked her.

She had not. My mother grew up in the era of obedience, that forgotten era of politeness and societal niceties when no one holding a position of authority was ever questioned. As a result, she is basically a passive soul who rises to the occasion only after she has been pushed a few too many times. I, on the other hand, arrived in this world on the heels of the rebellious sixties and I learned to question everyone and everything until I got the answers I felt I needed.

So, taking charge of the situation, I asked my mother for the telephone number of the nursing home and made the call myself. After being transferred three times, from one seemingly misinformed individual to another, I finally had a woman on the line who identified herself as the administrative director.

I wasted no time introducing myself and explained my relationship to her recent arrival. She received from me the Reader's Digest version of events surrounding my uncle's illness and his stepfamily's attempts to see to his demise. After hearing what I had to say, she told me that the facility would never have agreed to accept him had they known of the ongoing family dispute and the fact that he was taken there against his will.

"We don't like to get in the middle of family squabbles," she told me in a serious tone.

I assured her that Pasquale's family in Pennsylvania would do everything possible to see that he was eventually brought back home.

"In the meantime, see to it that you take *very* good care of him," I warned her.

In the following days, my mother took to calling the nursing home herself since she no longer trusted Nora's mind to keep the facts straight.

"Please tell my brother I called to ask about him," she pleaded with the nurses. My mother was afraid that Pasquale would begin to feel abandoned and that without his siblings' emotional support and constant presence, he might actually give up and concede to Julie's death wish. That was unthinkable. My mother thought that if Pasquale was at least made aware that someone from home was phoning to check on him, that knowledge might provide some measure of comfort and encouragement for him to battle on.

For several days after my initial contact, my mother called the nursing home and the nurse on duty freely spoke to her regarding Pasquale's condition. That is, until Julie learned of it and gave orders to the director to stem the tide of information flowing into Pennsylvania. That news resounded throughout the homes of Pasquale's siblings with renewed alarm since it was naturally taken to mean that Julie was again attempting to see to Pasquale's imminent demise.

As much as we all wanted to rush protectively to his side, it was not feasible given the distance. We determined that we would wait another week, allowing Old Man Winter to loosen his grip on our part of the world before making the trip to Virginia by car with as many of Pasquale's siblings who felt they could handle the journey. Until then, we could only pray for Pasquale's recovery and hope that my conversation with the director would see to his protection from Julie's ill will.

In an attempt to allay the family's fears in the interim, my sister phoned a friend, a nurse in Maryland, to find out what else could be done to ensure Pasquale's welfare from a distance until we could get to him in person. Carla learned that in some states, the local hospice organization will step in and monitor a patient's care. However, she was unsuccessful in locating such an organization near Norfolk.

As the days wore on, Pasquale's siblings began to make tentative plans to visit him in Virginia. Uncle Sal thought he would travel down there with his family in a month or so. Pasquale's sister said she would try to make the trip during the summer months if one of her sons agreed to do the driving. My mother still worried that Pasquale may not make it that long so I promised her I would take her to see him in a few weeks. I simply could not see my way clear until then to take leave of my real estate business. There were just too many irons in the proverbial fire. At the time, I had a number of properties on the market for sale and others already under agreement pending settlement. I did not feel comfortable leaving such a large caseload and the endless details for someone else to tend. Besides, I did have the administrative director's promise that Pasquale would receive the utmost care until she heard from me again.

With the matter temporarily settled I resumed my daily life, seeing to clients and the details of real estate transactions by day and continuing to unpack and settle into my cottage in the evenings. That routine continued uninterrupted until the phantom attacker visited my bedroom that dark, chilly night.

As I sat in my living room draining the last of the tea from my mug, waiting until I was certain my sister would be free to help me talk through the nightmare I had just experienced, it suddenly occurred to me what Pasquale was trying so desperately to communicate to me during my last visit with him. In fact, nothing was as clear to me as I visualized his lips forming the syllables that I could not audibly decipher at the time: *did you call my attorney?* I gave myself a mental kick in the pants for not realizing it at the time, but it made perfect sense.

Nora had already told him that she listed their house for sale and he wanted his attorney to stop her! That new knowledge, coupled with the previous night's dream, only served to impress upon me the urgency with which I needed to act.

Finally, the rising sun stole through the living room curtains, casting a lacy pattern across the floor. I greeted it with eyes burning from a lack of sleep then padded barefoot back into the kitchen to call my sister from the land line.

After I told her the details of my dream, she became quiet for a moment then said, almost to herself, "So that's what my dream was all about."

Carla went on to tell me about a dream she had experienced just days before. In her dream, she was standing on a street corner waiting for someone to collect her.

"I was standing there and I remember thinking that I had been waiting for such a very long time because the thought ran through my mind, *'Aren't they ever coming to get me?* Just then a Chevy Blazer pulled up," she said.

Those words sent a chill through me that raised the hair on my arms. In our family, only three of us owned such vehicles: my father, my brother, and me.

At the age of seventy-seven and with a weak heart, I knew my father would never attempt to drive the whole way to Virginia. My brother was another unlikely candidate as he had preparations underway for selling his home to complete his job transfer to another state. That left me. My heart sank with the weight of what I saw as my responsibility.

"Well, that confirms it," I told Carla. "I need to go and get Uncle Pasquale out of there. Damn her!" I yelled as I pounded a fist on the wall. "Damn Julie and her mother!"

◘◘◘

"If you need to go I can take care of Jette for you," Carla offered. "But I can't go with you. There isn't anyone to take care of my boys and they can't miss school."

"No, it's all right, I'll figure it out," I told her unconvincingly. "Thanks anyway, sis."

I put the phone back on the cradle, got dressed, fed and walked Jette, then left for work. During the drive to my office, my cell phone rang; it was Carla again.

"I forgot to tell you something. About my dream," she breathlessly announced. "I don't know if it's important or not but while I was standing there on that corner, I was holding a helmet in my hands."

"A helmet?" I echoed.

"Yes, but don't ask me why. Like I told you before, the whole thing made no sense to me until you called. And I didn't even remember about the helmet until just now."

Suddenly, goosebumps rose on my arms again as the words formed in my mind then fell from my tongue.

"The full armor of God," I finally realized, as my recent biblical training kicked in. "Helmet, sword, belt ... what does the helmet represent? Help me out, sis; my brain is a little hazy this morning."

"I don't know and Josh had my Bible last, so Lord only knows where it is now. If I find it in the next few minutes I'll call you back but I've got to leave for an appointment soon."

Carla did not call me again that morning and in the chaos of the workday, the matter of our dreams was, temporarily, put on hold. At the end of the day, as I made my way down the winding roads that led to home, the sense of urgency returned and I began to think through the problem again.

Jette and I shared a quick meal of leftover beef stew, after which I sank into my favorite over-stuffed chair and dialed my mother's telephone number. Before doing anything else on Uncle Pasquale's behalf, I wanted to gauge her reaction to the dream that haunted me. She replied that nothing Nora and Julie would do at that point would have surprised her. She went on to tell me about an incident that she had previously kept to herself.

One afternoon, when Aunt Eleanor and Nora were alone in Pasquale's hospital room, Nora unexpectedly and in a disconcertingly nonchalant tone said to Aunt Eleanor, "You know, there are things that can be given to people in his condition to put an end to this."

Nora's remark rendered Aunt Eleanor speechless. When she told her husband what Nora had said, he reminded her about the stories, whispered years before, that Nora's mother spent the last years of her life in a hospital for the mentally ill. There were also rumors that Nora may have had something to do with her first husband's death. There was no way of knowing if there was any truth to the gossip. However, the fact that mental illness appeared to run in the family would certainly explain Nora's own recent decline.

I also found it more than a little coincidental that after one of Julie's outbursts at the hospital, in the days after Pasquale was admitted, Dr. Simon muttered half to himself as he walked away from her, "That woman isn't right."

If the facts could be taken at face value, it appeared we were dealing with a family with a history of mental issues. Who knew what they might be capable of?

Before my conversation with my mother ended, she again voiced her conviction that the only reason they took Pasquale away was so they could control the speed of his demise.

By the time we hung up, it was almost 10 p.m. There wasn't much more I could do that evening, but I headed for the loft anyway and pulled the local telephone book off the shelf. I began sifting through the yellow pages, scanning the names under the heading, *Lawyers*. I randomly selected three, left messages on each of their office answering machines, and hoped at least one would return my call in the morning. Then, the more I thought about it, I decided that it might be best to hire an attorney who practiced in Pasquale's hometown. That way, he could continue to represent Pasquale once we succeeded in getting him back to Pennsylvania and, at that time, I remained optimistic of that accomplishment.

With that end in mind, I phoned the home of my good friend, Brenda, who still lived in the Smithton area. Her husband had been a police officer on the city force for a number of years. Surely, I thought, she or her husband would know the best attorneys. There was no answer at Brenda's home and I did not want to leave a lengthy message on her recorder, so I went on to the next person on my list, my younger cousin Emily.

I remembered Emily as a precocious, fun-loving teenager who always took an interest in the welfare of others. Today, she is a caring, competent member of the medical profession: a highly regarded physician assistant who never hesitates to become involved when someone in the family is ill. Emily had visited the hospital where our uncle was confined on many occasions. In the days immediately following his stroke, she would walk into the hospital still wearing her white lab coat after completing her own shift at a hospital across town.

Because Pasquale's attending physicians were familiar with Emily and recognized her as a competent professional, they had had no problem allowing her access to Pasquale's medical records. However, Julie *did* have a problem with that. A confrontation arose one afternoon when Julie happened to walk past the nurse's station and saw Emily standing there behind the desk next to one of Pasquale's physicians.

They were reading Pasquale's medical charts together, a sin of dire consequence in Julie's mind. After all, Emily was a member of the *other* side of the family, the side that had been kept in the dark, intentionally, at her command. A shouting match erupted after Julie called the doctor to account for sharing Pasquale's records with Emily. It ended with the doctor throwing the records down onto the desk and declaring that in all his years of practice he had never witnessed anything as ridiculous as the lengths to which Julie had gone just to keep family members from finding out about Pasquale's condition.

Having had even that brief opportunity to view the records and get a bearing on the seriousness of Pasquale's condition, Emily expressed her surprise, as we spoke that evening, at the irresponsibility displayed by his attending general physician, Dr. Barton, in allowing Pasquale to be transported to Norfolk, Virginia.

When I told Emily that my mother and I had decided a rescue was in order, she gleefully shouted, "You go, girl!" Then, in a more serious tone she asked, "How are you going to do that?"

"Darned if I know," I admitted. "If I can't find an attorney to take up our cause and get it done legally, I may have to pull off the bluff of the century to get him out of there. Either way, if I make the trip, I'm not coming home without him!" I vowed.

I knew I would need documentation to back up our claims of ill treatment if I was to convince the nursing home director in Virginia to release Uncle Pasquale. With that in mind, I asked Emily if she might be able to obtain a copy of Pasquale's medical records.

Unfortunately, that was out of the question. Emily explained that she could get into serious trouble making such a request. She could only obtain access to his records if he had been a patient at the hospital where she worked. That door was closed for the time being, but Emily could still provide first-hand testimony by telephone, if necessary, based on what she saw in those charts.

After the call to Emily, I made one more attempt to reach my friend Brenda by telephone. It was almost 11 p.m. Brenda was generally a homebody, but there was still no answer at her end. I hung up the telephone on the kitchen wall and aimed my weary body toward the bedroom, having decided that there wasn't anything more I could do but get to bed, try to make up for the previous night's loss of sleep, then resume my inquiries in the morning.

Suddenly, I remembered the helmet from my sister's dream. My pace quickened as I entered the bedroom. I pulled my Bible off the nightstand and sat on the edge of the bed as I flipped the pages of the concordance looking for the word helmet. There it was, and there was the verse that had nagged at my subconscious throughout the day. It began in the book of Ephesians, chapter six at verse eleven: *Put on the full armor of God so that you can take your stand against the devil's schemes.* A chill ran through me as I continued to read: *Stand firm then with the belt of truth buckled around your waist ... with the breastplate of righteousness in place ... take up the shield of faith. Take the helmet of salvation and the sword of the Spirit which is the word of God.*

The helmet of salvation. As the words sank in, I realized exactly what they meant. Uncle Pasquale really did need me to save him. That was the confirmation I sought, the green light that would get me off the mark.

Filled with elation, I lifted my eyes heavenward and shouted, "Yes!"

I sank to the floor, hugged Jette, and joyfully told her, "Uncle Pasquale is coming home!"

◘◘◘

My telephone was already ringing at eight o'clock the following morning. I trailed puddles across the floor as I bolted from the shower to the kitchen to answer. It was the first attorney I had called. Unfortunately, he was a personal injury attorney who felt that Pasquale's situation did not fall in his area of expertise. He suggested I locate a general attorney to take on the case.

A second call came on the heels of that one. That attorney also declined, recommending that I phone the bar association and ask for the name of an attorney who specialized in elder law. And so it went. In all, I spoke with five attorneys that day and none wanted to tackle the case.

It was no wonder that Pasquale's siblings had thrown up their hands, calling it a lost cause after their earlier attempts to engage counsel. I, too, began to feel frustrated, but was determined to forge on feeling certain that I was on the right track.

"Okay, God," I said aloud. "If you want me to do this you need to start opening doors and showing me the way."

That evening, an old friend from my high school days came to mind. Ironically enough, we had caught up with each other several years previously when mutual friends told me that he and his wife had also relocated to eastern Pennsylvania. In fact, they lived a mere seven miles from my home. They are good people whose company I enjoy; however, life and careers kept us all busy and, regretfully, I had not visited with them for the better part of the preceding year. We had always been on good terms though, so I looked up Eric's telephone number and within minutes time fell away as we chatted like the old friends we had always been.

Before long, I had filled him in about Uncle Pasquale's predicament and what I was attempting to do about it. Yes, Eric told me, he still had contacts in Smithton and without hesitation, he recommended an attorney he was certain would help.

"Tom's a real door-buster," Eric proclaimed. "It sounds like that's what you need." Then, in his typical brand of humor he added, "If you want, I can lend you my .32 rifle and you could just blow her away."

"Thanks, Eric, but no," I said. "If anyone lands in jail over this I'd really rather it was Julie instead of me!"

He laughed.

"Well, keep in touch and let me know how it turns out."

During my first conversation with Attorney Tom Cavanaugh, he appeared to be everything Eric had promised he would be. Tom was the first attorney I had spoken with who listened attentively, seemed to take the situation seriously, and offered a preliminary game plan. Within an hour of my first conversation with him, he had called me again to let me know that he had made contact with the Norfolk area bar association and felt that he had found a capable attorney in Jonas Maxwell, who would assist us in Virginia. Tom said Jonas had agreed to contact me before the day was through.

In my office later that afternoon, I heard from Jonas and he immediately put me at ease when he said, in a typical genteel Southern manner, "I would be pleased if you would call me Max; everyone does."

Max not only expressed a genuine interest in Pasquale's situation but also seemed fascinated by the details Tom had communicated to him. He asked me, almost apologetically, if I would mind starting from the beginning and relating the sequence of events again just to make sure he had it clear in his mind. After I did so, Max advised me that we would be able to pursue one of two options.

The first, and by far the best scenario, would depend on Uncle Pasquale having regained his ability to speak clearly by the time I arrived in Virginia. If that were the case, it would be a relatively simple matter for Uncle Pasquale to revoke the power of attorney he had previously granted to Julie. Nora, he advised, was not even a consideration; the dementia that plagued her was a documented medical fact. Legally, she could not stand in our way. Therefore, in spite of any opposition she would undoubtedly voice, we would be able to take Pasquale back home the same way he got there.

A second option came into play if Pasquale was clearly unable to express his desires. In that event, we would need to appear before the clerk of courts in Norfolk, state our case, and pray upon the court to upset the power of attorney by providing proof that Julie and Nora had not been acting in Pasquale's best interest.

If we had to go that route, it would take time—weeks or perhaps even months. I bit my lip at the thought of a protracted battle. Pasquale had already languished in a nursing home for over a month, his recovery stalled by the stepfamily. A lengthy delay in securing his release could result in irreversible damage; we simply had to get him out of there soon.

I ended the conversation by telling Max that I would pass the information along to the rest of Pasquale's family, then get back to him. To my surprise, I received a second telephone call from Max before the workday had ended. He was disturbed enough over Pasquale's circumstances and the lack of information about his welfare that he had contacted Norfolk's Department of Social Services to enlist their help. He told me I would need to contact them myself to file a formal report and set the wheels in motion, so he gave me the name and telephone number for a caseworker who awaited my call.

This, I felt, was extraordinary and certainly went above and beyond the attorney's call of duty. We had not even officially retained his services yet and already he was taking steps to help by securing a watchful eye via a local caseworker. Max was scoring major points in my book!

Immediately after ringing off with Max, I contacted the social services agency as he directed. I could not have asked for better results. Twenty-four hours later, a representative of that agency made a visit to the nursing home to see Pasquale for herself. She reported back to me that it appeared Uncle Pasquale was being well cared for; his stomach tube was still attached, giving him sustenance. However, he was in a groggy state during her visit so she was not able to freely converse with him. She filed a report with her agency, she told me, and then placed him on the list for weekly visits to monitor his progress.

That information allowed all of us to rest easier. It was a comfort to know that someone would be our eyes and ears until I could manage to get there in person. Jonas Maxwell was indeed turning out to be a godsend. Doors were opening and the weight of the ordeal was beginning to lift.

In the meantime, I enlisted my mother's help in mustering the troops and obtaining the consent of Pasquale's brothers and sisters to hire Max. She promised to call everyone together for a meeting at her home the following Sunday afternoon.

While she tended to that detail, I placed telephone calls to several trusted friends who I knew would spread the word through their church's prayer chains that a battle was raging and we needed prayer partners to uphold us. If there is one phenomenon that has awed me again and again over the years, it is the power of collective prayer. Some say it is simply the power of collective consciousness, and I can certainly attest to those efforts as well; others claim there really are spirit forces in the world that are able to come to our aid when called upon.

The Jewish people and kabbalists, among others, believe that if you pray at the grave of a righteous person, their spirit will come to your aid. I also remember a friend telling me that when she needed something accomplished, she would pray to her deceased grandmother and whatever she needed would be provided. As a mere mortal, I cannot claim certain knowledge about the validity of any of those practices, but I do know that something moved in my own spirit that day. I felt absolutely certain that while the ground troops were being put into place, special forces in the etheric realms would be gearing up for the battle as well. I was confident that I was no longer an army of one and that was a tremendous morale booster. I also knew, without a doubt, that one way or another Pasquale would indeed be going home.

CHAPTER SIX

Battle Lines and State Lines
Monday evening, April 5

*"So do not fear them; for there is nothing
concealed that will not be disclosed,
or hidden that will not be made known."*

—Matthew 10:26

The long drive was finally coming to an end. Ben and I exited I-95 and began heading southeast on yet another four-lane highway for the last leg of our journey. My eyes were burning from the highway monotony and Ben was getting restless. He toyed with his cell phone, then setting it aside, he thrust a hand into a paper bag on the floor to find an apple to munch on. Afterward, he tossed the core out of the window and pulled one of the maps from where we had stashed them between our seats. After opening it, flipping it over then back again and not finding what he was looking for, he refolded it and pulled out another. After flipping to the reverse side of the second map, he found the area he sought.

"Maybe we should call Max and get the rest of the directions," Ben suggested. "According to this map, we're less than an hour away from Norfolk."

Nodding my assent, I directed him to the compartment in my purse that contained the pocket-sized address book with Max's telephone number. Ben's cell phone had registered a signal only intermittently since we had crossed the state's border, so I handed him my cell phone as well. Such were the days of limited cell phone coverage and roaming charges. After punching in the number, Ben returned the phone to my open hand.

I glanced at the digital clock on the dashboard. It was already 5 p.m., the hour we were supposed to meet with Max. I had not spoken to him since the day before, and hoped he hadn't left his office thinking that perhaps we were not coming. However, he was there patiently waiting for us, as he had promised to be, and he certainly sounded much more calm than I was feeling. I made introductions then handed the phone back to Ben so he could write down the directions. We had driven a long way; one last stretch of highway stood between us and Uncle Pasquale.

Whether from exhaustion or anticipation, I did not know but suddenly I felt giddy and once more floored the accelerator to try to squeeze maximum mileage out of minimal time. No sooner had I done that when the engine coughed and sputtered and the car lurched forward. Ben shot a raised-eyebrow glance in my direction.

"Are we going to make it?" he asked with alarm in his voice.

"I sure hope so," was my uncertain response. Then, as reassurance for both of us I added, "Probably just the EGR valve again. It seems to be an intermittent problem. I'll have it checked out in Norfolk before we head back home."

In spite of the engine's protests, I pressed on. We had no idea what time the nursing home closed for the night and I wanted to make sure we made our first contact that evening. I figured we would have a better chance of seeing Uncle Pasquale alone, without Nora and her daughter there to interfere, if we arrived toward the end of the day.

As if he were reading my mind, Ben asked, "If Julie is there, what are you going to tell her?"

Without hesitating, I replied, "Same thing I told the neighbor who refused to keep her dog from defecating in my yard: I can be your best friend or your worst nightmare; your choice."

Ben snickered then egged me on, "So, what happened with the neighbor?"

Grinning mischievously as I recalled the incident, I continued.

"She called my bluff and I called the cops. After that, her children launched a name-calling crusade that lasted for a few weeks until I had a fence installed. Then the kids began to climb the fence so I had to ask the cops to pay another visit. I figured the last thing I needed was for one of her undisciplined brats to fall into my yard and tangle with one of my dogs. We battled on for another month until she surrendered, sold her house, and moved away. Then I held a block party to celebrate."

"Did you really?" Ben asked. He threw his head back in laughter at that part of the story.

"No," I chuckled. "No block party. I made up that part. But I probably should have!"

Just at that moment, I spotted a vanity license plate on the tailgate of a sporty looking two-door coupe. As we cruised alongside it in the passing lane, I nudged Ben and pointed to the plate.

"Check it out! Should we flag them over and see if they'll swap plates with us?"

Ben grinned as he read it aloud: S U R P R I S E.

"Surprise! Yeah, won't ol' Julie be surprised when she sees us! I'll bet she never expected the family to follow them so soon."

"Yeah, she'll probably think she is having a nightmare! But that's okay. As long as she behaves herself, it'll all be over before long. Then she can crawl back under her rock and we'll take Uncle Pasquale home where he can live happily ever after!"

It was just a few minutes past 6 p.m. when we finally found Max's office a half block from the courthouse in Norfolk's business district. It was a modest looking ground-floor location in an antique brick building. The entrance was mostly glass with a large display area in the front picture window giving the general impression that it might have been used for retail purposes in another era.

Inside, the office bore all the standard marks of a bustling, established business: stacks of paper adorned the desks just behind the reception area, bearing testimony to various cases in progress. A row of older, mismatched metal file cabinets lined up like tin soldiers against one wall; books, files, and periodicals were stacked precariously atop. The term *organized chaos* came to mind but it was a comforting thought all the same as it only served to reassure me that we had hired a man of experience.

After introducing himself, Max led us into a small consultation room. It was tastefully furnished with the lawyer's trademark long and narrow conference table made of polished cherry wood, barren except for a small antique looking brass table lamp at one end. Several leather armchairs were companionably scattered on either side of the table in such a way that it appeared the previous occupants had taken their leave just moments before we arrived.

The man behind it all was not the man I had envisioned. Instead of the tall, muscular frame I imagined, there stood a man of average height and build. His hair, longish, but neatly trimmed with bangs that swept across his forehead, was the color of polished silver and was in striking contrast with his sun-burnished skin. Sparkling eyes the color of a brilliant blue summer sky made their observations from deep within well-defined bone structure that served to endow his face with rugged good looks that reminded me of the Western film star Charles Bronson.

Like Bronson, Max's eyes seemed to disappear when he smiled. But this man was no gunslinger. In fact, everything about him, his bearing, speech, mannerisms, the entire aura of his being, bespoke of a Southern gentleman. I was instantly captivated.

Before long, I found myself in the midst of a subconscious battle between the schoolgirl with a crush who lurked just below the surface and the proper business-minded woman who was in control most of the time. In my mind, the romantic miss cozied up to Max and strolled off with him, arm in arm, in the general direction of the sunset while Miss No-nonsense tugged in the opposite direction struggling to remain focused on the task before us. The sunset stroll scenario played like a motion picture in my head while the retainer fee and documents changed hands.

Max added his signature to the agreement already inked by Pasquale's brothers and sisters, then he left the room to make a photocopy for me. He returned just as I succeeded in shoving the little flirt back into the depths where she belonged.

Max led the way from his office to the nursing home, which was situated in a small town almost thirty minutes from the city of Norfolk. While we followed behind Max's car, traversing first the city streets, then open highway, then suburban residential avenues, that serious tone took hold of us again. This time Ben was behind the wheel and he petitioned aloud as he drove.

"Lord, please, don't let them be there. We do not need a fight with Julie tonight. Please just keep them away."

It was just after 7 p.m. when the three of us walked into the quiet entrance hall of a facility that looked relatively new. The interior decor managed to strike that difficult balance between regulation hospital cleanliness and the warmth of home. We entered through a bright, glass-enclosed patio furnished with white benches and old-fashioned high-backed rocking chairs placed near a gently gurgling miniature waterfall. A second door led to the carpeted entrance halls, the walls of which were adorned with seascapes done in pastels. Turning the corner at the end of the hall, we passed an inviting visitor's lounge with over-stuffed furniture and lush plantings. We could not help commending Julie for her good taste as we took it all in.

"At least she did *something* right," Ben quipped.

"Hmm, with Uncle Pasquale's money, no doubt," I added.

The residents were in their rooms at that hour with the exception of a lonely looking soul who navigated the corridor in a manual wheelchair, her slippered feet quietly shuffling her along. Two women in white uniforms sat busily writing behind an octagon-shaped desk, which appeared to be the nurse's station.

One of the women gave us Uncle Pasquale's room number and pointed us in that general direction. Like an eager child unable to contain his excitement, Ben paced off ahead and was the first to walk through the doorway of Pasquale's room. Max and I arrived seconds behind Ben, just in time to see Uncle Pasquale's face register first a question, then the surprise of sudden recognition.

Suddenly we heard the voice that had been silent for so long as Pasquale clearly exclaimed, "Oh, oh my! How did you find me? How did you know where to come?"

Uncle Pasquale had finally found his voice, and we were elated! Filled with joy and the thrill of being reunited, he reached up from his bed firmly taking each of us in turn, grasped our arms, and pulled us close for kisses and hugs, while tears spilled over his cheeks. Finally, he sat back against the pillows and shaking his head, he told us, "I thought I was a dead man."

Ben and I glanced at each other. Pasquale's disconcerting statement only confirmed our fears.

We gave him a brief watered-down version of the events that had preceded our arrival, beginning with the account of his brother Sal demanding that Julie tell where she was taking him and finishing with the alarming reports that led us to make the long drive from Pennsylvania. Then I asked him the ultimate question.

"Do you want to go home?"

I knew his response needed to be clear and articulate so Max could legally bear witness. That would put the wheels in motion enabling Pasquale to vacate the power of attorney document that got him into this predicament in the first place. Uncle Pasquale did not fail to deliver. Not only did he express his desire to get out of there verbally, but he also threw his right leg up over the bedrail in a physical attempt to climb out of the bed and walk out!

"Let's go," he urged us anxiously, mindless of the catheter bag he had disturbed in the process. "Hurry up before they come back," he insisted.

We knew that "they" referred to Nora and Julie, and it devastated him when I gently placed his leg back onto the bed, explaining that we could not leave right at that moment. I then introduced Max, who stood there silently taking it all in. I explained that Max was there to represent him and to draw up a new power of attorney document so we could get him out of there. Only after that was accomplished could we arrange for an ambulance to transport him back to Pennsylvania. Uncle Pasquale listened intently and after I had finished, he looked up at me and asked simply, "When?"

I sent a questioning glance in Max's direction, silently urging him to fill in the blank. In response, he stepped around to the foot of the bed and put a hand on my shoulder. I could see the thought process in motion as his eyes took on a faraway look.

After a moment, he skillfully avoided a direct answer, saying instead, "We'll get working on it. Cousin Ben, why don't you stay here and keep Uncle Pasquale company while Gina and I see what can be arranged." Then the hand on my shoulder steered me out of Pasquale's room.

Max spoke as we returned in the direction of the nurse's station.

"Let's find out who's in charge here and see what we need to do to get him released."

"Then you agree that he can revoke Julie's power of attorney?" I asked hopefully.

"It certainly seems to me that he is in control of his thoughts and I did clearly hear him express his desire to return home to Pennsylvania."

That was reassurance enough for me. I could barely contain my excitement. While Max made inquiries at the desk, my mind whirled with images, thoughts, and questions, not the least of which was whether or not we should phone Nora to let her know we were spiriting her husband away! By the time I settled my thoughts, Max was talking on a telephone handed to him by a nurse behind the desk. After hanging up he informed me that the administrator of the nursing home would be arriving shortly. She had already gone home for the evening but agreed to return and meet with us.

While we waited, I questioned the nurse about local ambulance services. She located a telephone book and offered it to me along with a chair and a telephone behind the desk. With that, I set about the task of trying to arrange transport. After making contact with a dispatcher and getting at least a tentative green light for service the next day, I returned both telephone book and chair to the kind, accommodating nurse. So far, so good, and if all the details continued to fall into place we could be back on the road and headed toward Pennsylvania by morning.

"You get things done!" Max approvingly declared as I moved out from behind the desk.

"Maybe you should hire me," I grinned playfully.

As I stood next to him near the desk, I shrugged my shoulders and explained, "We simply don't want to be here any longer than necessary. My uncle needs to be back home where he'll get the proper care to make a full recovery and Ben and I both walked away from our businesses to make this trip. The quicker we can all get back to our lives the happier we'll be."

I walked back to Uncle Pasquale's room to give him and Ben the update while Max waited near the nurse's station for the administrator's arrival. Ben occupied the chair next to Pasquale's bed and the two of them were chatting amiably. When I walked in, Uncle Pasquale again reached out his arm to me as he grinned from ear to ear. It was a sight that melted my heart and I smiled as I took his hand.

"When are we leaving?" Uncle Pasquale wanted to know.

"We'll leave tomorrow," I assured him. "We're just waiting for a call back from the ambulance service. The administrator of the nursing home is on her way here."

"Thank God," Ben sighed with relief. Then to Uncle Pasquale he echoed, "We're going to get you out of here. Everyone is waiting to see you back home: your brother, your sisters …"

Before he could continue the discourse, Uncle Pasquale interjected,

"Natalie? Did she come with you?" Then looking at me and cupping his hand behind his left ear he asked, "Is your mother here?"

"No, Uncle Pasquale, she's waiting for you back home."

I realized at that moment that Uncle Pasquale was not wearing his hearing aid and told Ben we would have to remember to speak louder so Uncle Pasquale could hear us. Thinking the device might be in the nightstand, Ben pulled open a drawer and rooted through the items inside before declaring it absent. Julie. I was certain she was at the bottom of it, just as she had denied my uncle other things in her efforts to thwart his recovery. The fact that he was denied even the use of his hearing aid fueled my fire. However, I took consolation in the fact that all would be rectified when we had him safely back home.

Just then, Max entered the room to announce that the administrative director, Fern Donnelly, had arrived. Ben remained with Pasquale while I followed Max down the corridor and into a small private office where the director of nursing, Talia Evert, sat expressionless behind her desk. Mrs. Donnelly occupied a chair opposite Talia while Max stood making introductions. Everyone exchanged obligatory handshakes and cursory half-smiles, but it was obvious that neither of them appreciated being called back to work at that hour. Regardless, Max proceeded to explain the reason for our visit and what we had hoped to accomplish.

He told them that he had witnessed Pasquale's expressed desire to return home to Pennsylvania and that he was prepared to assist in that effort. A lengthy discussion occurred over the legalities of signing him out in light of the fact that Julie held that darn power of attorney over him. I sat smoldering, arms crossed over my chest, while Max attempted to jump over every hurdle they presented, from legalities to questions about Pasquale's mental and physical state.

"Besides, we haven't heard Mr. DiAngeli state that he does not want to be here nor have we seen anything to imply that there is any animosity between him and Julie," Mrs. Donnelly argued.

Talia nodded in agreement; however, I found both of those statements difficult to believe. I recounted to them Pasquale's struggle with the ambulance attendants when he was taken from Pennsylvania; it did not thaw their icy stares. They remained silent while I spoke of how Pasquale cursed at both Julie and Nora during the days that preceded his forced relocation, especially after he learned they were selling off his possessions. There was no doubt, I informed them, that Pasquale's relationship with Julie was anything but harmonious. My argument fell on deaf ears. Then they dropped a bombshell.

According to Fern Donnelly, within days of his arrival, Pasquale had expressed the desire to have his intravenous feeding tube removed; he said he wanted to die. They had a copy of his living will on file, compliments of Julie, of course, but hesitated to allow his wish to be carried out, as they did not feel he was of sound mind. Uncrossing my arms, I jumped to my feet and launched into a tirade in my uncle's defense relating Julie's behavior over the preceding months and her motives for wanting him dead. In Julie's defense, the administrator claimed that one of the nurses attending my uncle had also heard him voice such a request. In my mind, it did not require scientific genius to deduce Pasquale's motivation for such a statement and I told them so.

"Well, wouldn't you?" I challenged them. "If you were lying helpless in a hospital bed at the mercy of a stepdaughter with whom you had been quarreling for years and found yourself suddenly torn away from the caring support of the only family members you trusted, wouldn't you want to just give up and die? If I were in such a seemingly hopeless situation I certainly would!"

They quietly thought this over as they exchanged guarded glances. Finally, the administrator spoke again.

"We thought Julie was his daughter."

"And that's precisely what she wants everyone to believe," I informed them. "It makes it easier for her to carry out her little scheme. My uncle has no children. Julie is Nora's daughter from a previous marriage and that power of attorney was given to her years ago when she and my uncle were on better terms. Julie only works part-time jobs and her husband doesn't seem able to hang onto a full-time job long enough to provide a steady means of support for either of them. The two of them call home to Pennsylvania regularly to ask Nora and my uncle for money. Just before his stroke, my uncle told his sister that he refused to send Julie any more money and that Nora was almost out of funds in her personal account. Do you understand what I'm telling you? If my uncle dies, all of Julie's money problems go away. And I can assure you that if he dies here, *your* problems begin!"

I could tell by their studied expressions they were thinking over the implications.

"We're going to have to contact Julie," Fern decided. "If she is willing to sign for his release we can let him go. If not, then we will need to order a competency test before we can allow him to sign himself out. Understand that we are not trying to be difficult, but we do need to cover ourselves. It's too late tonight to do anything so we'll have to get back to you tomorrow."

"Well, you ladies had better get working on it," I declared. "I have already placed a telephone call to schedule his ambulance ride and I'm not going back to Pennsylvania without him."

With that vow, I stormed out of the office and paced in the hallway waiting for Max to dispense with them and catch up to me. I dreaded having to deliver this news to Uncle Pasquale and gritted my teeth in fury as I waited. Max had no sooner exited their office than that door closed. Glancing behind him to make sure the staff was out of earshot he walked to where I stood.

"At least they've done something right," he said consolingly. "If it weren't for them, your uncle could be dead by now."

I had already begun to dislike them, but as much as I hated to admit it, Max was right. In spite of arguments that Julie had presented to the contrary, they had kept my uncle alive.

I should have thanked them, and instead, I nearly crucified them. I would have to rein in my temper if we were to make any progress with those two belles of the manor.

We could accomplish nothing more that evening so I promised Max I would call him in the morning and with that, he took his leave. I attempted to plaster a reassuring smile on my face before returning to Pasquale's room to collect Ben and tell Pasquale we would be back in the morning.

"Where are you going?" he asked with a look of alarm on his face.

"To the hotel across the road to get some sleep," I told him.

Ben reassured him that we would be back in the morning while I stroked his forehead and managed to muster a smile.

"Don't worry, Uncle Pasquale, we won't leave you here," I promised.

"Okay honey, you go," he replied resignedly. "I'll be here when you come back."

I smiled at the wry humor in that remark, leaned over and kissed his forehead.

As Ben and I walked out to the parking lot, I filled him in on the details of the exchange in the director's office. A dejected look crossed his face as he shook his head.

"Nothing's ever easy, is it?"

"We're not beat yet, cousin," I said, throwing my arm across his shoulder. "Just a little technicality. Nothing we can't handle."

That made him smile.

"I'm glad I made the trip with you, my little cousin," he said as he returned the hug. "You know, I've always prayed that God would use me to do something important for someone one day. When your mother told me you were coming here, I figured I was being given that chance and if I didn't take it, it might not come around again."

I pulled away from him in mock horror and said, "I sure *hope* something like this doesn't come around again. I think once is enough, don't you?"

The hotel across the highway had plenty of vacancies since it was still off-season for vacationers. Ben insisted on paying for the hotel since I had insisted on handling the travel expenses on the way down. We were both raised with generous, giving families and that attitude rubbed off. Practically from the moment we set out on our journey, we grappled good-naturedly for the bill each time we stopped for gas and food until it became somewhat of a comedy routine.

After carrying our possessions up to the third floor of the hotel, we made calls to family members, who anxiously awaited news. While I dialed my parents' telephone number, Ben checked in with his wife. My mother was overjoyed when I told her that her brother had regained his ability to speak and was ready to go home. I promised to call her again the next day with an update on our progress. Meanwhile, she, in turn, relayed the news to Pasquale's other siblings while I went on to phone my brother, who was one of the people on whom I relied to keep various people updated on our progress.

Ben and I knew at the outset that we might encounter opposition to our plans, so we had also lined up prayer partners before leaving Pennsylvania to ensure that "collective consciousness" would kick in when we needed it. My brother was one of the key links in that chain. He also promised to telephone our siblings and cousins to keep everyone in the loop, and so it went until Ben and I mentally checked off everyone on our *need-to-know* list and determined it was covered.

We were not quite out of the woods yet, but Pasquale's speech had been restored and that was key in our battle.

Before surrendering ourselves to much needed sleep, Ben pondered aloud, "I wonder if Julie will really allow us to take him home."

"This is my take on Julie," I began. "She may be bold and she may be quite the actress, but I don't believe she's all that brave. When she finds out we're here and we've hired an attorney, I think she'll back down."

"Boy, I hope you're right," Ben sighed. "It would be nice if we could get it over with tomorrow and take him out of there."

The next morning Ben was up and about early. He called me from the hotel's breakfast room while my hair still dripped from the shower.

"Do you think we should check out now," he wanted to know. "Or should we wait and see what happens at the nursing home today?"

"They have plenty of empty rooms," I optimistically replied. "Let's check out; that way if everything goes well, we can just leave from the nursing home instead of having to come back here."

Uncle Pasquale was sitting up in his bed when we arrived. His face lit up when we walked into the room.

"I thought maybe I just dreamed you were here!" he exclaimed.

Ben took Pasquale's out-stretched hand, kissed his cheek, and reassured him.

"You weren't dreaming; we're really here."

At that moment, a nurse walked in and cheerfully introduced herself.

"Hi! I'm Penny, Mr. DiAngeli's nurse."

She was pretty, petite, and thirty-something with short blond curls and wire-rimmed glasses perched atop a cute little nose. She exuded congeniality. Uncle Pasquale wasted no time introducing us to her. With hands on her hips in mock surprise and with a lilting Southern drawl in her voice, she declared, "Well, no wondah you're in such a good mood today!"

"Hasn't he been?" I ventured.

In response, she pursed her lips and slowly shook her head in dismay.

"Then you haven't seen the best side of him," I told her encouragingly. "He's really quite a lovable character once you get to know him. Right, Uncle Pasquale?"

He grinned up at Penny as she moved to the side of his bed to check his IV line then, winking at her, Uncle Pasquale said, "She knows I would never hurt her."

"Aww, you're jus' full of sunshine today!" She reached down to pat his shoulder adding, "You're mah buddy."

Then she disappeared into the corridor. As soon as she was gone, Uncle Pasquale again took up the matter of his return to Pennsylvania.

"Are you taking me home today?" he asked earnestly.

"I'm still waiting for the transport company to call me," I replied. "As soon as they have an ambulance for you, we can go."

Pasquale was silent for a moment, obviously thinking it over. Finally, he spoke again.

"How did you come?" he wanted to know.

"In my car," I replied. "We drove down."

I could see that those wheels of his were turning. He wanted out of there and he wasted no time putting together his own solution.

"Then I'll go home with you in your car," he insisted.

It was heart-wrenching to see the disappointment on his face when I explained that we could not take that chance as long as he had the PEG tube in his stomach and it was attached to a feeding line. For his own safety, he would have to be transported back to Pennsylvania the same way he arrived, by ambulance. He seemed to settle in to acceptance, then suddenly sat up again. Tugging at his hospital gown, he worriedly announced, "I don't have any pants!"

Ben and I smiled at the humor in that statement even though Uncle Pasquale was quite serious. After more than a month of lying in bed in a hospital gown, he wanted his dignity back. The hospital staff could question his sanity 'til the cows came home but Pasquale had all of his wits about him and he knew better than to venture outdoors with no clothes on. He wanted regular street clothes to travel in, not the flimsy gown he had worn; he wanted pants!

"We'll get pants for you when you get back home," I assured him. "You won't need them to ride in an ambulance."

I patted his arm reassuringly, then decided that perhaps a call to his sister would lift his spirits. I punched my mother's telephone number into my cell phone and at the sound of her voice, I grinned and asked her, "Would you like to speak with your brother?"

"Yes!" she cried.

I handed the telephone to Uncle Pasquale and watched with mixed emotions while the tears again flowed from his eyes upon hearing her voice.

"I'm all right," he assured her with sobs of relief. "I'm all right."

After their brief exchange, I excused myself to make a few more telephone calls.

Outside I settled into the passenger seat of my car, plugged the cell phone into the cigarette lighter, then phoned the ambulance service. The dispatcher told me they could definitely handle our request but they needed cash up front, a credit card number, or medical insurance information to guarantee payment before they would schedule the run. The cost, a mere $4,500, was enough to stop me cold. We did not have access to my uncle's bank accounts; Julie did. We did not have access to his medical insurance information; Julie did. Ben and I did not have that amount of cash between us and it was more than the credit line I had available on my credit card.

A frantic telephone call to my mother ensued. Her first thought was to telephone her local ambulance service, the one that transported Pasquale to Virginia in the first place. If Uncle Pasquale's medical insurance paid for that ride, then the ambulance service would have the information at their fingertips. It should be a relatively simple matter, she reasoned, for them to drive back to Virginia to retrieve Pasquale and bill his insurance carrier. She promised she would make that phone call then consult her brother and sisters.

While I waited for that issue to be resolved, I decided to walk back inside and check with the nursing home's administrator to see what progress she had made since the previous evening. What she had for me was one of those good news/bad news deliveries. She had consulted with their legal counsel, who advised her that Uncle Pasquale could be released without Julie signing him out so long as he passed a competency test. That was great news! That meant that Julie's undoubted dissent could be removed from the equation and after what we had witnessed for ourselves, there was no reason to think Uncle Pasquale would not pass some silly test.

The bad news was that the test could not be scheduled until later that day, which meant that if he did pass, the soonest they could arrange for his attending physician to sign a release would be another twenty-four hours later. Inwardly I groaned at the thought of having to spend one more night there.

At the time, I foolishly thought that Nora and Julie were still unaware of our presence and that we would be able to whisk my uncle away without a confrontation. The more time we had to spend there, the greater the chance that a confrontation would occur, and I wanted to spare my uncle the added drama, if possible. He had been through quite enough already.

By the time I left the administrator's office, my cell phone was ringing. My mother had made the necessary arrangements and the ambulance service in Pennsylvania would be at the nursing home by noon the following day, Wednesday. As it turned out, Medicare did not cover his transport to Virginia; Julie paid cash, undoubtedly from Pasquale's own funds, and they again required cash up front to make the trip. The good news was that the cost was less than half of the amount the Norfolk agency wanted. Pasquale's sister, Eleanor, and her family once again came through with the required funds. I was proud of my mom for working through that problem so quickly, and equally proud of the displays of unconditional love my entire family had shown as they continued to rise to meet each new challenge.

On the heels of my mother's telephone call came one from Jonas Maxwell. I brought him up to speed and promised to check in with him again after we had the results of the competency test that afternoon. Buoyed on by the way things were shaping up, I practically skipped back inside the building. It was already past noon and my stomach was roaring in protest over the coffee I had been pouring into it almost continually since the day before.

By the time I returned to Pasquale's room, the nurses had already pulled the curtains around his bed for his bed-bath ritual. Ben stood outside the room, hands clasped behind his back, in a stance that reminded me of his father.

"You're smiling! You must have good news," he surmised, returning the grin.

"I do! Duck behind the curtain and tell Uncle Pasquale we're going out for lunch. We'll see him a little later."

We found the Mexican restaurant, recommended by Nurse Penny, a ten-minute jaunt from the nursing home after traveling down a stretch of highway bordered on either side by flat, sandy-colored terrain from which sprouted a variety of trees and colorful shrubs already in full bloom. As we took in the scenery, we marveled at the contrast to the still barren winter landscape in our home state.

At the restaurant, a waiter led us on a tour through the crowded main dining area, down a short, windowed hallway, then down a few steps to a table in a sort of enclosed patio with greenhouse windows. The patio annex dropped a couple of feet below the main dining room with the two areas separated only by wrought iron railing so that immediately to my left was a rather humorous exhibition of the legs of other diners. Some were clad in trousers, others not, some hairy and others bare, some twisted like vines around the chair legs.

"All righty then," I laughed. "I hope the food is better than the view!"

Ben did not share in the humor and as he studied the menu, I noticed the increasing depth of frown lines that creased his forehead.

"You're awfully quiet," I observed aloud. "If you don't like the menu, we can leave. It makes no difference to me where we eat. I'm easy."

"Nah, it's not the food; I'm just worried about Uncle Pasquale."

The waiter came to take our orders then disappeared.

"Why? Did something happen while I was making phone calls?" I asked.

"No, I'm just worried about that test," he replied flatly.

The waiter returned, setting glasses of water, bowls of salsa, and tortilla chips on the table. Ben continued voicing his thoughts as he plucked a chip from the bowl.

"Penny wasn't able to tell me *(CRUNCH)* who would be testing him *(CRUNCH)*, his doctor or a psychologist. If it's a regular doctor *(CRUNCH, CRUNCH)* it may not be so bad. But those shrinks, *(CRUNCH)* you never know what they're going to throw in to try and trip him up."

"I'm sure he'll be just fine," I told him optimistically. "I haven't seen anything yet to make me think he's lost his mind. I'm sure it's all still there."

Then I leaned across the table intently as a memory came to the surface.

"Remember what he told us this morning?" I reminded Ben. "He said, *'I haven't had a piece of meat or chicken or anything else to eat in five weeks.'* Think about that. If I had been lying in a hospital bed as long as he has, I'm sure I would have completely lost track of time by now. Yet he knows exactly how long it's been ... he's amazing!"

The waiter returned to set plates laden with steaming food before us.

"Yeah, he always did have a mind for details," Ben agreed. "I hope you're right."

"Ye of little faith," I chided.

By the time we finished our meals, the main dining room had cleared out. Gone were the many and varied human legs; only the wooden legs of the chairs over which they once dangled remained. As I stood and craned my neck up over the wrought iron railing to flag our waiter, my eyes caught something on the far wall that had been hidden from our view by the bodies of the lunch crowd. My jaw dropped as I silently read the twelve-inch tall letters written in bold script across the wall: *With God, all things are possible.*

"Ben," I called for his attention, then pointed across the room. "Look at the wall on the other side of the dining room."

"Well, I'll be," he said as he stared at the words.

"I don't think we arrived here by chance," I told him. "We were sent here so we could see that."

Whether it was Penny purposefully sending us to the restaurant to give us that message or a sign from God himself, someone was telling us to hang in there; all would be well. That day, I believed it.

We still had almost two hours before Uncle Pasquale's competency test, which was scheduled for three o'clock. Ben wanted to do some exploring to see how far we were from the nearest beach. As it turned out, the beach was just another fifteen minutes down the road from the restaurant.

"What an unexpected treat!" Ben remarked enthusiastically. "Even when I looked at the maps before we left Pennsylvania, it just never registered in my mind that we would be so close to the ocean."

"Hmm, I know what you mean," I mused. "When you're in crisis mode, it's like wearing blinders. The only thing you see is where you need to go and what you need to do. Everything else is a blur."

We found a place to park, then traversed a short boardwalk that led directly onto the sand. I had not been on a sandy shore in decades, and the first thing that struck me was that the water did not appear to flatten out as it stretched away from the beach and disappeared over the horizon in the way I imagined it would. Rather, the swell of the water appeared to be higher than the land. So much higher, in fact, that it seemed as if the slightest tilt of the earth could bring it all crashing down in violent waves upon the shore without a moment's warning, swallowing up every living thing that stood in its path. We were both awestruck; the sight stopped us dead in our tracks. Finally, Ben poured out his thoughts.

"Looking out over this great expanse, I just know there is a God."

I simply stood there, taking in the soothing sound of the tide washing over the shore.

After another moment, Ben announced, "I'm going to find a dry spot to sit down so I can read my Bible and pray."

As I watched him walk off toward the sand dunes, I slipped off my shoes and socks, rolled up the legs of my jeans, then struck out in the opposite direction toward the water's edge, stooping occasionally to pluck a seashell from the sand and drop it into the pocket of my jean jacket. As I neared the water, the incoming tide came closer and closer until it lapped over my bare feet and sprayed at the hem of my jeans.

As it did so, the old familiar feelings of apprehension began to surface. I came close to drowning when I was just eight years old. Instead of getting back into the water after that incident, I remained on the banks of the river, day after day, watching my brothers and my friends laughing and splashing about without me. I allowed fear to take hold of me and burrow deep inside my soul until I could no longer wade into water even up to my waist without gasping for breath.

❈❈❈

Lost in those memories, I suddenly realized I had walked right into the onrushing surf. As it crashed in over my ankles then slipped back out under my feet, I caught my breath and stumbled backward. One day, I vowed to myself, I will beat this fear; I will drive it out of the very core of my being and finally be free. But on that particular day, it was my uncle's freedom that was foremost in my mind. His freedom not only from the physical bondage of a hospital bed, but also from the self-serving actions of his stepdaughter were more important than my release from the childhood fears I carried inside me.

A familiar biblical story came to me as I tracked across the wet sand at the water's edge. It was the account of Peter as he walked across the water, arms out-stretched, eyes fixed on Jesus. Before turning away from the ocean, I raised my eyes skyward and sent up a prayer for myself, for Ben, for Uncle Pasquale, and for everyone who was counting on us to bring him home: *We are at the water's edge; help us walk across.*

By 2:40 p.m., we were back in the nursing home at Pasquale's bedside. He was fast asleep, completely oblivious to our footsteps and our voices. He did not even stir in response to Ben's gentle nudging. Ben took Pasquale's hand and began to rub it between his own as he called out his name.

"Uncle Pasquale, we've come back to see you."

Nothing, not even the flicker of an eyelid, acknowledged our presence. We exchanged panic-stricken glances. It was as hot as a sauna in there and thinking that he was simply over-heated, I grabbed a small towel that lay near the sink in his room, soaked it with cold water, and began to swab his face, neck, and feet, while Ben fanned him with his hands. Finally, Pasquale stirred but still was not fully awake. The doctor was due in less than twenty minutes. Pasquale had to be completely alert or he would miss the opportunity to gain his freedom! Dashing out of the room, I went to find Nurse Penny. When I explained the predicament, she calmly responded in her syrupy Southern drawl, "Well, ahm not surprised."

As we matched footsteps back to Uncle Pasquale's room, she explained.

"He gets a sedative twice a day, 9 a.m. and 9 p.m., in with his other meds and pretty much sleeps through the afternoon."

"You have *got* to be kidding!" I exclaimed incredulously.

"No ma'am, I am not. Those are his doctor's orders and that's what he gets."

I continued to protest. "But he's supposed to be having a competency test in less than fifteen minutes! How is he supposed to respond to a test when he can't even keep his eyes open?"

"Well, we can't withhold medicine unless his doctor tells us to."

Penny walked back out into the corridor to consult a clipboard that sat atop a pushcart.

"There's nothing in his chart about a test. Maybe his doctor wasn't made aware."

Then walking back into Pasquale's room she offered apologetically, "I can turn on the air conditioner and see if that'll help but that's about all I can do."

Uncle Pasquale was still so groggy that when he did finally speak to us, it sounded like he had a mouth full of mashed potatoes; his words were completely unintelligible. We had serious doubts about his ability to respond to any sort of test at that point, let alone pass it, and we were not happy.

At 2:50 p.m., a gray-haired woman wearing a white lab coat, wire-rimmed glasses, and a morbid expression entered Pasquale's room and asked us to leave. Ben and I exited the room, me shaking my head in mind-numbing disbelief and Ben fuming in the face of apparent defeat. How could this happen?

"Why in hell would they give him a sedative today if they knew he was being evaluated?" Ben spouted off.

We stormed out of the facility and into the parking lot, where I immediately rummaged through my purse for a cigarette. It never failed; every time I thought I had quit the blasted habit some mindless idiot like Julie crossed my path and made sure I didn't. The night before, I made Ben stop the car at a mini-market so I could buy a pack. As soon as we were out of this mess, I vowed, I would finally lay aside the disgusting habit for good. In the meantime, the wheels in my brain engaged as I inhaled. My thoughts returned to a telephone conversation I had with my good friend Jeannie the week before Ben and I left Pennsylvania.

When I explained the nightmare that had me smothered under a blanket, Jeannie's immediate response was, "They're trying to shut him up."

Remembering her remark, I realized just how prophetic those words were. Julie knew my uncle was getting his speech back just days before she spirited him to Virginia. She had to have known that once he began to speak again, her little charade would be over and the only way to prevent that would be to keep him under her control, sedated, and away from his siblings who would, of course, help him. Ben paced quietly in the parking lot before finally breaking the silence.

"Should we call home and cancel the ambulance?" he asked.

I was still trying to move past the anger long enough to formulate a plan and did not respond immediately. Moments later, after collecting my thoughts, I angrily threw the cigarette butt onto the pavement.

"No, damn it!" As I ground out the embers with the toe of my shoe, I stated with resolve, "He's going home. C'mon."

We marched back into the building to the office wing. I rapped on the open door of Fern Donnelly's office, determined that she would either take the appropriate course of action to rectify what I viewed as her inept handling of the so-called test or I would be a twelve o'clock shadow over her desk for as long as it took to get it right. She was seated behind her desk, her perfectly coiffed and sprayed hairdo looking as starched and unruffled as it had the evening before, glasses perched on her nose and a sweater draped across her shoulders. I half expected to see a copy of Better Homes and Gardens lying open on her desk; such was the picture of domesticity that she presented.

When we confronted her, she claimed to have had no knowledge of Pasquale's sedation but what riled us even more was her statement that she did not know whether Pasquale's attending physician had been notified about the impending evaluation or not, she simply *assumed* so. We may as well have been asking Betty Crocker to manage the ER! Not trusting her to handle the matter, I demanded and was given the name and telephone number for Uncle Pasquale's attending physician. I was determined to see to the detail myself.

Anger is an exhausting emotion and by that time, it had completely sapped my energy. Ben and I withdrew to a quiet corner of the almost empty cafeteria where I took a deep breath, sat down, exhaled, and then punched in the physician's telephone number on my cell phone keypad.

"No, the doctor is not available," the voice at the other end informed me. "She's with a patient. Can I help?"

My first instinct was to say no and simply leave my cell phone number for the doctor to return my call but something urged me on, so I plunged in. I poured out my heart to that doctor's assistant with the details of Pasquale's circumstances and the blundered test. She confirmed that the doctor had *not* been made aware that an evaluation had been scheduled and *yes*, she would see that the doctor called the nursing home directly to stop Pasquale's sedation.

I could not help wondering who, then, was the woman in the lab coat if Fern Donnelly and Pasquale's own physician were unaware of her? One of Julie's cronies, perhaps? As I clicked off the cell phone, Ben reached across the table smiling and patted my arm.

"I'm proud of you, cousin, you handled that very well."

And I realized he was probably right. Maybe it was time to put away the bull-in-a-china-shop attitude and try a little diplomacy. Anger and indignation had not taken us far.

At 5', 4" and 127 pounds, I was often told that I looked ten years younger than my thirty-plus years. Climbing the corporate ladder in my twenties, I learned to adopt a confident, almost stern demeanor just to be taken seriously. That demeanor often bled through to my personal life so that my dual personae were constantly at war while I struggled to find the right tone for any given situation. That inner struggle continued as Ben and I fought for Pasquale's release.

We walked back down the long hallway past the visitor's lounge, past the octagonal nurse's station, to Pasquale's room. The door was open and the doctor, if she truly was one, was gone. Uncle Pasquale was more alert but still yawning. He said that someone was in his room but he did not know who they were or why they were there. That statement was more than a little disturbing and caused us to wonder if perhaps Uncle Pasquale's stroke had indeed left him somewhat confused after all.

From our conversations with doctors and nurses, we knew that a condition known as aphasia could exist for quite some time after a massive stroke such as the one Pasquale experienced. Ben and I would relay one more request to our prayer partners that evening, that Uncle Pasquale would be given clarity of thought and expression so he could voice his own desires.

While Ben and I sat there with him, Julie's frame suddenly loomed in the doorway. She silently glared at us for a moment, ducked out then reappeared a minute later with Nora on her arm. I was shocked at Nora's appearance. She was trembling, seemed to have difficulty walking, and looked even thinner, if that were possible, and more pale than when I had last seen her.

The two of them stood silently just inside the doorway and made no move to come closer. Finally, Nora broke the spell when she began to sob, turned and walked out of the room. Julie wasted no time ducking her head back inside the doorway to hurl insults at us.

"Bastards!" she hissed. "You're breaking up a marriage!"

Drawing my hand up to my chest, I shot back, "Us? We haven't done anything of the sort. We're only here to make sure he receives the care he needs to recover."

"And I have a doctor who will say my mother can take care of him," she challenged.

"Oh, please, Julie. Don't be ridiculous!" I waved her statement away, but she ranted on, undeterred and determined to have the last word.

"He's in a home, isn't he?" she retorted.

That did it. We had all had just about enough of Julie's pig-headed foolishness during my uncle's confinement and I did not intend to allow it to continue. I stood my ground, condemning her definition of the word "care." Making a sweeping gesture with my arm that ended over Pasquale's bed, I chastised her.

"This is how you take care of him? He isn't eating. He isn't getting any physical therapy. He has made no progress in his recovery whatsoever and he does *not* want to be here."

Julie continued her tirade, attempting to lecture me about family until I stopped her cold.

"Don't even go there, Julie," I warned her. "You have never acted like a member of this family. As a matter of fact, why don't we just leave it all for the attorneys to sort out?"

She finally dropped that argument then took up another line.

"My mother would like to say good-bye to her husband."

"Well, tell her to come in!" I said, rising from my chair in a welcoming gesture. "We have no quarrel with your mother."

At that, Nora reappeared in the doorway, head bowed, and made her way to her husband's bedside. She neither spoke nor made eye contact with me or Ben.

I moved aside and again offered the chair I had occupied but instead, she simply leaned over the opposite side of the bed and kissed Pasquale's cheek, telling him, "You know I love you."

Tears welled up in his eyes and his voice cracked when he responded that he loved her too.

Then, taking her hand in his, he told her regretfully, "I can't take care of you now. You know that."

Nora nodded and as she made her way back toward the door, she told him, "I just wanted you to know this wasn't my fault. They're all above me."

"I *know*," he empathized as he shook his head in anger. Pasquale knew exactly what she meant. Julie and her husband were in control and Nora felt helpless to fight them.

It was a heart-rending scene and for a fleeting moment, I wondered if Ben and I were doing the right thing taking Pasquale away from her.

After they were gone, Pasquale told us tearfully, "I love that woman, but that other one—her daughter—is no damn good!"

After Nora and Julie made their exit, I left Ben with Uncle Pasquale and headed back outside to call Jonas Maxwell. To my surprise, Nora and Julie had not left the building after all. Instead, they had seated themselves on a sofa in the visitor's lounge. My heart went out to Nora as I walked past them. She looked absolutely pitiful with her head bowed and hands in her lap as if she had just lost the last friend she had in the entire world.

I truly felt sorry for her and all she'd had to endure in the preceding weeks, but my complete lack of trust in her daughter compelled me to continue my efforts to get my uncle out of there and away from their influence. I consoled myself with the thought that perhaps Nora would relent and move back to Pennsylvania once Uncle Pasquale was on his feet again. Outside in my car, I phoned Max and gave him a recap of the day's events, including the botched test due to the standing order for sedatives. He said he would contact Pasquale's doctor, as well as Fern Donnelly, and see if he could get the doctor to release Pasquale anyway. Max repeated what he had told Fern the previous evening—that he would stand as witness to Uncle Pasquale's lucidity.

As he observed, it appeared that Pasquale was at his best toward the end of the day after the morning dose of drugs had worn off and Max felt that if the doctor could see that for herself, she might be inclined to release him. If we could get the attending physician on our side, he thought, we would have a leg up in getting him released by the time the ambulance arrived the next day.

Julie and Nora were still seated in the visitor's lounge when I walked back inside, and it made me wonder what they were up to. Nora had come to say good-bye to her husband, or so she said, and she had already done so. Why were they hanging around, keeping a grim, silent vigil? It was unnerving, but then, maybe that was the point. Ben was standing in the hall outside Pasquale's room while a nurse emptied his catheter bag and changed his bed linens. After I told Ben of our adversary's encampment in the lounge, we quickly concluded that we could not leave Pasquale alone for a moment until he was safely onboard the ambulance.

"I feel bad for Nora," Ben said, echoing my own sentiments. "But that Julie gives me the creeps. Every time I look at her I see nothing but evil in her eyes. I wouldn't put it past her to do something to Pasquale yet."

Ben and I came up with a game plan by which I would go back to the hotel to freshen up and grab a bite to eat, then return to spend the night with Uncle Pasquale while Ben slept at the hotel. I would curl up in a chair in Pasquale's room if I had to, but he would not be out of my sight.

Ben agreed to drive my vehicle back to Pennsylvania the next afternoon, following behind the ambulance carrying Uncle Pasquale and me. As the designated driver, I felt it was important that Ben get a good night's rest in a comfortable bed. By the time we had agreed on that plan, the curtain around Pasquale's bed had been drawn aside and we were able to rejoin him. He asked us again when the ambulance would arrive, seemed satisfied with the plans we had made, and then quietly settled back into the pillows.

Nurse Penny had finished her shift over an hour before and another nurse had taken her place. By that time, it appeared the entire staff had been made aware of our presence and Pasquale's impending departure. Julie had apparently agreed to sign for his release after all. As they entered his room attending to his care, members of the nursing staff gave him congratulatory winks and smiles while they bustled about. Always the gentleman, and never taking the efforts of others for granted, Pasquale hugged each one in turn, thanking them for taking care of him.

During a moment when we were alone, Pasquale asked me if I had a few dollars he could borrow, small bills, he specified, promising, "I'll pay you back when we get home."

I handed over all of the ones and fives I had in my wallet, knowing perfectly well that he intended to tip the nursing staff on his way out the next day, and I grinned as I watched him gleefully tuck the money under his pillows. The look of utter contentment on his face was repayment enough for me.

Later that evening, Max informed me that Uncle Pasquale's physician was not able to make it to the nursing home due to a previously scheduled engagement.

Nevertheless, he too, seemed to think that the nursing home's directorial staff had seen the light. We knew that Nurse Penny was on our side and had been documenting Pasquale's lighter moods and his more vocal opposition to Julie since our arrival. Though we still were not certain of Fern Donnelly or Talia Evert's allegiance, Fern did tell Max that she would again talk to Julie about signing for Uncle Pasquale's release, indicating to Max that the nursing home was just as anxious to send him home as we were to take him there. I guess they, too, had finally had enough of the drama.

As I told Max how the nurses had stopped in to say good-bye to Uncle Pasquale, it certainly seemed to both of us that Pasquale's release had already been accomplished and we would be on our way by noon the next day. I thanked Max for his help, expressed how truly delighted I had been to make his acquaintance, and we said our good-byes as well. It appeared that the hard part was over and there was nothing left for me and Ben to do but carry out our watch during the night as planned.

※ ※ ※

At 7 p.m., I left the hotel parking lot and looped around a circle to access the drive-thru for the fast food restaurant across the highway. I ordered a burger and milk shake, collecting them at the next window as the attendant spoke to the customer in the car behind me through his headset. While he took their order, he missed not a beat as he simultaneously collected my money then handed a bag to me through the window without as much as a nod in my direction.

As I pulled away, however, the young man's head and shoulders suddenly shot through the tiny drive-up window as he called out after me, "Thank you, ma'am, have a nice evening!"

I grinned. I was in the land of Southern hospitality where no customer gets away without a proper thank you, even if it means yelling out a window or chasing the customer down the block to deliver the message. Another thought occurred to me just then. What in the world was Julie doing there? She had not an ounce of solicitude in her entire body; how did she manage to fit in for so many years? Then a realization hit me. It was the perfect setting among some of the most polite people on the planet for a manipulator like Julie to operate. It was certainly clear that she had done a number on the nursing home staff before Ben and I arrived to set things straight. Who else had she conned?

I pulled into the nursing home parking lot just before 7:30 p.m. to relieve Ben. He promised to telephone the relatives in Pennsylvania to let them know everything was going well and that we would be back home late the following evening.

While I sat with our uncle that evening, he cried at times, still regretting the whole situation and his necessary parting with Nora. Then, sobering up again, he declared war on Nora's son-in-law, Dan.

"I'd like to choke him," Pasquale angrily declared.

He then proceeded to tell me that he knew Dan had orchestrated the entire affair, from selling his car to raiding his bank accounts to putting his house up for sale. Pasquale recounted to me the names of the banks where he had accounts and how much money had been in each one. According to Pasquale, his stepfamily had already stolen hundreds of thousands of dollars from him—his life savings.

On the evening of our arrival two days before, Pasquale had related the same story to Ben while Max and I argued with the nursing director and administrator down the hall.

When Ben asked Uncle Pasquale how he knew what Dan had done, Uncle Pasquale told him, "When I want to hear something I just …" He finished not with words but with a gesture indicating feigned sleep as he folded his hands together, placed them against his cheek and closed his eyes. Ben told the story to me later that night in the hotel.

"That's just like him," Ben shook his head and chuckled, "playing possum so they wouldn't know he was listening. I'll bet those idiots gathered around his bed and made their plans thinking he was asleep and he would never know what they were up to until it was too late."

That was one more item to add to our to-do list for Uncle Pasquale. As soon as we were back on home turf and he was in charge of his life again, we would need to take steps toward damage control and try to recover as much of Pasquale's assets as we could find. Uncle Pasquale still had a long road to complete recovery and would need the money for continued care and therapy.

Pasquale would also need a place to live after he was finally released from the seemingly endless string of nursing homes. I determined that I simply had to get his house off the market as soon as we got back to Pennsylvania and I prayed I would not be too late. No sooner had we thought the race was behind us when it became apparent Ben and I were simply rounding yet another turn and had a few more laps to go. We were both determined to leave Julie in the dust yet.

CHAPTER SEVEN

Best Laid Plans

WEDNESDAY, APRIL 7

*"The best laid schemes o' mice an' men/gangaftagley.
An' lea'e us nought but grief an' pain."*

—ROBERT FROST, TO A MOUSE

I awoke with a sore neck and burning eyes after a fitful night's rest on an old vinyl-clad lounge chair just outside the door to Uncle Pasquale's room. He seemed to nap on and off until just before midnight, when he finally gave in to a sound slumber. I remembered getting up at one point in the wee hours of the morning when Uncle Pasquale awakened me with his request that I move the lounge chair so he could see me without craning his neck. His room was too small for the chair to fit into the furniture scheme without becoming an obstruction for the nursing staff while they tended to Pasquale's care, so it was placed just outside the doorway. Pasquale still needed reassurance that I hadn't left without him, so I maneuvered the clumsy chair into his direct line of sight, after which he drifted off to sleep again.

By the time daylight crept into the hallway, Ben had returned and took up the post near Pasquale while I made a quick trip back to the hotel to freshen up and change my clothes. When I returned at 9:30 a.m., the curtain was drawn around Pasquale's bed while the nurses gave him his morning sponge bath. Ben paced in the corridor with a look of concern on his face.

"Something's going on," he half whispered. "I don't think they stopped the sedation. He's really out of sorts this morning and I can't understand what he's saying. Yesterday he talked so good; today it's all garbled and he's not making any sense."

That was definitely not good news, but we were still operating under the assumption that his release had been secured and we would be out of there by noon. As long as no one challenged us or Pasquale's ability to leave, we would proceed as planned.

No sooner had that discussion ended when I was summoned to meet with Fern Donnelly, the administrator. When I entered her office, the expression on her face told me I was not going to like what she had to say, which was, in a nutshell, that Julie had refused to sign for Pasquale's release.

Furthermore, without a competency test they simply could not allow him to sign his own release. That, she told me, was the advice from the nursing home's legal counsel. I was furious! Why had I been foolish enough to believe that Julie would release her meal ticket and allow him to return to Pennsylvania? Still, I refused to yield. Gritting my teeth to keep from screaming, I simply rose from the chair and calmly but firmly told Mrs. Donnelly that the ambulance was on its way and if she hurried she still had a few hours to arrange another test. With that said, I strode out of her office and back through the corridors to my uncle's room. As far as I was concerned, the entire mess was her fault; I was not about to let her off the hook. I felt that if I kept the pressure on, she would find a way to secure Pasquale's release in spite of Julie.

By the time I returned to Uncle Pasquale's room, he was sitting up in bed but obviously uncomfortable as he occasionally winced in pain.

When I told him that Julie had refused to sign for his release, he shrugged his shoulders and simply stated, quite matter-of-factly, "You do it."

I explained to him that it was not quite that simple. The power of attorney document that he had signed years ago complicated his release. I went on to explain the other options, telling him that we would not be able to leave that day but we might be able to do so in a few days. Hearing that news, he cried. It wrenched my heart to see his hopes dashed. Ben and I tried to reassure him, telling him not to worry and that we would remain in Virginia with him for as long as it took, but he would not be consoled. No sooner had we delivered that blow than Julie and Nora walked into his room. Gone was the forlorn, pitiful-looking Nora of the evening before.

She strode purposefully into the room, her gait still a bit wobbly, but with renewed determination. The previous day's mask of indignation was gone from Julie's face. Instead, she wore a look of smug self-satisfaction, and I hated her for it. Nora made her way to Pasquale's bedside and as she reached down to cup his face in her hands, Pasquale pressed his lips together tightly and turned his head away, refusing to kiss her. He would not even acknowledge Julie with a glance. Undeterred, Nora immediately began to fuss with his sheet and blanket. Ignoring me and Ben, she turned to Julie in mock exasperation.

"He's soaked! Feel this pillow," she announced.

She marched over to the window to turn on the air conditioning unit then returned to Pasquale's bedside and pulled the blanket back up over him. Ben and I shot raised-eyebrow glances at each other. If she intended to make a show of her ability to care for him, she blew it with her contradicting actions.

At that point, my cell phone rang; it was Laura from Good Shepherd Nursing and Rehab, the facility that was waiting to receive Uncle Pasquale in Pennsylvania.

"I hear you're having a little trouble down there," she said. "We've been told that if you try to take your uncle today, Julie will call the police."

Julie must have been waiting especially for that moment as she lurked in the doorway, arms folded across her chest, watching me intently. I had no intention of giving her even an ounce of satisfaction so I laughingly repeated those words back to Laura.

"She's calling the police, huh? Good! Then I'll call the local media and we can put this little charade in the limelight. There's nothing I'd like more than to have this whole story made public!"

Upon hearing my words, Julie huffed out of the room. I meant it too. If she were foolish enough to involve the police, I would not have hesitated to take the opportunity to call the local television station and publicly humiliate her. Then she would have had no choice but to release Pasquale or answer a lot of embarrassing questions—on camera! In the meantime, we needed to consult Max.

"Uncle Pasquale," I touched his arm. "We're just going down the hall. We'll be back soon," I told him. With that, Ben and I walked out, still shaking our heads in disbelief at Nora's pitifully incompetent attempt at playing nursemaid.

"Too bad none of the nurses were there to document *that*," Ben lamented.

As soon as we were out in the parking lot, I phoned Max.

"Looks like we're going to need your help today after all," I informed him. "Can you come?"

Yes, he could. In fact, anticipating trouble, he had cleared his morning appointments the day before. Max was an absolute treasure. He was always one step ahead and I continued to marvel at the lengths to which he went on our behalf. He truly believed in us and in what we were trying to accomplish for Pasquale. His steadfast faith in us meant so much in light of the continued opposition.

◘◘◘

Max arrived at the nursing home in due course. Since Julie and Nora had seemingly disappeared while Ben and I were away, Max took advantage of their absence and attempted to interact with Uncle Pasquale.

In a friendly, conversational way he reintroduced himself, to which Pasquale replied impatiently, "Yeah, yeah, I remember."

Max then asked Pasquale to tell him his name and where he was from. Pasquale's response was largely unintelligible since the sedation produced garbled speech, but we did manage to catch the name of the village, Greys Wood. Max had expected to hear him say Smithton, the city where Pasquale had lived just prior to his unexpected relocation. Instead, Pasquale named the village where he spent his childhood. It was not an incorrect answer; however, it was the type of response that might only serve to continue the controversy over whether or not a state of confusion still prevailed in Pasquale's mind. It would not do.

Once again, Ben remained behind to keep company with Uncle Pasquale while Max and I went to find Fern Donnelly. As we approached her office, we saw Nora and Julie seated in an adjoining office along with Talia Evert and another woman whose acquaintance we had not yet made. It appeared that Nora was being shown where to place her signature on a document. We stood there in the hallway observing the event until Talia spotted us at which point she rose from her chair and closed the door. I looked at Max with raised eyebrows but before I could share my thoughts Fern appeared, invited us into her own office then immediately closed the door behind us.

As soon as we were seated in front of her desk, Max again presented our position that Pasquale would not make a full recovery in her facility and that he needed, and indeed had expressed the desire, to return to his home state. Pasquale himself had stated that he refused to eat or participate in physical therapy as long as he was in Virginia. That was the only way he could protest his removal from Pennsylvania.

During Max's discourse, Talia Evert quietly entered the office and deposited herself in a chair against the wall to the left of where Max and I were seated. Fern continued her side of the argument, stating that she understood our concern but legal counsel for the nursing home advised her not to allow Pasquale's release unless the person holding power of attorney, Julie or Nora, signed for his discharge or a new attorney-in-fact was appointed, or Pasquale proved, by way of a competency test, that he was sufficiently cognizant to release himself.

Fern then began questioning me about my heated exchange with Julie in Pasquale's room the previous afternoon. I gave it to her verbatim and as I spoke, I could not help noticing Talia's change in posture. Her body language, arms and legs crossed, toe tapping against the chair leg and eyes rolling skyward sent the clear message that she did not believe a word I was saying. In fact, when I finished the account she sat forward in her chair and voiced her objection with an accusatory tone.

"That conversation never took place!" she cried.

I was flabbergasted. Talia had not been present to hear the argument herself; how dare she pass judgment and call me a liar. In defense, I returned her challenge.

"Oh, you were there?" I asked sarcastically. "I didn't see you in the room."

She harrumphed but made no further remark. Determined to prove that I was telling the truth, I asked Max if he had a polygraph machine in his office or if he knew someone who had one.

"I'm ready!" I told him. "Hook me up; then we'll see who is lying."

Then, I shot back at Talia in condemnation of her biased attitude.

"And why are *you* taking sides in this anyway, Talia?" I charged. "You're supposed to be a health care *professional, unbiased* in your opinions and looking after the welfare of your patient, not the welfare of his lying stepdaughter!"

She was caught and she knew it. Fern shot Talia a look that caused an immediate change in Talia's physical demeanor. She slumped back in her chair and relaxed the angry expression on her face before coyly backpedaling on her stance.

"I was simply trying to prevent any further angry confrontations for the sake of the facility," she lied. Unwilling to let her off the hook so easily, I once again admonished her, telling her that she should be more concerned about the effect of such a confrontation on her *patient*, the "facility" be damned, and that she could be assured he was not happy about being prevented from leaving. I further told her that if she did not believe me then she could walk down to his room and see him crying for herself.

Fern coldly reminded me that they still had no documentation in their records of any dispute between Pasquale and Julie and that they were simply attempting to get at the truth of the matter. And that's where the problem lay. When Pasquale arrived at the nursing home, Julie presented Fern and Talia with a story about her *father* that they had no reason to question until Ben and I came along. Now, Fern and Talia were in the difficult situation of having to determine who was telling the truth and Julie already had two weeks lead-time to get chummy with them.

As I had come to learn in the previous month, Nora and Julie both possessed chameleon-like qualities. They could easily don the mask of oppression when it was necessary to win an ally then turn around and hiss like asps when they felt their position was threatened. Add Nora's almost perpetually pitiful demeanor and it was easy to see how the people who sat in front of us in that room had been taken in.

Finally, Max suggested that we attempt to resolve the matter directly with Julie, and so our little council disbanded while Talia went to find her to see if she would agree to a meeting.

By 1 p.m., we had assembled in the conference room across the hall from Fern's office. In attendance were Jonas Maxwell, Julie, Talia Evert, Fern Donnelly, and me. Max took the chair at the head of the table; I sat at his right and Julie at his left. Talia and Fern kept a discreet distance, as was appropriate for what should have been their impartial position in the feud, at the opposite end of the long conference table. Max opened by introducing himself to Julie then, maintaining a polite, nonthreatening demeanor, he began to question her. He asked her if she understood the issue surrounding Pasquale. She claimed she did. Max asked her what her relationship was to Pasquale to which Julie replied,

"Daughter." Then, quickly correcting herself, she added, "Stepdaughter."

Max got right down to the business at hand.

"Is there anything that would induce you to sign a release and allow Mr. DiAngeli to return to his home in Pennsylvania?" he asked Julie.

Without hesitating, Julie replied with a single word, "No."

Max tried a different avenue when he posed his next question.

"May I see the power of attorney form that Mrs. Donnelly has in her file?"

"Yes," Julie immediately responded then, after glancing over her shoulder at Fern and Talia, she reversed herself, quickly adding, "Talk to my attorney first."

If I had any doubts as to whose side Fern and Talia were leaning toward, that action confirmed it for me. I glared at them, silently communicating to them that I knew that what was being said to my face and what was being done behind my back were two very different scenarios. Max's third and final question was put to Julie.

"May I ask why you will not allow Pasquale to return to Pennsylvania?"

Her short, undoubtedly coached, response was, "Talk to my attorney."

With that, the interview concluded. Julie followed Fern and Talia out of the conference room. Max closed the door behind them and he and I remained to reflect.

"So, what do you think?" I asked him as I drummed my fingers on the tabletop.

He cast his eyes toward the ceiling, crossed one leg over the other and thought for a moment, then carefully chose his words before giving his opinion.

"I think one of two scenarios applies. One, she really does have something to hide that may come to light with Pasquale's release and subsequently cast blame in her direction. Or, two, she's just plain stupid."

Option number one was something I had already surmised. Number two, however, took me by surprise so I asked Max to elaborate.

"If she was smart," he reasoned, "she would have answered, *'Yes, if the family signs a statement to the effect that I will not be prosecuted for my prior actions, I will sign for his release.'* That would accomplish two things: first, it would make this whole mess go away and I really do believe Julie wants it to go away and second, she would get to keep any of the money your uncle claims has been stolen from him without fear of prosecution."

I hadn't thought the matter through to that conclusion and in my mind, Max's rating just went up another ten points. But then, that's what legal counsel is for: to out-think the opposition and find a way to break the impasse. After hearing his synopsis, I had to admit that Max's opinion was, more than likely, right on the money, no pun intended. Julie did not appear to be as bright as her mother had always claimed she was.

Max, on the other hand, was brilliant as he continued to come up with one idea after another. One piece of advice he gave us was that we could contact the State Department in Pennsylvania since the governor does have the authority to vacate a power of attorney. He also suggested that we try to rent a video camera and begin taping Pasquale's more coherent moments. As long as Pasquale's doctor insisted on showing up when it suited her schedule instead of timing a test to coincide with Pasquale's most lucid period of the day, between 4:30 p.m. and 7 p.m. when the sedative began to wear off, Pasquale might have difficulty passing any test to the nursing home's satisfaction. Whereas if Ben and I were to videotape our conversations with Pasquale to prove that he did indeed carry on intelligent conversations when he was not drugged, then we might be able to sway the nursing home administration into allowing him to sign for his own release.

In the interim, Max planned to head back into the city to seek out the Clerk of Courts and see about scheduling an immediate hearing for guardianship. Just as we walked out of the main entrance of the nursing home, the ambulance from Pennsylvania pulled into the parking lot and tears welled up in my eyes. Max put a hand on my shoulder consolingly.

"Dear lady," he said, "I wish there was something more I could tell you to ease your pain."

"It's all right, Max." I gave him a reassuring half smile. "I have faith in God. And in you," I added, mustering a smile. "Between the two of you, we'll get him home yet."

Ben was already standing outside under the canopy when the ambulance pulled in. Simultaneously we walked toward it as the doors opened and two attendants hopped out. Ben and I introduced ourselves then apologetically explained the circumstances since it appeared they had made the trip in vain. Ray, the driver, took it in stride, going so far as to say they enjoyed the trip since it took them out of their normal routine for a day.

Though Julie had already stated she would not sign a release, we still held out hope that the issue might be resolved somehow within the next twenty-four hours. With that in mind, we asked Ray if he and his partner could remain in town overnight to give us some time to work it out. He wrote down my cell phone number.

"I'll check with the dispatcher in Pennsylvania and let you know," he said, but he did not sound hopeful that our request would be granted.

In the meantime, Ben told them they might as well have lunch near the beach since they had come so far. He pointed them in that direction and we watched them drive away.

Ben and I walked back inside the nursing home with heavy hearts, talking through our options as we went. When we crossed the threshold and started down the main corridor, the melodious sounds of an organ drifted down the hall to meet us. The residents had gathered in the community room and they were singing Amazing Grace. It brought tears to my eyes.

We were almost at Pasquale's room when Ben suddenly remembered that he needed to recharge his cell phone. He walked back outside to the car while I proceeded to Uncle Pasquale's room alone. I entered to find Pasquale crying and writhing in pain. The sight sent a chill through me and I quickly threw my purse and jacket at a chair then rushed to his side.

"I can't take it … hurts like hell!" he moaned.

"What hurts," I asked frantically, "show me!"

"Here," he said. He had his arm across his stomach then immediately drew it up to his head so that I was not certain from which part the pain radiated. I asked again.

"Is it your head that hurts or your stomach?"

I could not get a direct answer from him. Instead, he continued to moan in pain.

"I called the nurse twice," he said, flinching. "Nobody came."

That was all I needed to hear to send me flying into action like a mother hen protecting her baby chick. Talia Evert's office was roughly twenty yards straight down the hall from Uncle Pasquale's room and that's where I ran to. She, in turn, called for Nurse Penny and the two of them sprinted back to his room before me.

A short while later, after a liquid painkiller had been administered through the feeding tube in his navel, he was beginning to feel some relief. By then, Ben had returned from the car and I filled him in on what had just occurred.

"You know," I told him, "it's probably a good thing Uncle Pasquale was not put in that ambulance after all. Can you imagine if this had happened on the road today? If the ambulance attendants did not have medication onboard, he would have been in serious trouble."

"Everything happens for a reason," Ben agreed.

As we learned later, the ambulance attendants were not permitted to remain in Virginia to wait out our standoff with Julie. Instead, their dispatcher required them to turn around and head back to Pennsylvania. They returned with an empty ambulance and our family had incurred the expense in more ways than one.

Beads of sweat still glistened on Pasquale's forehead after the painful episode. While I mopped his face and neck with a damp towel, Ben tied the nurse call button to the bed rail where Uncle Pasquale could reach it with his good hand. He watched with curiosity while Ben worked.

"What's that for?" Pasquale asked him.

Ben explained how to use the call button so Pasquale would not have to shout for help the next time he was in pain. Pasquale then told us that he had not been feeling well all week and had tried to tell the nurses but they did nothing. The more we heard, the more we witnessed in that place, the more determined we were that we absolutely had to get our uncle out of there. No matter what it took.

▣▣▣

In the turmoil that mounted over the course of that morning and afternoon, neither Ben nor I had taken the time to eat. Not that either of us could have even thought about food, but as the day wore on, the acid churning in our stomachs reminded us of our oversight. After making sure that Pasquale was resting comfortably, we headed out for an early dinner around 4 p.m.

We settled into our seats at a nearby restaurant and as we sipped our beverages, Ben and I marveled at the irony of the fact that Pasquale seemed surrounded by so many incompetent people, yet he was the one they insisted needed to pass a competency test. The nursing home's administrative staff had obviously swallowed Julie's story, hook, line, and sinker when she claimed that Pasquale had a violent history. All they needed to do was consult the medical records that should have arrived with him from Pennsylvania and they would have seen it was untrue. The only 'violence' that Pasquale had previously displayed was his attempt to physically protest his sudden, unannounced removal from the nursing home in Pennsylvania.

And was it any wonder that they had no documentation of any animosity between him and Julie, no inkling that he did not want to be there? The answer was perfectly clear to us: Pasquale had been so heavily sedated since his arrival that he was only lucid for a few hours in the evening *after* the regular daytime nursing shift was gone and *after* Julie and Nora went home. It did not take a rocket scientist to figure that one out, but there seemed to be a serious lack of common sense among the nursing home staff.

Shortly after 5 p.m., we were back on the beach, standing at the water's edge soaking up the peace and tranquility in the one spot where we knew we would find it. That was where both of us felt we could clear our minds and connect with the higher power that sustained us during those turbulent days. Once again, we separated near the edge of the water, each of us going our own way to reflect, talk to God, and try to gain some sense of direction.

As I ambled barefoot across the sand I began, once again, to pick up shells that had been tossed ashore by the waves. The first one I picked up bore a distinct resemblance to a duck's foot. I found some measure of humor in it so I held onto that one for times when I would need to remind myself to laugh. While I walked, I prayed for peace between the warring families, a softening of Julie's stony heart, and that the eyes of the nurses would be opened and Julie's deception revealed. We were on a roller coaster ride and I could not get a clear sense of where it was all heading, so I sent yet another plea skyward. *The waters are treacherous, Lord, help us find our way across or make it clear that the time is not now and send us home.* That was my petition.

When we returned to the nursing home early in the evening, our uncle was feeling much better physically but had sunk into a depression. With a weary look on his face, he told us that he simply wanted to die. We scolded him, telling him he should not give up and say such things, but he was pouting, shook his head and said he had nothing left to live for—everything had been taken away from him so he may as well die. That was exactly what Julie was hoping for and it angered me. I knew Pasquale had a fighting spirit; the Pasquale I had known from my childhood would never just lie down and let his opponent trounce all over him. He was a proud man and he simply needed to be reminded of that fact.

"Do you want Julie to win?" I asked him. "Do you want to see her and her husband keep everything that you worked so hard for all your life? You're already so much better than you were when you left Pennsylvania. I know it's difficult, but you can do it."

That seemed to snap him out of it and he lay there thinking. His eyes searched the room, and then he shared another profound thought.

"You know, I couldn't even talk to you a few weeks ago," he reminded me.

I beamed as I recalled that day in March when I visited with him before he was taken away. That was the day he tried so earnestly to tell me to find a lawyer for him but I did not understand. Tears welled up in my eyes at the thought—he remembered!

And that was the man of whom Julie had said earlier that day, "He doesn't know what he's saying. If you sit and listen to him long enough he'll tell you the moon is made of green cheese!"

That was just another serving of Julie's deception spoken to us in the hope that we would eventually believe her and simply return to Pennsylvania without our uncle. She did not know us nearly as well as she thought she did. We are not the type of people to throw up our hands and simply walk away from a loved one.

After Pasquale had calmed down, I walked out to the parking lot to telephone Max and let him know that we had checked back into the hotel after deciding we would stay on for another day or so. While I tended to that task, Ben remained with Pasquale to repair his eyeglasses. Earlier, on our way to dinner, Ben stopped at a drug store and purchased a set of nose pads. Pasquale had a sore on one side of his nose where the cracked bridge of his eyeglasses rubbed his skin raw. From the looks of it, the sore had not been acquired overnight but apparently, no one, not his ever-loving, doting wife nor his caring stepdaughter nor the many nurses and aides who floated in and out of his room, saw fit to remedy the situation.

As a result, Uncle Pasquale stopped wearing them, which meant that everything around him was out of focus. We noticed that without his eyeglasses, Pasquale would sometimes mistake one nurse for another, which only added to the illusion that he did not possess all of his faculties. When a tall, thin, short-haired woman with thick eyeglasses entered Pasquale's room earlier that day, he refused to speak to her. She was the physical therapist, who made persistent attempts to work with Pasquale, but he mistook her for Nora and refused to cooperate with her. When I pointed that out to the therapist, she acknowledged that she had assumed as much and her admission only led to another question: then why hadn't someone repaired Pasquale's eyeglasses so he could see clearly and avoid the confusion? It seemed like such a simple matter. Yet it was just one more item on the growing list of things that irked us about the level of care he had been receiving.

When I got to the parking lot and called Max on my cell phone, he delivered yet another blow and there was simply no way to soften the delivery: the Clerk of Courts needed a statement of competency from a physician before he would schedule a hearing to challenge Julie, the current attorney-in-fact. My chin dropped onto my chest and I closed my eyes in a gesture of defeat as I realized we were back to square one. We needed that blasted test before we could go forward, sideways, or in any direction at all for that matter. As always, Max tried to point out the bright side, explaining that even if Pasquale failed the test, that failure would actually play into our favor as it would open the door to the need for an emergency hearing. I told him I would speak to Fern about it in the morning and try to determine when another test might be scheduled. That meant that I would have to take a deep breath and put on the diplomat's hat again, and I just hated having to placate people whom I viewed as incompetent asses.

As I walked back across the parking lot toward the building entrance, I sent a hopeful gaze skyward along with a single silent plea: *Set my uncle free!* Somewhere in the back of my mind I thought I heard a small voice answer, *Keep your eyes on me.*

⌧⌧⌧

Later that evening, after Ben and I returned to the hotel and had an opportunity to review the day's events, I learned that while I was outside in my car consulting with Max, Ben had an opportunity to question Pasquale's roommate, Gene, about the botched competency test from the day before. Gene is a veteran sailor who regaled us with stories of his days in the Navy during the hours we spent with Pasquale. Gene had acute diabetes and was living at the nursing home only as a temporary measure until his condition stabilized so that he could return home to his family. He was a congenial fellow with sparkling eyes and a round face that always wore a welcoming smile. We truly enjoyed Gene's company when he was in the room, and I could not help thinking that if Uncle Pasquale had not been so heavily sedated for such prolonged periods, they probably would have been terrific company for one another, sharing war stories.

Ben told me that according to Gene, a doctor walked into their room on the day of the test, stood at the foot of Pasquale's bed and without introduction or any form of explanation began firing questions at Pasquale: *What's your name? Do you know where you are? What's today's date?*

"Hell," Gene admitted, "I don't even know what today's date is and I've only been away from home a couple of weeks!"

When Ben asked him if our uncle had responded to the questions, Gene said he did not. Pasquale just stared at the doctor with a frown on his face as if he did not know what she was saying or why she was there. According to Gene, the doctor was not in the room more than five minutes. So, that was the big test. One more item was added to the next day's to-do list: talk to Fern about finding a more competent doctor!

Back at the hotel that evening, I quietly mulled over the day's events and attempted to form our strategy for the following day. When my head finally touched the pillow that night, I slept peacefully remembering Ben's earlier words, *Everything happens for a reason.* I hoped he was right and that whatever the reason may be would soon become clear to us, for only then could we find a way to get Pasquale out of his predicament and back home where he belonged.

CHAPTER EIGHT

Blood, Ink and Red-tape

THURSDAY, APRIL 8

I awoke with a song running through my head. It was the upbeat refrain from a popular Christian tune often sung at the church I attended back home: *We will dance on the streets that are golden ... Sing aloud for the time of rejoicing is near!* Through the words of that song, I felt God was telling me that the enemy's fortress was being dismantled, brick by brick, and we would soon reach our goal. I shared those words with Ben while we sipped coffee in the hotel's breakfast room. It seemed to brighten his mood as well and we both walked out of the hotel with lighter steps that morning.

By 7:45 a.m. we were on our way to the nursing home. While Ben drove I was already punching numbers on my cell phone keypad, getting started on the list of tasks that needed to be accomplished that day. The first telephone call was to the office of Uncle Pasquale's attending physician. We were not certain if the order to stop his sedation ever came through and we did not want to risk another bungled competency test. With that in mind, I left a firm, but tactful, message with their answering service. I delivered the same message, in person, to the nurse on duty outside Pasquale's room when we arrived. She had not yet administered the morning dose of medication and I extracted a promise from her that before doing so, she would check with his doctor regarding the change in orders.

While I spoke with the nurse in the hallway, Ben proceeded to our uncle's room ahead of me. Pasquale, seeing that Ben was alone, asked with concern, "Where's Gina?"

"Right here, Uncle Pasquale," I answered, sailing into the room moments after Ben.

"I just needed to talk to your nurse for a minute," I told him.

It had been so long since I last heard him say my name that I was beginning to wonder if he remembered it. Each one of those little triumphs meant so much to us as it proved that his brain had healed since the stroke and his memory was resurfacing intact.

Pasquale looked better that morning, more refreshed and with a little more color to warm the ashen pallor that his face had taken on in the preceding weeks. Though he appeared more relaxed than the previous day, he let us know immediately that his suspended release from the nursing home still weighed heavily on his mind.

"I just want to be out of here and on my own again," he complained. Then he asked,

"Who else is coming to visit?"

Ben explained to him that we weren't sure if anyone else would be able to make the trip any time soon, to which Pasquale replied hopefully, "Maybe I can go home next week."

At that point, Ben excused himself to telephone his wife to find out how she was coping with their business. While he was gone, Nora and Julie arrived. It was just after 9 a.m. Julie entered Pasquale's room first, noiselessly, like a scout advancing ahead of the troops. She addressed me, coolly, from just inside the doorway.

"Can you please leave so we can spend some time alone with him?"

"Sure!" I responded cheerfully. *Keep smiling so she won't know what you're up to.* The last thing I needed was for Julie to interfere with my latest attempt to have Pasquale's sedatives withheld.

■ ■ ■

While I did a slow burn on the inside, outwardly I projected nothing but sunshine and sweetness. Beaming a smile in her direction, I arose from the chair and assured Uncle Pasquale that Ben and I would return later. After the confrontation with Talia Evert, I was determined to make a concerted effort to be as solicitous and cooperative as possible so that no one would have grounds to accuse me of being the aggressor, which was more than I could say for Nora that morning. She entered on the heels of her daughter spewing venom and with pure hatred in her eyes.

"I want to sit by my husband!" she shouted at me. "I'm his wife!"

"Sit," I told her. "No one is stopping you."

With that, I calmly made my exit and went to find Ben.

Not long afterward, while Ben and I sat in my car in the parking lot, we noticed Julie getting into her car and driving off without Nora. Ben and I exchanged knowing glances—we could handle Nora—then scrambled out of the car and headed for the building.

In weeks past, while Pasquale was still in Pennsylvania, his siblings had noticed a distinct pattern: when Julie was at her mother's side, Nora became sullen or aggressive. In Julie's absence, Nora's mood seemed to return to the congenial nature that existed in her prior to Uncle Pasquale's stroke; she became, once again, the woman we knew and appreciated. With that in mind, Ben and I boldly walked back into the building and made our way to Pasquale's room. We had agreed beforehand that if it looked like Nora was still in the mood for a fight, we would simply excuse ourselves and drive to the beach. Thankfully, that wasn't necessary.

❈❈❈

As we entered the room, Nora's weary glance acknowledged our presence. She was seated next to Pasquale's bed, holding his hand. To our relief, she again appeared serene without Julie's influence. Uncle Pasquale invited us to sit so Ben cautiously took the chair on the opposite side of his bed, across from Nora. Before I could settle into the chair next to him, Nora addressed me in a weary tone.

"Gina, what is going on?"

"What do you mean?" I asked innocently.

"What are you doing here?" she wanted to know.

I did not want to talk over my uncle and risk another angry scene in his room so I invited her to walk out into the hallway with me, which she did. Before I could begin to speak, she again addressed me.

"I have always liked you, Gina," she sounded sincere. "Why are you doing this to me?"

I chose my words carefully and tried to be gentle with her, still mindful of the fact that her mind wasn't what it used to be. I still felt that her daughter bore more of the responsibility for the way all of this had turned out and I did not want Nora to feel as though we were pointing a finger at her.

Taking a deep breath, I told her that I meant her no harm. I then explained that my mother became alarmed during their last telephone conversation when Nora told her, "This will all be over in another month."

"Don't you see?" I attempted to reason. "His sister thought he was dying. When he left Pennsylvania he was recovering, according to his doctors. Then, to make matters worse, Julie gave the order that the nurses were not to speak to my mother again so she had no way of finding out what was really happening to her brother. We had to come."

Nora thoughtfully considered what I had told her and said she remembered the incident. She claimed that Pasquale was having such a bad night that she thought she was about to lose him. She told me that she had even called in a Catholic priest from a nearby parish to administer last rites (*Again with the priest!* I inwardly groaned).

Nora and I chatted, almost amiably, and I hated to stir up the waters, but I didn't want to mislead her as to my intentions so I simply laid it all out and told her that if my uncle wanted to go home we did intend to honor his wishes and take him. However, I also told her that she was welcome to come with us. Hearing my offer, she cast her eyes to the floor and appeared to be thinking it over. I told her she could let us know later, hugged her, and then gently steered her back into the room where I could already hear Pasquale asking Ben where Nora and I had gone.

Nora took up her place once more next to Pasquale's bed and as she did so, he reached out and took her hand.

Choking back his tears he looked at me and said, "I love this woman, but I don't want her daughter anywhere near me and I'm not living with her."

Tears spilled down over Nora's cheeks as well at Pasquale's heartfelt confession.

"I don't know what to do," he cried. "I want to be with her but I know I can't take care of her anymore."

"And I can't take care of you either," Nora surprisingly admitted.

It was a heart-breaking scene and I sympathized with both of them. It was truly a difficult situation and there were no easy answers. I just wanted both of them to be safe and happy so I offered up the only solution I could think of.

"Why don't all of you move back to Pennsylvania? Maybe if Julie moves in with you there, Uncle Pasquale, the two of you may be able to iron out your difficulties."

"It isn't as if she or her husband would be leaving a promising career," I added.

Nora was hesitant. She said Julie would have to work and would not be able to be at home with them throughout the day when they would need someone the most. I reminded her that she had given Julie two hundred *thousand* dollars before they left Pennsylvania and that my uncle's resources would be sufficient to support them all. Julie could work part-time in the evenings if she wanted to and hire an evening nurse. Nora stated that Julie lost her most recent part-time job while she was in Pennsylvania immediately following Pasquale's hospitalization.

As a matter of fact, the reason Julie left her mother alone that very day was that she had an interview for another job. Hearing that, I could not help wondering if that might have been the reason why Julie was in such a hurry to move my uncle to Virginia. But then, she did not own a home there and had no other ties to that state. If she had lost her job as well, and only a part-time position at that, why couldn't she have simply relocated back to Pennsylvania as she claimed she would do the previous November? It was Julie's husband who insisted they move to Virginia and right or wrong, Julie indulged his every whim until talk of divorce surfaced. It certainly seemed to me that I was still missing a piece of the puzzle and, so far, no one was offering to fill in the blank.

"Why," I wondered aloud, "did Julie insist on putting everyone through so much anguish when she could have lived comfortably under my uncle's roof?"

"Julie won't move back there," Nora replied, sadly.

"Then I will," I declared. "I'll uproot myself, if necessary, to help both of you."

I was so desperate to do something, anything, to ease their pain that the words tumbled out of my mouth before I had even considered what I was saying. I had just relocated myself into a new home and had a thriving real estate business. I loved where I lived and worked and would terribly miss both! Much as I hated the thought of uprooting myself again, I knew I would do it if they asked me to. After all, they were family and that's what family does.

"You've always been like my own daughter," Uncle Pasquale said through his tears as he reached out and took my hand.

"And I always will be," I promised him.

"I can't decide," he cried out in anguish, shaking his head.

"You don't have to decide today," I consoled him. "Rest now. It will be clear to you in a few days. Whatever you want to do, we'll be here for you and we'll respect your wishes. Right, Ben?" Ben nodded and hugged him.

"We love you, Uncle Pasquale," he told him.

We left the two of them alone, holding hands, so they could discuss their circumstances and try to come to a mutual conclusion. In the meantime, Ben and I went out in search of lunch. Along the way, I took the opportunity to call my mother. The news from home was not good. Aunt Eleanor had collapsed the previous day when she was told the ambulance had returned to Pennsylvania without her brother. The stress of the situation was too much for her to bear and it appeared that she might have suffered a slight stroke as well. The family suddenly had one more to worry about.

"Try not to worry, Mother," I reassured her. "Everything will turn out all right."

The more I thought of Aunt Eleanor, the stronger the urge was to call her. I thought that if she heard my voice, heard for herself that we were still upbeat and convinced that we would be able to bring her brother home soon, it might help to ease her mind.

■ ■ ■

When I made the call, I could hear her strained voice in the background while I spoke to her son, my cousin Seth. I stressed that the situation was far from hopeless and in fact, was more good than bad. I told Seth about the episode when Pasquale was in so much pain and that I felt it was a blessing we had not been traveling with him at the time. I also told him that we finally succeeded in having Pasquale's sedation stopped so he could coherently express his own wishes, an issue of utmost importance in gaining his freedom. It really did appear that circumstances were coming around in our favor.

"It's just taking a little longer than we expected, that's all."

The day before I would not have been so self-assured, but the way events were unfolding, I was certain Julie would be exposed and moved out of the way so she could not threaten Pasquale again. If we had been able to simply walk in there and take Pasquale home, that task would not have been accomplished. I wasn't sure how it was happening but it was a fascinating process to watch as events seemed to be intentionally orchestrated to further our cause.

Each time we encountered a stumbling block, it appeared the obstacle had been purposefully put there so that during the removal process, Julie's ulterior motives would be further exposed and Pasquale would be elevated to a new level of respect in the eyes of the nursing home staff. It humbled me to realize just how privileged I was to have been given a glimpse of the supernatural play-by-play that was unfolding. Then I knew what that disembodied voice meant when it said, *Keep your eyes on me*. There truly is a higher power that can lay out a plan that will be much more effective than any plan a human mind can conceive.

By the time Ben and I were seated at a restaurant for dinner that evening, I was already engaged in the third telephone call of the day to Max, our faithful ally. He was not only our valued counsel but had quickly begun to feel like a member of our family. I could not wait to tell him that Uncle Pasquale had called me by my name that morning.

"How wonderful to hear!" Max enthusiastically proclaimed.

After I told him about the healing conversation that took place with Nora, absent Julie, he thoughtfully replied, "It makes me wonder how it came about that Nora put all of her trust in Julie with the whole DiAngeli family offering to help her and Pasquale."

"Dementia." It was the only answer I could come up with. "And coercion. In Nora's current state of mind, she's like an impressionable child."

And Julie was a rotten influence. The increasing boldness she had begun to exhibit was unnerving. It was as if that power of attorney document had been a key to a golden city that she would guard with her life, if necessary. Shortly after we met, Max told me it had been his observation over the years that there is no more powerful motivator than the prospect of found money; not even sex, he had said. Perhaps I was simply naive, but I would not have believed it if I hadn't seen the greed factor in action with my own eyes. Unfortunately for Pasquale, his life savings equated to a lot of *found money* for his needy stepdaughter and her husband.

During our conversation, I asked Max if, in light of Pasquale's improved cognizance, it would be possible for Pasquale to legally appoint a new attorney-in-fact and vacate Julie's authority. Max said he would not be opposed to attempting it and that he would prepare a new document, for medical purposes, naming Ben and me as attorneys-in-fact. If we were successful, we could use the document to gain Pasquale's release. Max also expressed his regret at not being able to lay hands on a copy of the existing power of attorney document. If he was going to draft a new one, he wanted to ensure that all terms of the existing document would be covered. I wasn't sure I could do anything about that, but it continued to weigh on my mind all the same. Before hanging up, we made plans to meet again at the nursing home at eight that evening.

On the way back to the nursing home, my vehicle reminded me that I had failed to tend to the engine's misfire after we sprinted down the interstate highway days earlier. Feeling we might be left stranded if I did not immediately see to the problem, I dropped Ben under the portico at the entrance to the nursing home, then drove back down the highway to a nearby service station. In doing so, I missed an event that would prove to be a momentous turning point in our efforts to free our uncle.

As fate or heavenly intervention would have it, Ben's return to Pasquale's room was perfectly timed to precede Nora and Julie's arrival by mere minutes. During our absence, Uncle Pasquale had been dressed, placed in a wheelchair, and was seated alone in the hallway outside his room. He was out of bed for the first time since his stroke! Ben pulled up a chair and joined him there. While they sat engaged in conversation, Nora and Julie made their way down the hall toward them. As was her usual method of exerting her authority, Julie immediately asked Ben to leave so she and her mother could visit with Pasquale alone.

Ben promptly rose from the chair, prepared to obey, until Pasquale's left hand shot out and grabbed Ben's arm with a strength that surprised everyone, including the nurse who happened to be dispensing pills from a push cart just a few feet away.

In a loud and clear voice, Pasquale expressed his displeasure at Julie's demands.

"You stay here!" Pasquale commanded Ben, "Don't you leave me with them!"

Then he delivered a few choice words to Julie and Nora, equally loud and clear.

"You two, get the hell out!"

Apparently, some unpleasant business had transpired between the three of them earlier in the day after Ben and I left for lunch, something that set Pasquale off and continued to rile him. His wrath was directed at *both* of them at that point, not just Julie.

Not wanting to get in the middle, but concerned about Pasquale's agitated state, Ben attempted to placate everyone by remaining near enough to reassure Pasquale but out of sight to Julie and Nora.

"Don't worry, I'm not leaving you," Ben assured him. "I'll just go and sit inside your room while you visit with them."

Julie was not happy with that arrangement and frankly, neither was Pasquale and he continued to spout off at *the two of them* until Nora chimed in.

"You love them more than you love me," she said to Pasquale with resentment.

Her remark seemed to get Pasquale's attention and although he was still steaming, he did allow them to sit down next to him, Julie on one side and Nora on the other.

That was the scene I spied from the opposite end of the corridor when I returned from the automotive service station. Of course, I had no idea what had just occurred.

I only knew that Ben was gone, Julie and Nora were in residence and the expressions on their faces, even from a distance, told me they were not having a happy visit. I decided they were probably best left alone, so instead of continuing on my course, I simply detoured left down another corridor and exited the building into a rear courtyard.

Not knowing that Ben was captive in Pasquale's room, I went off in search of him. Eventually, I covered the interior of the building, carefully avoiding the vicinity of Pasquale's room, as well as the grounds. Having no luck finding Ben, I returned to the courtyard, slumped down onto a park bench, and remained there. Periodically, I walked around the exterior of the building to the front parking lot to see if Julie's car was gone yet. The minute I discovered it was, I beat a path back to Pasquale's room to get the scoop.

Ben and I had become an almost constant presence in that nursing home and most of the nurses and aides began to greet us like old friends. However, there was one old battle-axe (every nursing home seems to have one) who never spoke a word to us and acknowledged our visits with a scowl on her face. It caused us to wonder if perhaps she had taken Julie's part in the ongoing feud or if she was simply one of those people who dislikes their job but plods on anyway purely out of mean determination. Fortunately, the "battle-axe" was not on duty when the shouting match took place between Pasquale and *the two of them* or I am certain the incident never would have made it into Pasquale's medical record.

According to Ben, after Julie and her mother finally left, he asked Nurse Penny if she had heard the exchange.

"Yup, ah couldn't believe it," Penny declared in her slow Southern drawl. "And ah wrote down every word!"

With both Penny and Nurse Lisa on our side, Fern and her sidekick, Talia, would get the documentation they claimed was heretofore lacking and I sent up a silent *thank you* that the important detail had finally been tended to.

By the time I rejoined them that afternoon, Uncle Pasquale was tucked back in his bed, resting quietly against the pillows, and Ben was seated next to him. I dropped into the chair on the opposite side of Pasquale's bed. A few moments later, Nurse Lisa returned to tell us that the standing order for sedation had finally been revoked, only temporarily, until the next competency test, but revoked nonetheless! When Lisa spoke to us, I recognized her accent.

"You're from Boston, aren't you?" I asked her with a grin.

She was and she went on to tell us that many of the nursing home's employees were transplants from other states, Nurse Penny being one of the few exceptions. I had traveled to Boston several years before and shared with her my memories of the sights I had particularly enjoyed. Getting into the spirit of the conversation, Lisa entertained us with a story about her last trip to the city with her children. They returned to Boston during the previous Fourth of July weekend to escape the summer heat in the South only to find that by some fluke of the weather it was even hotter in the North. So hot, in fact, that the fire department resorted to hosing down the crowd during an afternoon event at one of the stadiums. Ben and I laughed but Pasquale made not a sound. He lay there quietly with a look of suspicion on his face. After Lisa finished her tale but before she exited the room, Uncle Pasquale looked at me questioningly.

"What's that? What did she say?" he asked.

I repeated the story to Uncle Pasquale and as I did so, the tension in his face relaxed and his frown broke into a grin.

That incident finally brought home to us the solution to one of the biggest issues delaying Pasquale's release. Fern and Talia were convinced that Pasquale was unable to clearly communicate and that impression, we then realized, was born largely of the fact that because Pasquale could not hear what was being said, he simply did not respond even though he was certainly able to. Taking advantage of Lisa's witnessing this incident, Ben explained that Pasquale's hearing aid seemed to have gone missing.

However, if everyone spoke loudly enough, Pasquale could and certainly would answer them. Lisa was not even aware that he required a hearing aid.

"Nope—it's not even in his charts," she reported after flipping through several pages attached to her clipboard. This too, made it into the nursing home's records that day.

After Nurse Lisa left the room, Ben pointed out something that I had missed when I first arrived. Tacked to the bulletin board on the wall to the right of Pasquale's bed was a small 3" by 4" piece of notepaper on which had been scrawled a message by obviously trembling hands. It read simply: *I love you. Your wife, Nora.*

Apparently, Nora had placed it there before she left the nursing home that day and we could not help but wonder if the message was there for our benefit more than Pasquale's. It seemed to be an act of one-upmanship to counter our triumph after Pasquale made it known whose company he preferred earlier that afternoon.

Much as I sympathized with Nora's position, the impish child in me could not let an opportunity pass, so, I set about making up my own little sign with paper and a black magic marker borrowed from the nurse's station. When I had finished, I taped the sign to the cover of the lamp hanging above the headboard of Pasquale's bed. It read: *Please speak loudly. I have lost my hearing aid!*

Just as Ben and I read between the lines of Nora's love note, we hoped Nora and Julie would do the same with ours. That little notice was meant not only as assistance in restoring Pasquale's credibility, but also as a message to Julie that we were onto her scheme and would do everything possible to see that those attending Pasquale were no longer fooled by her attempts to make him appear incompetent.

Later that day, when I conferred with Fern about other matters, I brought up the fact that Pasquale had been unable to hear the entire time he had been there and that her nursing staff was not even aware that he had a hearing problem. I demanded that either Pasquale's hearing aid be located or a new one be ordered *immediately* so he would have it before the next competency test was administered. She promised to telephone Julie to find out if she had Pasquale's hearing aid at her home. Fern and her staff were looking more like Julie's saps with each passing day, and it was a fact that was no longer lost on Fern Donnelly.

When I spoke of these events to my mother later that evening, she let out a sigh of exasperation. She told me that Pasquale had both a new pair of eyeglasses and his hearing aid when he left Pennsylvania. She had gone to Pasquale's eye doctor to pick up the glasses herself the week before Pasquale was spirited away and she had seen Nora tuck both items into her purse when she cleared Pasquale's possessions from the room. What happened to them? Were they purposefully being withheld from Pasquale to put him at a disadvantage? We certainly thought so.

While I worked to rectify those issues with Lady Fern, Ben took up another concern. Pasquale had had no physical therapy at all since his arrival in Virginia. His right hand, the one he lost control of during his stroke, was still immobile. When the time came to sign for his own release he would need the use of that hand. Each time we visited, Ben sat next to Pasquale and patiently massaged that hand while he talked to him. At one point Ben put a pen in Pasquale's left hand and attempted to help him practice writing, but it was no use.

As Pasquale resignedly admitted, "I can't do it."

While Ben continued his attempts to restore movement to Pasquale's hand, I returned to the privacy of my car to call Max. Nurse Penny had warned us the day before that she had seen Julie and Nora standing quietly in the corridor outside Pasquale's room, hidden from our view and eavesdropping on our conversation.

Penny's confidence confirmed what I had suspected: she had taken on the role as our ally and was not only doing everything in her power to help Pasquale, she was also watching our backs.

With Penny's warning in mind, Ben and I had taken to inspecting the hallway before launching into important matters with Pasquale, and we never spoke on the phone with Max inside the building lest any spies be listening and carry the words back to Julie.

I settled into the driver's seat of my car and punched in Max's telephone number. Since Uncle Pasquale was unable to pen his name on a new power of attorney document and we would see the results of the second competency evaluation the following day, I saw no reason for Max to visit the nursing home that evening. Much as I enjoyed seeing him, I had to keep in mind that with every telephone call and every trip to the nursing home, his meter was ticking. I felt that I owed it to the family who had so graciously paid the legal retainer fee to be a good steward of that money.

When I reached Max, I told him we might as well wait it out and see what happens. He was relieved at the thought of ending his day early for a change and did not feel the least bit uncomfortable telling me so. His absolute candor was one of the qualities that caused me to place such complete trust in him. As I have said, we thought of him as family at that point. During less intense conversations concerning Pasquale, Max and I were even able to share some of our personal interests and glimpses into each other's family lives. I was beginning to feel as though I would be leaving a friend behind when the time came to return to Pennsylvania.

Just as Max and I were about to end our call that evening, Ben suddenly appeared at the passenger door of my car. As he climbed in, he hit me with Julie's latest power play.

"We've been barred from the home," he announced sarcastically.

"Hold on a minute, Max, we may need you again," I said into the phone. Then to Ben,

"Repeat that?"

"Well, not exactly barred," he admitted. "Julie said our visiting hours have been restricted. We aren't allowed to go in before 9 a.m. and we have to leave by 6 p.m. because it's too stressful for Uncle Pasquale when we're there all day."

"That's a farce—that *is* all day! As if she really cares about his level of stress anyway," I laughed.

"False alarm," I announced into the cell phone. "You get the night off, Max! I think we can handle this one."

That evening, Ben decided he wanted to skip dinner, fast for the rest of the day, then attend a service at a Catholic church he spotted a short distance from the nursing home. Until he mentioned it, I had completely lost track of the days and the fact that the Easter holiday was quickly approaching. It would have been a nice gift to the family if we had been able to bring Pasquale home to them by Easter Sunday but that remained to be seen.

While Ben attended the church service, I remained at the hotel to meditate and relax. Ben invited me to go with him, but having left ritualistic religion behind so many years before I was no longer comfortable in that venue. For me, simple, quiet meditation was the avenue for collecting my thoughts and moving forward.

After meditation and a quick trip outside for a cigarette my body was craving but my brain told me I really did not need, I made the nightly telephone call to my mother. Pasquale's siblings were weary of the rollercoaster ride we had all been on and it was taking a toll in elevated blood pressure, loss of sleep, loss of appetite, and Aunt Eleanor's recent trip to the hospital. In an effort to reduce everyone's stress, my mother made the decision not to give her siblings daily updates anymore. At least, not until Ben and I managed to secure concrete proof that Pasquale was, in fact, going home.

"We keep giving them hope and then we let them down," she lamented to me. "It's just too stressful and I'm not going to do that to them anymore."

I couldn't blame her and told her that I hoped to be able to give them proof of his return soon.

I had set the cell phone on my nightstand and picked up the TV remote when I suddenly remembered that I had not called my own home since leaving Pennsylvania. Twelve messages were waiting on my answering machine.

One message was from my good friend Jeannie, who simply said, "I don't know where you are or what's going on, but you were on my mind today so I just wanted you to know I've been lifting you up in prayer."

That message blew me away as it meant that even in the midst of battle, that higher power was still calling prayer warriors to stand in the gap for us. Then a sudden chill ran through me when I realized that if warriors were still being called, then the battle had to be intensifying not abating. If the events of the preceding days could truly be compared to a rollercoaster ride, I thought, then we must be reaching the point on the track where the cars turn upside down just before they are sent hurling down the home stretch. The implication was disturbing.

Good Friday, April 9, dawned overcast but with a warm, almost tropical breeze. When we had left Pennsylvania earlier in the week, spring had not yet officially arrived there. Daytime temperatures had barely reached the forty degree mark and there was little sign of new life in the trees and flower beds. In Virginia, on the other hand, the trees were in leaf and flowering shrubs were practically in full bloom. The air was sweet with a pungent, flowery fragrance, and it was getting hot. According to this girl's Northern body clock, it was *way* too hot for a day in April!

I was beginning to feel uncomfortable in the denim jeans and long-sleeved shirts I had packed for the trip, so I convinced Ben to visit a local department store with me that afternoon, where I purchased short-sleeved shirts and hair combs to lift my shoulder-length locks off my neck.

Ben, too, was beginning to feel the effects of what, for us, was a drastic change in climate. He made his way to a local barber shop first thing that morning for his ritual springtime "unveiling." Off came the beard; off came the three-inch long ponytail tied at the nape of his neck. He looked like a different man when I saw him afterward.

Ben laughed at the expression of surprise that must have registered on my face.

"Didn't recognize me, huh?" He grinned, and then in a more reflective tone, he voiced another thought as he rubbed his cleanly shaved chin. "Gee, maybe I shouldn't have done that yet. The way Uncle Pasquale has been lately maybe he won't recognize me!"

We still had half an hour before we were permitted to visit Uncle Pasquale that day. Ben had been caught off guard by Julie's stunning announcement the previous evening and did not think to ask her if the visiting hour restriction was her ruling or that of the nursing home. He voiced his regret over that lapse while we waited. I did not feel it was an issue either way and couldn't help wondering if Ben had misunderstood. After all, we still had the entire day with Uncle Pasquale so I simply shrugged and let the matter roll off my shoulders.

When Ben complained that the restriction was just another of Julie's ploys to regain control over Pasquale, I smiled benevolently then recited for him one of my favorite Bible verses: *Do not curse your enemy but pray for them and I will heap burning coals on their heads in your name.*

"Just picture Julie with flames shooting out of her hair and you'll be all right," I told him as I laughed and patted his arm.

Everyone has an Achilles's heel, and God knows exactly where it is. That's why it is better to gracefully walk away and leave the business of vengeance up to him. In light of our uncle's circumstances and Julie's maddening actions, it certainly wasn't easy to follow that advice, but I vowed to make an attempt to be as humble as possible. Patience and humility were virtues that did not come naturally to me.

Over coffee that morning, Ben told me about his conversation with the woman who had cut his hair and shaved his beard. She recognized his Northern accent, which struck us as humorous since we never thought of our speech as having any sort of accent at all. We had heard a variety of accents from New England to New York, Ohio to the Carolinas. Come to think of it, Pennsylvanians are surrounded by people from other states who speak with a distinct diction, but Pennsylvanians? Nah! In any event, the hairstylist asked Ben what brought him to the beach so early in the season.

He gave her the Reader's Digest version of our adventure with Uncle Pasquale.

"Mah werd! Sounds like a story for Sixty Minutes!" she exclaimed with a Southern drawl. Then she quickly added, "Don't fergit where ya got yer hair cut!"

Everyone wants their sixty seconds of fame. All we wanted was to wheel Uncle Pasquale out of that nursing home and get him back to Pennsylvania where he belonged. To that end, Pasquale's second competency evaluation was scheduled for that very afternoon and it was to be performed by a neurologist instead of the general practitioner who handled, or should I say bungled, the first test. This was definitely a step in the right direction. Providing Pasquale passed the exam, he would be able to sign his own release immediately and we could be on our way twenty-four hours later.

If the neurologist determined Pasquale was not legally competent, then we would simply take a copy of his report to Max, as Max instructed us to do, and the battle would continue in a court of law.

Ben and I arrived at the nursing home promptly at 9 a.m. and found Pasquale in an unusually deep slumber. *Not again!* We groaned. After the sedating drugs were withheld the preceding day, he was so much more alert that finding him practically unconscious again took us by surprise. When Nurse Lisa told us that the order from Pasquale's attending physician had definitely been changed, she also warned us that the order stipulated that his medication could be withheld only so long as Pasquale did not become agitated. If he did become agitated then he was to be given the formerly prescribed sedative dosage immediately.

We understood that the order was given in that manner to protect our uncle. His brain was still healing from the massive stroke and the last thing any of us wanted was for him to suffer another episode. However, as we observed the deep, almost comatose state in which he appeared to be submerged, we could not help wondering if, after Ben had been forced to leave the premises the previous evening, Julie had purposefully set him off so that the nurse on duty would be compelled to sedate him.

I put my hand on Pasquale's forehead to see if I could detect a rise in temperature. As I was doing so, the nurse we had dubbed the battle-axe came into Pasquale's room demanding to know what we were doing there. When we answered that it was our turn to be there, she informed us, practically gloating, that our visiting hours had been restricted to the hours of 4–6 p.m., not the nine to six time frame that Ben thought he had heard the previous evening. The battle was intensifying all right. The enemy was losing, they knew it, and they had resorted to such pitiful measures as severely restricting our visiting hours in an attempt to regain control.

As we took our leave, it was Ben's turn to wrestle with anger as he verbally abused Julie and my turn to offer solace.

"We cannot allow anger to get in our way anymore," I told him. "If we do, we'll be playing right into Julie's hands."

Months later, after obtaining a copy of the nursing home's records, we would learn that Julie more than likely *was* the author of my uncle's drug-induced stupor. The night nurse made this notation at 10:30 p.m. on the day that Ben had been tossed out of the nursing home: *Resident is crying; states "my nephew is gone." Will continue to watch for signs of agitation.* Why did Pasquale believe we were gone? Who but Julie would have had a reason to tell him such a lie?

With our visiting hours restricted, it certainly would have been easy enough for her to get away with such a ruse, upsetting Pasquale in the process and guaranteeing another dose of sedation. I would not have put it past her to tell him that we had gone back to Pennsylvania and would not be returning.

It was only ten o'clock in the morning when we were tossed out of Pasquale's room for the second time in two days and with nothing better to do, Ben suggested we go exploring. He had spotted a pier and some house boats off in the distance during one of our many trips down the highway in the preceding days and he wanted a closer look. After exiting the highway and meandering down a few residential side streets, we found the road that led to the pier. We walked to the edge, removed our shoes, and sat there like two kids with our bare feet dangling in the water, chatting amiably.

After leaving the pier, Ben and I headed for the beach, the one place that had become our refuge. It was there that we felt closest to God, there where we heard his voice in the thunderous crashing of the waves and saw the magnificence of his being sparkling across the water. Within minutes of sinking our feet into the sand, Ben stooped to retrieve one of the shells I had come to call duck feet.

"Here's another of the ones you like," he called out to me. "Want it?"

"Nah, keep it for yourself," I replied.

"Nope," he stubbornly declared as he tossed it back onto the sand. "I'm not picking up any more shells. I've collected enough already and there's no more room for them in my suitcase!"

"Bet ya dinner you can't resist taking another one before we leave here today," I laughingly challenged him. With that, we took our separate contemplative paths.

Life abounded there, both on the sands and in the water. Evidence of creation was everywhere, from the dolphin twins arcing in unison over the waves to the children playing in the sand down to the most minute, fingernail-sized seashells that lay on the shore. Some of the shells were so tiny and fragile I could not help thinking it was a miracle they arrived on shore intact. But they did. The comparison to my uncle's recent tossing about on the waves of life did not escape me and I marveled all over again that he too had washed ashore largely intact.

As I strolled along, barefoot, jeans rolled up to my calves, I ran my fingertips over the ridges of a pearl-gray seashell I held in my hand while I tried to center my mind. I needed to get a sense of where that day would lead us.

Before long, I found myself humming the melody from another popular Christian tune. Eventually the humming gave way to words until I found myself singing softly while I walked: *And step by step you'll lead me and I will follow you all of my days.*

Just then I spotted the edge of a solitary seashell protruding from the sand. I sank to my knees and began to clear away the fine, pebbly grains until I uncovered an odd looking shell with a beautiful mother-of-pearl coating. It was shaped like a miniature footprint. I stood, walked to the water to rinse off the sand then turned it over in my palm as I studied it. A footprint, one footprint. Suddenly I remembered the popular poem and the significance was not lost on me. Like a broken record, one line of that poem, *Footprints*, echoed over and over again in my mind: *when there was only one set of footprints, I carried you.*

One set of footprints. I mulled that over in my mind. Okay, the poem says when there is one set of footprints, the footprints are God's. God alone. But, what did that mean for Ben and me or for Uncle Pasquale? And then it hit me like a wave breaking over the rocks: Ben and I were finished there; we were being released and sent home.

The feeling was unmistakable but I could not help asking, *why?* Could it be that Pasquale was going home after all? Or was there something else happening that we were unaware of, something going on behind the scenes that we were not meant to be a part of? I could only trust that God would do the rest; he would carry Pasquale alone.

Still somewhat confused yet excited nevertheless, I quickly backtracked and ran across the sand to find Ben. I felt an urgent need to get back to the car and check in at the nursing home.

It was already past noon when we got back to the lot where Ben had parked the car. My cell phone had been left there to recharge the battery and I reached for it as soon as I opened the passenger door. When I pulled it from the charger I saw the *missed call* display plus the little icon that indicated a message had been left in the voicemail box.

While Ben drove I dialed into the mailbox to retrieve the message. Max's excited voice boomed into my ear.

"I need a phone call from the Irresistible Force as soon as possible!"

That was the moniker I had earned in the preceding days. Max took to calling me the Irresistible Force when he discovered, during our first evening at the nursing home, my dive-in-and-take-charge approach when confronted with a problem. Put me on a task and if it's something I believe in completely I'm like a bloodhound on a trail. I won't give up until I've found the body! Dutifully, I dialed the number for Max's office.

"You must have a *very* good friend," he began.

He went on to tell me that when he arrived at his office that morning, his secretary handed him a set of documents that had come through their fax machine. The documents were photocopies of Pasquale's living will and the power of attorney document that Julie had refused to allow Max to see. When a door is closed, we open a window! The day Julie denied Max access to those documents, I had pondered the problem and come up with a brainstorm. What I did was not illegal and I did not lie to procure the copies; I simply omitted a few facts. The documents did not come from anyone on the nursing home's staff and that is all I am permitted to say, having been sworn to secrecy by Max himself.

The important thing was that Max did receive them, took the time to study them, and having done so, was able to render an opinion. More importantly, if and when we reached the point where he would be able to draft a revocation, he could now do so, carefully countering every point detailed within the original document.

The second piece of news he delivered was that Nora had collapsed at the nursing home late that morning and was taken away by ambulance. Was that God's mighty hand moving her and her daughter out of our way?

When I asked Max how he came about that bit of knowledge, he declined to elaborate, saying only that he could not reveal his sources. It appeared that he, too, had a very good friend!

After my conversation with Max, I decided to check in with Fern Donnelly to find out exactly what time Pasquale's competency evaluation would take place. Ben and I needed to make some decisions and the evaluation played a crucial role. I got Fern on the phone in short order but to my complete bewilderment, she informed me that the test had been postponed, rescheduled actually, for April 16, a full week later! She refused to give me any further details, stating that I would have to obtain reasons for the delay directly from Julie.

Julie, it appeared, had been busy indeed. Not only was she showing no signs of relinquishing control over Pasquale, but she appeared to be attempting to tighten the noose around his neck. She gave the order to delay the test for a specific reason; that much was certain. The big question was why? What was she up to now?

I hung up with Fern and repeated the information to Ben. In light of the delayed exam, we determined that we would drive back to Pennsylvania for the weekend, take care of personal business, pick up a week's worth of clean clothing, then return to Virginia the following Monday. However, we did not want to leave without having the opportunity to see Pasquale and it would be hours before our appointed visitation period began. Hours that would mean the difference between our arrival in Pennsylvania before midnight or well into the wee hours of the following morning. I began to think aloud as I reasoned my way through the dilemma.

"Fern doesn't know that *we* know that Nora and Julie aren't there," I said to Ben.

"I'll bet if I called her again and told her that we just want to duck in and say good-bye to Uncle Pasquale, she'd allow it."

Ben agreed it was worth a try. We would have worried ourselves sick through the weekend if we had not been able to tell Pasquale, in person, that we had to leave but would definitely return in a matter of days.

Donning the diplomat's hat once more (this was really getting to be a habit) I redialed the nursing home's telephone number and got Fern back on the line.

"I know we aren't supposed to visit my uncle until four o'clock," I began in a compliant tone, "but since his test has been rescheduled for next week, Ben and I have decided to return to Pennsylvania for a few days. We would really like to see our uncle before we leave."

I played to her sympathy telling her that surely, by that time, she had seen his attachment to us and knew that it would upset him greatly if we were to simply disappear without an explanation. To my surprise, she actually told me about Nora's fainting spell then stated that since it was unlikely she and Julie would return that day, we were welcome to visit. I feigned shock and politely expressed regrets over Nora's sudden illness. I should have received an Oscar for that one.

After voicing my gratitude for her gracious benevolence, I replaced the receiver and grinned at Ben.

"We're in!" I told him, unable to suppress my glee.

By 12:30 p.m., we were at Pasquale's bedside. Whether the result of some medication or a side effect of being weaned from sedatives we did not know, but he rambled incoherently. There was no way a test could have been administered that day. As we attempted to engage him in conversation, Pasquale seemed to jump from one emotion to the next in a profound state of confusion. At one point, he shook his head and cried like a frightened child.

"I just want to die," he moaned.

Then the angry man who had been subjected to the whims of others for too many months fought his way to the surface, yelling, "*I* want to be the boss!"

Ben kept trying to talk him through it while I was mopping his face with a damp cloth in an effort to bring him around. Finally, the Pasquale we knew emerged from the fog and took my hand. Remembering the offer I had made to him and Nora the previous afternoon he meekly asked, "Will you move in with me?"

"Yes, of course I will," I reassured him.

He promptly flip-flopped, once again groaning amidst the emotional turmoil that engulfed him.

"I don't know what I want to do!" he cried anxiously.

It was an awful position for anyone to be in, but particularly difficult for our aging uncle.

He had no children of his own to care for him and the family he did have for the previous eighteen years had suddenly turned against him. Pasquale was such a proud man that it killed him to ask anyone else for help. Even though he wanted to return to Pennsylvania to spend his final years in a place familiar to him, surrounded by the brother and sisters he had always been close to, part of him still struggled with the love he felt for his wife. He knew he would be leaving her behind, perhaps just for a little while but possibly forever. It was a difficult decision; one that only he could make. Ben and I remained with him for more than an hour until he finally appeared to be in control of his emotions again.

After we collected our jackets and prepared to leave, he kissed us both.

"You come back next week and then I'll tell you what I'm going to do," he told us.

Ben climbed into the driver's seat to handle the first leg of the journey while I made one final telephone call to Max.

"The saints are heading back to Pennsylvania," I informed him light-heartedly.

I told him that Pasquale's test had been rescheduled and that we would return the following week.

"I'll telephone you as soon as we get back in town," I promised him.

After hanging up, I leaned back against the headrest and closed my eyes. The week's events had sapped our energy and I was grateful that Ben had offered to take the first few hours behind the wheel. Later, we traded places during a brief refueling stop in southern Maryland. As soon as I was behind the wheel again, I pushed the car's engine until it screamed in an attempt to get us through the Washington, DC, beltway before rush hour traffic was in full swing. We did not make it.

At several points I was forced to reduce our speed well below thirty miles-per-hour, a relative crawl in comparison to our previous rate of progress. Ben and I shook our heads at the sight of eight lanes of solid bumper-to-bumper vehicles, thankful that we chose to reside in less populated cities.

Hours later, we pulled into a rest area. A bank of stainless steel vending machines glimmered under the floodlights outside the visitor's center, reminding us that we hadn't eaten a thing since breakfast. We greeted the sight, a multitudinous variety of snack foods, ice cream, candy, and beverages, like two wanderers coming out of the desert.

"I've never been so happy to see junk food in my entire life," I declared as I gleefully plunked quarters into the slots. "And I don't even like the stuff!"

Ben again took the wheel for the last leg of the journey while I called his wife, Annie, who was en route across the state of Pennsylvania. She planned to intercept us near Harrisburg, Pennsylvania, then return west, taking Ben home with her while I continued east to my own little house in the country. By the time we reached the rendezvous point, we were exhausted. I hugged my cousins, wished them a safe journey, then climbed behind the wheel again. As I watched them drive away, I silently wondered how each of us would find the energy to cover the last hundred or so miles.

I did not know whether it was the caffeine from the last cup of coffee, the adrenaline rush that kicks in to give us that second wind, or the refreshing return to a cooler climate, but I was wide awake by the time I pulled into my driveway just minutes after midnight. I carried my suitcase and bags of seashells into the house, stripped off the denim jeans I had worn for a solid week—we had originally intended to be gone for just a few days—then slipped into a soft flannel nightshirt, relishing the comforting touch and clean fragrance as the fabric cascaded down over my body. I filled the tea kettle and placed it on the stove then filled the kitchen sink with water.

After washing the dishes I had hastily piled into the sink earlier that week, I sank into the over-stuffed chair in the living room with my Bible in my lap and a steaming mug of green tea on a side table.

I was thankful for the small victories we had experienced that week and prayed for my uncle's protection during our absence. Who knew what Julie might dream up while we were gone? As I randomly opened the Bible to the book of Psalms, the amazingly comforting and appropriate words of Psalm 107 appeared before me and I was overcome with emotion.

Give thanks to the Lord, for he is good. Let the redeemed of the Lord say this—those he redeemed from the hand of the foe, those he gathered from the lands, from east and west from north and south ... they cried out to the Lord in their trouble and he delivered them from their distress.

Tears were streaming down my face as I read the next part. *He brought them out of the darkness ... and broke away their chains ... for he breaks down gates of bronze and cuts through bars of iron. He sent forth his word and healed them; he rescued them from the grave. He stilled the storm to a whisper; the waves of the sea were hushed ... and he guided them to their desired haven!*

After reading that, I no longer had even a shadow of a doubt that we would be bringing my uncle home soon.

CHAPTER NINE

Freedom takes Another Form
SATURDAY, APRIL 10

"A man is what he thinks about all day long."
—RALPH WALDO EMERSON

The day dawned bright and clear, bringing with it a fresh, pine-scented fragrance heralding springtime in the Pennsylvania countryside. I skipped down the sidewalk that bordered the flowerbeds in front of my cottage then hopped the few steps down to the driveway. I was on my way to retrieve my beloved companion, Jette, from her veterinarian's care and I could not wait to greet her with a hug and bring her home.

When I arrived at the veterinary hospital, Jette's doctor told me she had managed reasonably well during my week in Virginia, considering the effects of her illness, but she had taken a turn for the worse just the previous day.

Words, however, could not have prepared me for what I saw when Jette was brought to me in the waiting room. Though she perked up her ears and managed a feeble wag of her tail at the sound of my voice, I could see that something was terribly wrong. Her fur was as lustrous as I remembered but her eyes were not as bright as they were the day I dropped her off. The shock came when I saw that her happily wagging tail protruded from a sling that girded her lower abdomen and was held aloft, above her back, by one of the hospital's technicians. Both her doctor and the technician walked beside her as Jette tentatively made her way to where I knelt on the floor, slack-jawed, tears welling up in my eyes.

She nuzzled into me, whimpering, while her doctor explained that Jette needed help walking now as her hind quarters had weakened considerably. The tumor that had been slowly invading her spine during the preceding months had finally done its worst: Jette was no longer able to walk completely under her own power.

I was stunned by the news, but all I could think to do was take her home and hold her close to me. With the technician's help, and arduous effort on Jette's part, she climbed into the back seat of my car and we headed for home.

In my driveway twenty minutes later, I tried to coax her off the rear seat but she refused to move. I squatted down outside the rear door to meet her gaze and spoke softly to her, but by then her breathing had become labored and a more distant look appeared in her eyes. I slid one arm under her chest and the other around her shoulders, attempting to cradle her and help her out of the car, but Jette whimpered and dropped her head back down on the seat. I knew it was a bad sign, but I didn't want to acknowledge it. Instead, I left both rear doors open while I unloaded her bedding and food from the cargo hold, speaking to her all the while in the cheeriest voice I could muster, hoping that she would gather the will to move when she realized she was in familiar surroundings.

"Come on, big girl," I coaxed. "You're home now."

After the cargo hold was emptied, I made another attempt to assist her by kneeling on the back seat, grasping her hind quarters just above her hocks, then gently nudging her toward the door. She cried out in protest so I stopped, walked back around to the opposite door, and attempted to lift her from her shoulders. Jette again cried out then slid backward out of my reach. Prone on the seat again, she glanced up at me with pleading eyes, chin resting on her paws, then turned her head sideways to avoid my gaze. I climbed back into the vehicle and sat down on the seat next to her, stroking her fur, talking consolingly while I struggled with my thoughts and feelings.

"Okay, my big girl, we'll just wait here for a few minutes until you're ready."

Jette had earned the nickname boo-boo girl when she was a six-month-old puppy. Over-exuberant and all legs, she was fifty pounds of bounding, inquisitive energy that resulted in bumps, bruises, and bee stings. She also had a propensity for unintentionally inflicting boo-boos on me. One day while I sat on the living room floor during one of our play sessions, Jette ran circles around me and the sofa, intermittently hunkering down behind the sofa in a game of hide-and-seek, then jumping out with a bark as if to say, *found you!*

At some point during a lap around the sofa, she picked up one of the large soup bones that I had a habit of buying for her and that bone was my undoing. That bone had to be nine inches long and it was heavy. Firmly held between her teeth, it did as much damage as a baseball bat when she playfully rushed toward me and made a flying leap into my lap. The soup bone connected with my eyeglasses, pushing the right lens inward toward my eye and cutting a perfect arc just below my eyebrow. The wound required ten stitches to close.

Weeks later, stitches removed and the incident all but forgotten, we were once again engaged in play. And, once again, Jette sailed into my open arms and I discovered too late that she had again snatched her soup bone from the floor in the seconds before impact. That time it was a bulls-eye at the bridge of my nose. Thankfully, I was wearing contact lenses instead of glasses that time, but the result was a beautiful multi-color shiner that make-up could not hide.

As my good friend David once observed, "Dogs are a contact sport!"

Jette was also an imitator. When she saw me setting books and knick-knacks on the living room bookshelf, she decided that must be where we keep our things. So she followed suit, carrying her own toys one by one and placing them in a row on the bottom shelf. As if that were not enough, she made frequent attempts at imitating human speech often with comic results. Words like *mwaahm* (mom) and *howree* (hungry) were a part of her everyday language.

That particular canine trait, I have been told, is a sign not only of higher intelligence but also of the ability to think through problems. I had to admit she was a fast learner and had an amazing capacity for vocabulary. I could speak full sentences to her, never mind what the training manuals said, and she would always show me the appropriate response. I saw her problem-solving skills in action many times when a toy rolled out of reach. Jette would take up various comical postures or physically move obstacles until she finally figured out a way to retrieve the thing. However, if the object was simply impossible for her to retrieve on her own, she did not hesitate to come and find me. She would bark and tug at my sleeve until I followed her to the errant toy.

Though Jette delighted and amazed me, imitators can be dangerous in their own way. For example, when we played ball Jette was not satisfied to be solely a retriever, oh no, not Jette! She wanted a little variety in her game playing. To put a spin on our ballgames, Jette eventually learned that if she hit the oncoming ball with her snout instead of catching it in her mouth, she could send that ball whizzing back to me. The first time she did that, I failed to recover from the shock in sufficient time to avoid a line drive aimed at my head. Luckily, I suffered only a headache and not a concussion.

Her quick movements, natural curiosity, and a prey drive that kicked in for bumblebees as well as bunny rabbits, earned her a fair share of her own boo-boos. During her first summer with me, I watched her in a continual state of amazement and wondered, at times, if she would make it through puppyhood at all. Such were the adventures of life with Jette.

Those memories and more played in my mind like a moving picture show as I sat next to her on the back seat of my SUV that Saturday morning. There was no denying it, Jette and I had enjoyed a wonderful, adventurous life together; we were truly comrades. Much as it pained me to admit it, we had come to the end of that journey. We are not provided with perfect, immortal bodies, but I'm convinced there is another realm of existence beyond this one. An existence unencumbered by a physical body; a new life free from the devastating pain of progressive disease. A place, as the Bible says, where every tear will be wiped away.

And that, I finally determined through my own tears, was where Jette needed to be. If this was really the end of her earthly life, then I owed it to her to see that she suffered no longer. Yet, in my selfishness, I did not want to let go of her.

I made one final attempt to help her move off the rear seat. Finally, using every ounce of strength that remained in her, she did it. However, she immediately collapsed panting and whimpering onto the ground. I knelt down beside her in the driveway, took her beautiful head into my lap, and wrapped my arms around her. I rocked her and sobbed, my tears splashing down over her fur.

"Please, not yet," I cried. "I still need her!"

Time stopped for a moment there in the driveway while I held her and cried, but I knew what I had to do. It would have been cruel to allow her to go on in that state. And go on, I knew she would for as long as I willed it. More than a year previously, I had watched my gentle Belgian shepherd waste away until she was a mere skeleton. Still, she too refused to give up and die; she refused to stop loving me, refused to cease living for me.

I was a coward when death came to call on that gentle girl. Instead of holding her lovingly in my arms while she was returned to God, I handed her over to her veterinarian and ran away to drown in my sorrow. Steeling myself against the pain in my heart and the gut-wrenching memories, I determined that would not be the case for Jette. I owed it to that special animal to be present for her to the very end and I felt bad enough that I had missed the last week of her life while trying to save Uncle Pasquale's. I knew that I had to hold her until she took her last breath.

Finally summoning the courage to do what needed to be done, I left Jette lying in the driveway long enough to run back inside the house, grab my phone, and alert her veterinarian. I pulled a soft flannel sheet off my bed before returning to Jette's side. Making the sheet into a make-shift stretcher, I rolled Jette onto it and summoned the strength to lift her onto the tailgate and slide her into the cargo area. Less than an hour later, the fatal injection administered, I held her in my arms and felt her body relax. With one last sigh, her spirit returned to God, and I was inconsolable.

Jette was borrowed for a season then returned with the same measure of love with which she had been given to me. No more would I feel her cold, wet nose nudging me awake in the morning. Gone were the days when we would romp through the snow together. There would no longer be a warm, companionable presence curled up on the sofa with me to watch movies on a rainy Saturday afternoon.

I returned afterward to an empty house, devoid of that gentle, loving, silly spirit that had inhabited it with me. As long as she was at my side, there was no reason to fear anything. Now, with the sun setting and Jette gone from my life, I found that devil called fear lurking just beneath the surface, threatening to destroy my sense of peace.

For years, I fell asleep in a suburban townhouse village with neighbors on either side of common walls. Eighteen-wheelers screeched down the four-lane highway less than a football field's length away from my backyard. During the summer months, the noise from the highway made it impossible to fall asleep with bedroom windows open.

But after moving to the cottage, well off the beaten path, I found myself lying awake in my bed at night blissfully absorbed in the sound of the wind rustling the leaves on the trees in the pitch-black stillness outside and murmuring through the windows. Only Jette's constant presence kept my imagination from conjuring images of woodland gnomes making their way stealthily across the yard to peer in through my windows and disturb my slumber.

Fear can be a useful emotion when it keeps us from taking unreasonable risks, but it can be a terrible, debilitating weight when the wrong kind of fear is allowed to take root in our souls and flourish unchecked. Fear can hold us captive for months, years, even a lifetime if we allow it. Some people who have had near-drowning experiences never step into the water again. One person I know was attacked by a dog when they were young and allowed that one experience to deprive them of the joy of living with an animal companion.

I have known people who feared crossing bridges to such an extent that they drove many miles out of their way to avoid them and if there was no way to avoid a bridge, they simply would not make the journey. Some people will not visit the sick or elderly in hospitals because they fear they will contract a disease. Fear is as varied and nameless as the people whom it possesses. It is one of the most destructive emotions we humans possess and as long as we employ a safety net and avoid confronting whatever it is we are afraid of, we will never rid ourselves of it. We will never experience the joyful freedom from fear. Jette was my safety net, and now she was gone.

As I sat in my living room that evening alone with my thoughts, memories and yes, my fears, that little voice that nags at my subconscious and serves to pull me back to reality said, *Why are you afraid? Don't you know that I am still here with you?*

That higher power that many of us call God was still with me even though Jette was not.

Why did I allow myself to believe that I would not be safe while alone in the dark?

I was suddenly ashamed. Ashamed at my lack of faith, ashamed to admit that I had allowed fear to take root in me so completely that it blocked my ability to see that God had always been there for me. He, not Jette, had been my protector all along. It was he, not Jette, who gave me the spiritual courage to face every situation in my life.

By the time I arose from my chair that evening, turned out the lights and made my way down the dim hallway to my bedroom, I realized that I was no longer afraid of the dark, no longer afraid of the unknown. In Jette's passing, I too had been set free.

CHAPTER TEN

Almost Home

Thursday, April 15

*"Contend, O Lord, with those who contend
with me ... may those who plot my ruin
be turned back in dismay."*

–Psalm 35

The Easter holiday weekend had come and gone with Pasquale still held captive in Virginia. As it turned out, we were unable to return to him as soon as we had initially anticipated. After conferring with the family in the days following our return to Pennsylvania, Ben and I determined that we needed reinforcements. In the event we had to resort to a lawsuit to secure Pasquale's release, his siblings would need to give first-hand testimony about the lengths to which Nora and Julie had gone in an effort to prevent Pasquale's recovery in the days immediately following his stroke. That testimony would be vital in convincing a judge to vacate Julie's power of attorney and appoint another family member in her place. Of Pasquale's siblings, my mother and Uncle Sal were also the best candidates for being able to withstand the long journey by car. Neither one, however, was able to depart on that Monday morning due to previously scheduled doctor appointments.

They were in their golden years. Considering the entourage of specialists, more frequent trips to the family general practitioner, and the seemingly endless parade of pills and doctor bills, I cannot help wondering just whose "gold" is referred to in that adage. In any event, missing a doctor appointment is like getting out of the popcorn line at the movie theater. You have no choice but to go to the end of the line and wait your turn all over again. Neither my mother nor Uncle Sal wanted to get back in line to see their respective doctors, so Ben and I had no choice but to wait until the Thursday after Easter.

As my mother cheerfully noted after we had settled on a departure date, the day we returned to Virginia would be Pasquale's birthday. We had hoped that Pasquale would receive his long-awaited release to mark that milestone. Meanwhile, we could only trust that a higher power as well as our ally, Nurse Penny, would protect him from the wiles of his stepdaughter and keep him from getting anxious when we failed to return to him on Monday as promised.

Ben and I used the several days' reprieve to tend to our own businesses. While we bided our time in Pennsylvania, Julie, too, we would find out later, was tending to certain details in her battle to keep Pasquale right where she wanted him. Months later, after we had obtained a copy of the attendant care records from the nursing home, we discovered just how desperate Julie and Nora had been to prevent Pasquale from returning to Pennsylvania. Indeed, the implications were that not only had they attempted, once again, to prevent his very survival *legally*, by virtue of the living will, but it also appeared they had side-stepped all legal and medical authority and literally had taken the matter into their own hands.

Playing into their scheme, however unknowingly, was the attending physician who made her weekly visit to Pasquale during our absence. She had first recorded her observations and a dire prognosis immediately following Pasquale's initial arrival in Virginia. Echoing those sentiments weeks later, she again made notations in his medical record that appeared to sound the death knell: *Patient combative, prognosis poor, no potential for rehabilitation.*

■■■

In later months, we would bear witness to other cast-off souls in other nursing facilities where the general intent appeared to be one of simply keeping the residents comfortable and quiet. Translate that: sedated and unable to complain even if they wanted to. Toward that end, we discovered, the attending physician typically uses one or a combination of mood-altering drugs that happily achieve the desired effect. For a brief period in my life, I worked as a volunteer attendant care aide in a nursing home. The sheer volume of drugs administered to just one invalid during the course of a day boggled my mind! The more I thought about that scenario as I waited impatiently in Pennsylvania, the more concerned I became.

It is hard to know exactly what Pasquale was thinking after Ben and I left him just before Easter, but the day after we departed, the attending nurse noted that Pasquale was *becoming anxious and confused*. Again, he stated that he just wanted to die. His stepfamily, latching onto the fresh opportunity, took his statement literally and continued to badger the nursing home administration into allowing him to do just that. We can only surmise, based on the records, that Fern Donnelly had decided against euthanasia and that her sudden unwillingness to comply with Julie's demands prompted an even more malicious attack against Pasquale.

By the afternoon on Easter Sunday, Nurse Penny's notations in Pasquale's medical chart stated that Pasquale had been trying earnestly to tell her something but most of his words were unintelligible thanks, no doubt, to the drugs poured into his body at regular intervals. The words Penny was able to understand were *Smithton*, the city he hailed from in Pennsylvania, *brother* and *machine*.

Later that week, when Penny spoke of this incident to Ben and me in person, she said that she had been able to figure out that Pasquale wanted to call his brother and that he had actually given her the seven-digit telephone number but Pasquale could not remember the area code. That was no surprise to us. Pasquale's hometown was still a semi-rural, sparsely populated area. Residents were not yet required to dial the full ten-digit telephone number to reach someone across the street, as was already required in metropolitan cities. The human mind does not automatically remember things it does not deal with on a daily basis. Had it not been for that missing piece of information, just three numbers, Penny would have placed the call for him.

My mother was in Pasquale's room with us when Penny told this story and she was able to enlighten us further about Pasquale's use of the word *machine* in place of the word *telephone*. Pasquale's mother, an Italian immigrant who never quite got the hang of the English language, always referred to the telephone as *la machina*. According to Penny, it all made perfect sense. Pasquale's post-stroke, aphasia-afflicted mind would have caused his memory to waver between past and present.

Until Pasquale moved beyond that stage to the point where he would be able to think and express himself more clearly, he would probably continue to use the incorrect words for whatever it was that he was trying to convey. However, the fact that Pasquale had even attempted to contact his brother by telephone at all was a significant sign of his continuing recovery. It was a sign, we were certain, that also posed a fresh threat to Julie's plans. Pasquale was making more of an effort to make himself understood. That was something Julie could not allow. He was even beginning to make demands about his living conditions and personal care that countered the intentions of his stepdaughter and Julie meant to thwart that progress in any way that she could.

The good news was that the *machine* incident was one of the significant events that helped to convince Fern Donnelly that Pasquale was indeed coherent and really did want to go home. For the remainder of that day and for several days that followed, the attending nurses continued to record copious notes of Pasquale's behavior and verbal requests. What was more, they actually began to take a more active role in obtaining for Pasquale the things that he needed: his hearing aid, his new eyeglasses, a set of regular clothing to get him out of the hospital gown during the day—and Julie was clearly feeling the heat of his progress breathing down the neck of her obstinacy.

Also on Easter Sunday, a representative from the local social services agency, an ombudsman per the nurse's notes, made his weekly visit to check on Pasquale's care as Jonas Maxwell had directed that agency to do weeks before. According to the notes, the ombudsman met Nora and Julie for the first time during his brief visit. He left while they were still in attendance at Pasquale's bedside. Sometime after Nora and Julie departed, the nurse noted in the record: *CNA (Certified Nursing Assistant) reported to me that resident's PEG tubing wasn't wrapped around the triangle part of the pump. Replaced tubing.* The nurse was referring to the tube that periodically sent vital fluids directly into Pasquale's stomach. Because he still was not eating solid food, it was necessary to sustain him with nutrients delivered via that PEG tubing.

On that particular day, someone had obviously tampered with the tube and it wasn't a stretch to guess just who that may have been. What did they think they were doing? Were they trying to cut off the flow? Did they try to add something toxic to the mix?

As Penny declared when she told us about the episode several days later, "That thing didn't unwrap itself from the pump!"

 ￭￭￭

The time of day that the event occurred had not been noted, but it must have been late in the evening as the nurse on duty entered the next notation at 10:45 a.m. on Monday morning: *Alert and cooperative; PEG tube patent; wife at bedside; HOB increased 30 degrees; meds down G tube without difficulty; vital signs stable.*

The notation entered in the record at 6 p.m. the same day implies that by that time the nursing staff was sufficiently suspicious of the sudden difficulties with Pasquale's feeding tube that they were keeping close tabs on the situation. The nurse wrote: *Tube feeding was leaking. Recapped the plug. No difficulty with tube since. Wife at bedside most of the day. She has gone from the facility at this time.*

It was disturbing to read that record, even months later. I could not help wondering if Julie had attempted to introduce a toxic substance into Pasquale's feeding line to aid in his demise. As I read the account, I thought back to the episode the previous week when I walked into Pasquale's room to find him writhing in acute stomach pain. Just prior to that incident, Julie had begun her practice of evicting us from Pasquale's room so she and her mother could visit with him—*alone*! I could not help wondering if our eviction was more than just a power play on Julie's part after all.

Perhaps she only wanted the privacy to ensure there would be no witnesses to her devious actions. I sincerely doubt that Nora's trembling hands could have managed to drop a substance into such a small tube, but there was no doubt that Julie could have and would have been perfectly capable of attempting such a foul deed.

As I read those nursing records, it was significant to me that in more than two weeks of notations that was the first time when a nurse actually recorded Nora and Julie's departure time, leaving no shadow of a doubt that they had finally fallen under a cloud of suspicion and their actions were being closely monitored as a result.

Also significant is the fact that Pasquale's attending physician chose to visit him that Easter Monday morning (she had just been there the previous Thursday) and finally gave the order to stop administering sedatives altogether. That event initiated Pasquale's vital return to a more alert state so that coherent thought and speech quickly followed. Those events were precisely what Julie had fought so hard to prevent. Add to that Pasquale's sudden interest in using a telephone and, as I am certain Julie realized, the possibilities would have been endless.

Pasquale, himself, would have then had the power to strike a major blow against the designs of his stepdaughter. He would have been able to give voice to events she would much rather have kept under wraps and all her careful planning would have come undone. There is little doubt that by that time, Pasquale would have passed a competency exam with flying colors, and that, I suddenly realized while I read the account, was why Julie had decided to delay the test. No test, no proof, no release! Julie must have thought she could keep Pasquale in limbo indefinitely as long as she refused to allow the test to be administered.

Tuesday, April 13, marked another flurry of anti-enemy activity in Pasquale's little realm. The incident was recorded by not only the nursing staff but also by the resident social worker in a separate record. Things must have been getting pretty interesting for social services to get involved. In the record, the social services administrator made note of a meeting between the nursing home's administrative staff and Julie (no mention of Nora). Though the specific reason for that meeting and its eventual outcome were not recorded, it does not require a great leap of imagination to realize that it had to have centered on Pasquale's desire to get out of there and away from his stepdaughter.

When I looked back on the entire sequence of events months later, the reason for the footprints-in-the-sand message became obvious to me. Ben and I *had* to be taken out of the equation so other forces could take over and unmask Julie for the spoiled, conniving, manipulative person she was. Had we remained in Virginia over the Easter weekend and continued our visits, as Ben and I had at one time contemplated, we too could have fallen under suspicion. Out of the picture and at a safe distance in another state, no one could cast blame in our direction. From the printed records in my hand, it was quite clear that the misguidedly kind, complacent management staff at the nursing home had a real eye-opening weekend and suspicion fell right where it belonged.

That said, we will never really know just who wanted Pasquale dead. It is easy to favor Julie or her husband since they had been Pasquale's primary antagonists all along. However, considering Nora's mental decline due to the dementia that ravaged her brain, one could reasonably speculate that she may have had a hand in it as well. In a twisted sort of innocence, perhaps Nora truly believed she was merely helping her husband toward his expressed wish to die. Julie's irascible and condescending manner toward her mother would serve to solidify her position of power and also ensure Nora's compliance in achieving that end.

While Ben and I had taken Pasquale's moaning desire to die as nothing more than the figurative ramblings of a man in the throes of physical and emotional distress resulting from his circumstances, Nora may have taken his remarks quite literally. Although tremors would have made it very difficult if not nearly impossible for her to manipulate the small PEG tube mechanism, those trembling hands could also account for the fact that the tube cap had been displaced and left that way.

One thing is certain, without the careful attention and intervention of the nursing staff, the deed might never have been discovered and Pasquale could have suffered irreparable damage. Without the heightened vigilance of Penny and the other nurses in attendance, Julie's plans might have succeeded that weekend, in which case we would have journeyed back to Virginia only to retrieve our uncle's lifeless body.

Tampering with Pasquale's feeding tube was not the only measure undertaken by the stepfamily to derail Pasquale's plans for escape. The social services administrator recorded a telephone call from Pasquale's attending physician that day during which the doctor informed her that the psychological evaluation scheduled for April 16 had been canceled altogether at Julie's request. Julie no longer played about with postponements; she would simply not allow it. Period.

Later on that same Tuesday afternoon, the nursing home's social worker recorded in her notes that she had telephoned Julie to advise her that the director of nursing, our former nemesis, Talia Evert, had scheduled a hearing test for Pasquale. Since Ben and I had informed the nursing staff of Pasquale's deficiency during our visit the preceding week, they intended to rectify the situation by ordering a hearing aid for him. Julie, however, did not intend to spend any more of Pasquale's money on his personal needs. It must have irked her no end, but at that point, she had no choice but to surrender the "lost" device. The social worker recorded: *Julie found hearing aid and will bring in.* That was one more victory for Pasquale and another chink in Julie's armor.

On Wednesday, April 14, only one notation was made in the records by the nursing home's social services administrator but it was a significant one as it confirms that the staff was indeed watching Nora and her daughter very closely: *Res* (resident) *continues on m/c* (medical) *H* (high alert) *coverage due to nursing* (ordered by the nursing staff). *Res has tube feed.*

That was, by far, the most damning piece of evidence contained in the records as it pointed directly to the staff's suspicions that either Pasquale's wife or stepdaughter and no one else, had made an attempt to interrupt the life-sustaining fluids he received. It is also interesting that a notation in the nurse's notes for April 13 states: *blood was drawn* (from Pasquale) *for FH 5 problem.* The specific nature of the problem and exactly what they were looking for in the test results is not clear from the notes but FH is an inherited condition, whereby a chromosome mutation results in dangerously high cholesterol, translating into heart attack or stroke. It also affects the tendons of the feet and hands. In their belated attempts to aid in Pasquale's recovery, the nursing staff may have been looking for a reason why he still did not have use of his right hand, aside from Julie's intentional withholding of physical therapy.

What is very clear is that Julie's facade as the well-intentioned, loving stepdaughter was quickly falling away as she began taking what amounted to desperate measures in her attempt to ensure she did not lose control over Pasquale or the money that would come to her upon his death.

◫◫◫

On a lighter note, between the lines of drama, the record showed that without the influence of the previously administered sedatives and mood-altering drugs, Pasquale was showing signs of his former jovial nature. The nurses were seeing a different side of him and they were obviously enjoying their interactions. On Wednesday, April 14, the attending nurse recorded: *10:45 a.m. Alert, laughing, Pt* (patient) *did state that we could yell at him, that it would be fine because he did not have his hearing aid in!*

She further recorded that Pasquale had told her quite plainly, "I don't know where it is; I had them one time."

She recorded her response to Pasquale: *Encouraged him that we would find them. Will speak to family.*

She made good on her promise and must have telephoned Julie immediately. Her next notation in the record just fifteen minutes later: *11 a.m.* (Stepdaughter) *states that hearing aids were at his bedside drawer. She stated that she brought them in yesterday. Applied hearing aid to L* (left) *ear. He can hear without having to raise your voice. He continues to be alert and cooperative. Call light is in reach.*

I did another slow burn, even months later, when I read those notes. How typical of Julie to take Pasquale's hearing aid to the nursing home but simply deposit it in the bedside drawer and tell no one. If there truly is such a fiery place as hell, I hope there's a little compartment there with Julie's name on the door.

◫◫◫

Thursday morning, the day of our return trip to Virginia from Pennsylvania, finally arrived. By 7 a.m., Ben, my mother, Uncle Sal, and I were in my parent's driveway tossing luggage into the trunk of Uncle Sal's car. Six hours later, we were pulling into the parking lot of the hotel where Ben and I had stayed the week before.

As we unloaded the trunk and made our way inside, Uncle Sal, fed up with the drama of the preceding weeks, shook his head and said, "I still don't understand why he put Nora and Julie on that power of attorney document in the first place. If it weren't for that, he wouldn't be in this mess!" Shooting a glance at my mother he added, "Why didn't he trust one of us to take on that responsibility for him?"

"Who knows!" my mother lamented.

"That's not so hard," I interjected in Pasquale's defense. "You're supposed to be able to trust the person you married. Nora was a natural choice."

"Well, that's true," Uncle Sal admitted. "But why Julie, of all people?"

"I'm sure he didn't count on Nora coming down with dementia," I surmised. "He probably figured she would keep her daughter in check if he was ever in a position where they needed to use those documents."

Mother agreed. She stated that in spite of the many instances when Nora pitied her daughter and willingly mailed a monthly stipend to her, there were also times when she expressed her impatience with Julie's never-ending neediness.

We could have conjectured about the hows and whys all evening, but it did not change the circumstances. As Ben observed the previous week, everything happens for a reason. We just had to trust that was so and move forward as best we could.

Nurse Penny was preparing to go off duty when we arrived at the nursing home that evening. She greeted Ben and me like old friends but those greetings paled in comparison to the joyous, tearful reunion that followed when Pasquale saw his brother and sister enter the room.

"Sal! My brother!" Pasquale exclaimed when his eyes met Sal's.

Pasquale reached out his arms to embrace him. My mother's arthritic hip kept her a few paces behind us but when she finally caught up and made her entrance, Pasquale's face again rendered surprise, then elation, as he cried out, "My baby sister!"

"She isn't such a baby anymore!" Sal said as he laughed.

Pasquale tearfully hugged and kissed his sister and brother again. Finally, emotionally spent, he sat back against the pillows, placed his hand against his forehead, and looked at Sal.

"I'm not sure if this is reality!" he exclaimed, echoing the thoughts he had expressed when he saw Ben and me enter his room for the first time. After the emotional rollercoaster ride he had experienced and the recent weaning from sedation, it was no wonder Pasquale did not feel he could trust his senses. Sal did his best to reassure him.

"This is real," Sal told him emphatically through his own tears. Then taking Pasquale's hand in his own as physical confirmation, he continued, "*I'm* real. Do you know how far we had to come to see you?"

Pasquale was still wiping the tears from his face and shaking his head in disbelief.

"Do you know where you are?" Sal asked him. "You're in Virginia."

Pasquale was not wearing his hearing aid and misinterpreting his brother's question, Pasquale gruffly declared, "I'm not going *there!*"

"I've got news for you, buddy," Sal grinned, gave Pasquale a good-natured poke with his finger and informed him, "You're already here! But we're going to get you back home, don't you worry!"

Unfortunately for Pasquale and his siblings, the battle-axe replaced Nurse Penny for the night shift. As a result, the happy reunion lasted no more than twenty minutes before Julie's threatening figure loomed in the doorway of Pasquale's room.

Unbeknownst to us, the battle-axe had been Julie's spy all along. She must have called Julie within minutes of reporting for her shift after she found us in Pasquale's room, and there Julie stood, eyebrows furrowed in rage, dark eyes blazing! A terrible row occurred when Julie demanded that we leave immediately.

"You aren't supposed to be here after 6 p.m.!" she angrily charged.

While she lashed out at us, Pasquale defended his family and shouted back at her.

"Get the hell out and leave us be!" he demanded.

In an attempt to defuse the situation and make Julie shut up and go away, I feigned ignorance, passively expressed regrets, and pretty much said, "Oops, I forgot!" That did not go over well and she continued her raging tirade, insisting that she would have us *thrown* out if we did not leave immediately of our own accord.

Pasquale, still in the fray, formed a united front with his siblings and smugly informed Julie from his bed, "I'm not going with you."

Julie knew exactly what he meant and it was the last straw. Before Ben and I took it upon ourselves to drive down South and crash her party, Julie had planned to use Pasquale's money to buy herself a house, promising Pasquale and Nora that they would then move in with her and she would take care of them. It was her "happily-ever-after" ruse. Julie was taking care of things all right, but the purchase of a house had nothing to do with Pasquale or, we would later find out, Nora. That was simply another lie intended to pacify Pasquale while Julie waited impatiently for him to die and leave all of his assets, willingly or not, to her. Our unannounced arrival impeded those plans and made it necessary for Julie to move up the timeline; she had run clean out of time and patience!

Hearing Pasquale's rebuke, Julie hissed the same accusation at Sal and my mother that she had flung in my face the previous week, "You're breaking up a marriage!"

Having heard that one already, Ben and I simply rolled our eyes at the absurdity of the statement. The remark did not even merit a response as far as we were concerned, but Pasquale's sister could not resist a sarcastic retort.

"Oh, and if he's dead that wouldn't be breaking up their marriage?" my mother replied.

By that time, the battle-axe reappeared and it was clearly time to retreat. After a six-hour road trip, I was in no mood to contend with Julie. In the preceding seven weeks, she had given our family a million reasons to send a well-aimed fist flying in the general direction of her big mouth, but there was only one reason not to. Pasquale's health was still fragile and we could not risk his suffering another stroke due to embittered emotions raging unchecked in his room.

For that reason alone, I was prepared to simply walk away and call it a night. My mother, however, seized the opportunity to unleash almost two months' worth of rage and animosity she had been storing up for Julie and Nora. She proceeded to give Julie a tongue-lashing that reverberated down the hall outside Pasquale's room and did indeed get us thrown out of the nursing home. Taking my mother by the arm, I had literally pulled her away from Julie.

"If I thought you wouldn't be able to behave yourself," I admonished her, "I wouldn't have asked you to come!"

"I just needed to tell her what was on my mind," she cried out in her own defense.

"Anger isn't going to get us through this," I told her. "And it won't help your brother either!"

By that time, tears were streaming down my mother's face; Uncle Sal was wiping his cheeks as well. I hated to yell at her but I knew we had to get out of there and allow Pasquale to quiet down. Tomorrow was just around the corner and the battle would simply have to wait until then.

After we had gone, Julie struggled to regain control as she turned in anger back to Pasquale's room to finish the confrontation. As the battle-axe noted in the nursing records, Pasquale threatened to commit suicide if Julie would not allow him to leave. Had it not been such a sad state of affairs, that remark might have been funny as Pasquale was in no condition, physically, to do an injury to anyone, not even himself.

However, during the shouting match that commenced, Julie apparently got close enough to his bedside that Pasquale was able to take a swing at her with his good arm, after which Julie issued a new challenge.

"You can go up to Pennsylvania," she shouted, "but mom will stay right here and I'll see to it that she divorces you!"

The nurse further noted for the record that she immediately telephoned Pasquale's attending physician, requesting and receiving an order to administer sedation at once.

Further details of the exchange were not recorded by Nurse battle-axe as I am certain Nurse Penny would have done had she been in attendance. However, the end result was now a matter of record and that was of primo importance. Perhaps, Julie had only meant to use her mother as a pawn and blurted out the divorce threat in a final effort to regain control over Pasquale, but whatever her intentions, Julie's verbal attack unwittingly accomplished two things on Pasquale's behalf.

First, she verbally agreed to Pasquale's release, a fact that was duly noted by the battle-axe herself, amazingly enough. Second, Julie's outrageous behavior apparently had a frightening effect on her former ally, Nurse battle-axe. The nurse's later notations were full of caring concern for Pasquale and seemed to take on the tone of one who had clearly defected to the other side of the conflict.

After that showdown, no one in our little traveling group felt like going out for dinner. However, I insisted that it would do everyone some good to sit down and relax. Besides, I tried to reason with them, a light supper would help to absorb the acid I was sure had been churning in everyone's stomachs, including mine.

Early the next morning, I called Jonas Maxwell to relate the incident with Julie and to request that he begin legal proceedings at once to vacate Julie's power of attorney citing abuse as the cause. We agreed to meet Max at his office at 2 p.m. to sign the necessary papers. After hanging up with him, I had another brainstorm while thinking back on events of the previous evening and Nurse Penny's tale of Pasquale's attempt to reach his brother by phone. I saw an opportunity arising from that incident and made another phone call to my recently acquired (if still somewhat reluctant) ally, Fern Donnelly.

Once again donning the demeanor of an obedient servant, I voiced my family's concern about Pasquale's recent attempts to get out of bed on his own and phone his brother. In my speech to her, I sympathized with Fern's position right smack in the middle of the warring families, telling her that I completely understood the nursing home's legal stance and agreed they had to protect themselves.

After all, I told her, there was no telling on whom Julie's wrath would next fall. With that little seed planted, I continued my discourse telling Fern that we were *very* concerned that Pasquale might hurt himself in his attempts to get himself out of there if he grew impatient with our progress. If that occurred, it would look bad for the nursing home since they would be, she had to admit, at least partially responsible for holding him there. The few seconds of silence that followed my little speech were priceless. I knew the seed had taken root and was sprouting little tendrils of wisdom all through Fern's brain cells!

Finally, Fern found her voice. She told me that she was not aware of Pasquale's attempts to call his brother but that she would look into it immediately. Her admission floored me. This woman was supposedly running the place—and it was not exactly a mansion with seventy rooms—yet time and again, she was left out of the proverbial loop on the care and progress of a patient in whom she should have taken the utmost interest under the circumstances.

Fern actually thanked me for calling. In my mind, I envisioned varying shades of crimson spreading over her face as she did a slow burn on her way to the nurse's station in search of Talia, Julie's yet unrelenting defender. I knew I had made an important point in the argument for Pasquale's release.

Since we were unable to visit Pasquale until 4 p.m. and had nowhere else to go that morning, the four of us sat commiserating at a table at the hotel's complimentary breakfast bar until the hotel staff began to close up at 11 a.m.

While we sipped the last drops of our coffee, Ben suggested a diversion to the beach and I quickly agreed. The serenity of the shore had calmed us during the previous week's frustrations and I hoped it would do the same for Uncle Sal and my mother.

At first, Uncle Sal demurred. He really was not a fan of sandy beaches and salt-water spray, he said, and he was reluctant to join us. Once we arrived on the shore, however, it was fun to watch as he eventually got into the spirit of the beach atmosphere and began to examine and collect seashells alongside me.

My mother, however, had difficulty walking on the uneven sand as it shifted under her feet and challenged her arthritic hip. She would only proceed so far on Ben's arm before turning back to find a bench to sit on. Even so, she seemed to relax there as she took in the sun and the sea air. It had been an arduous battle to that point, sucking the vitality out of each one of us in the process and we needed to gather our strength for the final skirmish.

In spite of the pleasant diversion, we kept our eyes on the clock and left the beach in time to arrive at Jonas Maxwell's office precisely at 2 p.m. as scheduled. We were anxious to hear his plan of action and hoped the session with him would prove to be fruitful. We waited only a few moments before Max appeared in the lobby to greet us with a welcoming smile spread across his handsome, sun-tanned face. His beautiful blue eyes crinkled in a smile all their own.

After ushering us into a conference room, he informed us that he had been working on Pasquale's case earlier in the day and was awaiting a telephone call from Julie's attorney. The four of us sat there, leaning forward in our seats, eyes glued on Max, intensely absorbing every word as we wondered just how he intended to secure Pasquale's release.

Just as Max began to outline the legal action he would need to take to achieve a revocation of Julie's power of attorney, his secretary opened the conference room door to tell him that the caller he had been waiting for was on hold. Max excused himself to take the call, leaving us to sit there and speculate. Approximately ten minutes later, he reentered the conference room.

Standing just inside the doorway, he beamed at us and asked quite simply, "How soon can you get an ambulance here?"

Four sets of jaws gaped speechlessly, except for my mother who managed a one-word exclamation.

"What?" she cried incredulously.

"Julie has agreed to release Pasquale," Max calmly announced, still beaming like a proud father. As I have said, he was like family to us and that was what I liked most about him. This was not just another case to him. It was obvious he took a genuine interest in Pasquale's plight and I had a feeling that it was not just Pasquale, not just our family that garnered his interest and received such careful attention. I would have been willing to bet that absolutely everyone he represented was seen by Max first as a person and then in the context of his job.

My mother and Uncle Sal sat there with tears of relief streaming down their faces while Max excused himself once more to sew up the details of Pasquale's release, details that would include immediate restoration of our *unrestricted* visiting privileges.

When we asked Max how he managed it, he replied cryptically, "Let's just say Julie had a change of heart."

"Yeah, right!" Ben snickered. "I don't even think she has a heart!"

We all laughed, drunk with victory, at the time. Later, when I had an opportunity to reflect quietly, alone, I found that I actually pitied Julie as much as I had pitied her mother. She was obviously a miserable soul devoid of the simple joys of life with little or no experience to tell of the measure of love our own family felt for one another. I did not know it then, but my new-found pity for her would last less than forty-eight hours.

By 4 p.m., we were back at the nursing home. All was calm on that front; the stepfamily was nowhere in sight. Pasquale was more than calm. In fact, he was enshrouded once again in a deep slumber, snoring soundly and completely oblivious to our presence. I pulled a small notebook from my purse and added another task to the growing list of things to do after we returned with him to Pennsylvania: get Pasquale's doctor to wean him off the blasted sedatives—permanently!

It was incredibly disappointing, especially for Pasquale's brother and sister. Almost twenty-four hours had elapsed since their arrival and they had visited with their brother a total of twenty minutes. Their only consolation was in the fact that he was going home. This time there was no doubt about that.

Since there was no point in sitting there watching Pasquale sleep, we returned to the hotel, collected newspapers, tourist pamphlets, and magazines from the lobby displays, then settled into chairs under the colorful outdoor patio umbrellas. When the sun threatened to sizzle our flesh, we retreated to the indoor poolside patio.

We had no choice but to wait until Max sorted the various details and legal red tape, clearing the way for Pasquale's exit. While we waited, Ben and I made the usual round of telephone calls to check on business affairs and update the relatives. My mother called her sister back in Smithton to arrange for Pasquale's ambulance ride. Again.

Later that evening, we decided to treat ourselves to dinner at a nice restaurant and celebrate Pasquale's pending homecoming. We piled into Uncle Sal's car and were no sooner out of the hotel parking lot when my cell phone rang. It was Max, calling to confirm the conditions of Pasquale's release and to relate the liberal visiting schedule he had worked out with Julie's attorney. We still did not have full, unrestricted access to my uncle, but it was enough. Besides, I figured it was Julie's last hurrah. Just that one last tenuous thread connected Pasquale to her and that thread would be severed in a matter of hours.

※※※

On a whim, I suggested to Max that he join us for our celebratory dinner. To my surprise and delight, he hesitated only a moment before accepting so we drove back into the city to retrieve him at his office.

Max led us to a rustic-looking structure on the edge of a canal. There, we enjoyed a wonderful dinner of Southern fare, including fried green tomatoes, on a canopied deck overlooking the sun-dappled water. Mother and Uncle Sal, mostly Uncle Sal, regaled us with stories of his and Pasquale's childhood escapades, peppered with memories of immigrant parents who always seemed to be in the kitchen feeding the neighborhood.

Their father, my beloved grandpa, was well-known for his culinary skill and Uncle Sal's friends would bring all manner of small game to him, taking him up on his standing offer, "You bring; I cooka for you!"

Everyone was welcomed at my grandparents' home for as long as they wished to stay. Uncle Sal laughed as he recalled those times.

"I never knew who I'd find sleeping on the sofa when I got up in the morning!"

After dinner, we exited the restaurant through the backdoor and onto the boardwalk. The stress and worry of the previous weeks had finally lifted. It was good to see Uncle Sal and my mother relaxed and laughing. On the way to the car, which had been parked a couple of blocks away, Max treated us to a nickel and dime tour of some of the beautiful architecture in that charming, older section of the city. It was a memorable evening, one that we would still be talking about weeks later.

The next day, we learned that the ambulance service would not be arriving from Pennsylvania until the following morning. We had one more twenty-four hour stretch to see Pasquale through before he would be on his way home. While we waited, we found day-trip diversions to occupy us between our morning and evening visiting hours with Pasquale.

The knowledge that he was finally going home elevated Pasquale's spirits to new heights. He joked and laughed with us as well as the entire nursing home staff. Without the influence of sedation and with his siblings at his side to bolster his confidence, the Pasquale we had always known and loved had finally reemerged. The nursing staff marveled over his transformation and took extreme pleasure in Pasquale's witty and sometimes sarcastic interactions with them.

The only thing Pasquale still worried about was that he had no street clothes. Echoing his complaint to me and Ben the previous week, he sent a mournful glance in Uncle Sal's direction and in all seriousness he declared, "I have no pants!"

We chuckled over the humorous note in his remark at the time, but later, after his return to Pennsylvania, we would learn just how prophetically sad a statement that was.

Nurse Lisa was on duty during our visit that morning and told us she had documented the difference in Pasquale's moods and level of cooperation after Ben and I had arrived in Virginia.

"You were good for him," she told us. "I could tell he was uplifted by your visits."

Nurse Lisa was one of the allies who took up Pasquale's cause. We thanked her, told her how much we truly appreciated her efforts to see that Pasquale was respected, and had what he needed to feel comfortable and cared for. Were it not for Lisa and Penny, their initial belief in us, and the lengths to which they went in making certain we had the documentation we needed to further Pasquale's cause, it is likely the battle for custody of Pasquale would have raged on for weeks, even months, longer and the damage to his health might have been irreparable.

When I bumped into Penny later that day, I thanked her for telling us about Pasquale's request for *la machina*. Apologetically, I told her about my telephone call to Fern and expressed my hope that I did not cause her any trouble in the process. In my view, Penny was a top-notch nurse with a bedside manner all medical professionals should strive to emulate. In addition, she was not afraid to stand up and be counted among the righteous and for that, she will have our undying gratitude. Penny was incredibly gracious about the incident with Fern and told me yes, Fern had confronted her about it earlier in the day.

In her sweet, Southern belle demeanor, Penny said, "Didn't bother me none; ah told her it was all in the record. All she had to do was read!"

We left Pasquale at 11 a.m., promising to return at four. Ben once again donned the demeanor of a twelve-year-old on vacation and insisted that we go off exploring. I got a kick out of that side of his character; it only confirmed for me what I have always thought: there's a kid in all of us that will come out to play if we let him.

That afternoon's destination, Ben decided, would be another beach he wanted to see, then a plantation roughly forty minutes from our hotel. Uncle Sal moaned good-naturedly at the mention of another beach.

"You know I'm not crazy about the beach," he warned us, "but I'll go."

Natalie's hip was feeling better that day, so she didn't mind where we went as long as she didn't have to sit at the hotel in a chair all day. After a few false starts and wrong turns, we finally arrived at the beach and found a parking spot near a boardwalk. Uncle Sal stepped off the boardwalk and onto the sand.

"This is about as excited as I get," he informed us. "I'm here; I've seen it. Let's go!"

We laughed. Then he continued in a more reflective tone.

"Now, last night—that's something I enjoyed. I could have walked those bricked streets and city sidewalks for hours just taking in the architecture. That's what I enjoy."

I had to admit that I agreed with him. As much as the beach had meant solace and a place for centering ourselves the previous week, I didn't feel that I would want to call it home. I am a country girl at heart. Like my uncle, I prefer walking on more solid ground. I would much rather follow the paths that wind through deep, ancient, pine-scented forests, where new surprises await at the passing of each season, than spend my days under the burning sun, skin uncomfortably taut from salt-water spray.

When we returned to the nursing home at 4 p.m., we found Pasquale moaning as he struggled against sleep. His doctor had finally stopped the previous standing order for sedation, but a long list of other drugs still made their way into his IV tube on a twice-daily basis, and their combined effect prevented him from being fully alert.

"I can't wake up," he complained to us as we hovered near his bed.

A blast from the air-conditioner and some cold, damp towels finally pulled him out of the stupor so that by five o'clock, he was alert and conversant once more.

Pasquale's conversation with his brother and sister centered on details about what he feared was his financial ruin at the hands of Julie and her husband, and worries about who would help him when he returned to Pennsylvania. He was reassured time and again that he did not need to worry so much; we would all help him and see that he had what he needed. That was not what Pasquale wanted to hear.

"*I'm* the oldest," he soberly reminded his siblings. "I'm the one who always took care of everyone. No one should have to take care of me!"

Finally, he settled down, winked and smiled at Ben, then reached out for his hand.

"You're good kids," he said to Ben and me. Then to my mother and Sal he added, "Kids today aren't like these two. Kids today don't care about anyone."

But then, I thought, there is only one Uncle Pasquale and we would have gone to the ends of the earth for him if we had to. It had nothing to do with being a good kid and everything to do with the kind of man Pasquale was.

"The family is coming in," Nurse Lisa appeared suddenly in the doorway, reminding us that the six o'clock hour had arrived. Her remark was also a reminder of the way Pasquale's siblings had been treated like outsiders instead of close members of Pasquale's family throughout the entire ordeal. My mother and Sal grumbled all over again at the implication that they were not a part of Pasquale's family. Julie, as always, took pleasure in being punctual so she could watch us leave.

Before Lisa had gone too far from the room, Uncle Sal caught up and questioned her about Pasquale's release. She advised him that Julie had not yet signed the document, but Lisa promised to see that Julie did sign it during her visit. Uncle Sal, however, was not satisfied. He wanted to wait right there and actually observe Julie putting her signature on that darn piece of paper. Before I knew it, my mother was chiming in and I sensed another battle brewing.

"How do we know she won't pull another fast one?" Uncle Sal speculated.

Then, to make the mutiny complete, Ben joined their ranks, even going so far as to call Max and leave a message on his answering machine asking him to step in again which, I was certain, would not be necessary.

I began to panic at the thought of another ground-shaking eruption in the halls of the nursing home. When we walked out of Pasquale's room, he was relaxed and in good humor. I did not want anything to upset him again. What was more, I was disappointed in my family's lack of faith. Hadn't their brother just been delivered into their hands? Hadn't they signed, just the day before in Max's office, the agreement with Julie to gain his release? Her signature was on *that* piece of paper, even if she had not yet signed the actual nursing home release form. She could hardly go back on her word now.

To pacify everyone and get them the heck out of there, I gave Lisa my cell phone number and extracted her promise to phone me as soon as the deed was done. Then, like dutiful but reluctant children, Pasquale's siblings finally left the building.

That evening, my mother and I lay on our twin beds in the hotel room, me channel surfing with the TV remote while she called my father. I put down the remote as soon as I saw George C. Scott appear on the screen in what I knew was the closing scene from *Patton*, one of my all-time favorite movies. Patton was quite the controversial commander. He was gruff, proud of the men under his command, but led in a manner that his own hierarchy would eventually challenge. A cunning student of war and triumphant in battle after battle, Patton kept his eyes on a higher power and was always confident of victory.

I could not help thinking it was a fitting culmination to our journey, so I continued to watch. At the end of the movie, George C. Scott narrates a description of Patton's Roman counterpart from another era: *"The victor rides in a chariot; his children, robed in white, ride with him. A slave stands directly behind the victor holding a golden crown above his head and whispers a warning in his ear, 'All glory is fleeting.'"*

I got goosebumps when I heard those words and reflected on Pasquale's recent battle. There I was basking in the glory of Pasquale's final victory over Julie, but I had no clue as to just how prophetic those words would be: All glory is fleeting!

CHAPTER ELEVEN

The Prisoner is Set Free

SUNDAY, APRIL 18

"Of all skepticism, the saddest is the refusal to believe in the possible."

—WILLIAM SALTER

It was a beautiful blue-sky morning with just a hint of a salt-water-scented breeze in the air; the kind of morning that makes you want to walk outside, stretch your arms out to the heavens, and inhale deeply. Having done just that, I strolled around the hotel to the brick patio at the rear, tucked my legs under myself, and settled onto a chair under an umbrella. Uncle Sal's car had pulled out of the parking lot just minutes before, with my mother and cousin Ben waving from the passenger seats. They were on their way to a Catholic mass. My mother had long since given up hope that I would change my mind and become a Catholic again, and I was happy we did not have to go there again that morning.

Instead, I sat on the patio and relished a quiet morning alone with my coffee, God, the butterflies, and the birds singing in the trees. It was not long, however, before I found myself thinking of Nora. The upcoming separation would not be easy for her or Uncle Pasquale, for that matter, and I sincerely hoped for an eventual reunion after Pasquale's recovery. In the interim, I hoped Nora's daughter would be more charitable in the future and see the error of her ways in her callous treatment of my uncle and his wife. Well, maybe I'm a sucker for lost causes but I believe that as long as the heart beats and there is breath in the body, there is hope that a person can change.

Early that morning, before my family ventured off to church, Uncle Sal had revisited his misgivings about Julie and wondered aloud whether she would actually sign Pasquale's release.

"She'll drag her feet," he declared, making no attempt to hide his resentment. "Same way she made me wait for two hours at the nursing home in Pennsylvania until she brought the address and telephone number for this place."

Though I had not yet received Nurse Lisa's telephone call as she had promised, I still had a sense of peace about it.

"It'll be all right, Uncle Sal," I reassured him. "Lisa might have simply forgotten to call me before her shift ended. I'm sure the release is already signed."

"I hope!" he replied, cynically.

While I sat there at the umbrella table, I too hoped I was not off base with my prediction. We needed additional drama that morning like we needed a case of the measles. No sooner had that thought formed in my mind when my cell phone rang. It was Jonas Maxwell calling to tell me that he would be on standby for us in case we encountered any last-minute opposition to our departure plans.

"You've done a great job for us, Max, and we are eternally grateful. But at this point, I'm simply trusting God to take us all the way home," I told him confidently.

"I have to tell you," Max said, "that one of my most cherished memories of this case is your cousin, Ben, stroking Uncle Pasquale's hair. I hope that when I am old and in a nursing home someone will be there to stroke my hair."

"Oh, I have a feeling you won't be disappointed," I cheerfully replied. Max was such a caring, compassionate individual that I found it hard to envision him spending his elder years alone.

Shortly after my conversation with Max, I received the anticipated telephone call from Nurse Lisa. Julie had signed the release; Pasquale was free to go! When my traveling companions returned from the church service, we wasted no time packing and checking out of our rooms.

It was Pasquale's big day and we were just as anxious to see him take leave of that place as he was to be finally going home. Shortly after 9 a.m., with suitcases and seashells stowed in the trunk of Uncle Sal's car, we were off.

Unfortunately, all was not sweetness and light at the nursing home. We arrived just in time to witness an argument between Pasquale, Nurse Penny, and a nurse's aide. The staff was attempting to help Pasquale out of his bed and into a wheelchair so they could take him down the hall to the showers in preparation for his journey. Pasquale was having none of it. Still suspicious of everyone who was not a blood relative, Pasquale lashed out at the nurses in protest, even attempting to scramble out of the opposite side of the bed to avoid their grasp. Having endured so much treachery at Julie's hands, he trusted no one but us and since we had not yet arrived, he was convinced that he was again being spirited away from us under Julie's orders. A frazzled looking Nurse Penny met us in the corridor as we advanced toward Pasquale's room.

"Ah am so glad y'all are here," she sighed. "He just will not cooperate today."

Uncle Pasquale could be a bit cantankerous at times, we knew. To us, that feistiness was a welcome sign. It meant Pasquale was feeling much better, knew his own mind, and meant to enforce his own wishes. I grinned at the prospect as we entered his room.

"Good morning, Uncle Pasquale!" I greeted him cheerfully as I crossed the room to deliver a hug.

"They're trying to take me somewhere!" he cried, glancing anxiously from one to the other as we stood around his bed. "And I'm not going with them!"

"It's all right, Uncle Pasquale," I reassured him. "They just want to give you a bath before the ambulance comes to take you home."

He was not wearing his hearing aid and apparently only heard the word, *home*.

"Are you going home?" he asked in alarm.

"Yes," I told him. "And so are you! You're coming with us today!"

"Don't you want to go home?" Sal chimed in.

Pasquale responded with a question of his own, "Are you taking me?"

"Yes!" Sal told him emphatically. "I'm riding with you in the ambulance."

Hearing that, Pasquale relaxed and smiled sheepishly at the nurses.

"You have to let the nurses do their job, Uncle Pasquale," I coaxed him. "It's a long ride and you'll feel better if you let them give you a bath and a shave before we go. Okay?"

"Okay," he said finally as he grinned and tugged playfully at my hand.

"You just behave yourself," Sal admonished. "We'll be here when you get back."

"Okay, okay," Pasquale repeated in resignation, waving Sal away.

"Let's go!" he ordered Nurse Penny with a twinkle in his eye. "I don't want to keep them waiting!"

"I told you he was a character," I reminded Penny.

"Yes, you certainly did and ah can surely see it!" she replied, shaking her head.

Penny wheeled a grinning Pasquale out of his room and down the corridor toward the showers, the two of them now chatting amiably as if nothing had happened. Pasquale signaled "thumbs up" while we stood there shaking our heads and laughing.

"I think this is going to be an interesting trip," Uncle Sal observed wryly.

Pasquale may have been down but he was certainly not out. His feisty spirit assured us he would eventually beat all of the odds and make a full recovery. We could barely wait to get him home and put that process in motion.

While Pasquale enjoyed a shower, we waited in the visitors lounge, comfortably ensconced in the plush, over-stuffed furnishings. Sometime later, Nurse Penny came to find us again.

"Do you want me to administer a sedative to keep him quiet for the trip?" she asked.

"Good Lord, no," I groaned. "Enough with the sedation already! He needs to be fully aware of where he is and where he is going, Penny. I don't want him to wake up six hours from now and wonder what state he's been taken to next. I want him to see the outside of this building when he leaves and the familiar surroundings when he arrives in Pennsylvania. There needs to be no doubt in his mind that he has been taken home."

My mother and Sal echoed their assent with, "That's for sure," and "I'll say."

"Okay, you got it!" Penny cheerfully responded. "No sedation."

To our delighted amazement, the ambulance and transport team arrived from Pennsylvania almost an hour ahead of schedule at just a few minutes past 11 a.m.

Ray, the driver Ben and I had met the previous week, made the trip once again but with a different partner. They were a welcome sight and we greeted them enthusiastically, beaming approving smiles while they transferred Pasquale from a wheelchair to the gurney, strapping him securely.

Fern Donnelly came to Pasquale's room to say good-bye. Pasquale would probably go down in their records as their most notorious case and I silently hoped the lessons she had learned through the previous month's experience would not soon be forgotten. The nursing director, Talia Evert, one of Julie's biggest fans, came to stand poker-faced next to Fern and Penny as the gurney carrying Pasquale was wheeled out of his room and into the hallway. Talia looked on in silence until the remainder of the staff began to take their leave. Then, with the smugness I had come to loathe in her, she calmly broke her silence and took the wind right out of our sails.

"Are either of you skilled nurses?" she challenged with her typical know-it-all affectation as she cast an appraising glance over the ambulance team.

Ray and his partner exchanged guarded glances and shook their heads.

"He has to have a skilled nurse in attendance," Talia continued. "Someone capable of monitoring his feeding line and vitals during the trip."

"We can take his vitals," Ray offered. "But," he admitted, "we aren't equipped for the rest of it."

"Well, that's what's required in order for him to be transported," she informed them with her arms crossed over her chest, obviously enjoying their discomfort as Ray nervously shifted his stance.

Her eleventh-hour announcement left us speechless and I'm certain that was her intent, but I refused to bow to her one last time. My mind raced with alternatives as I silently met her malevolent gaze. She was enjoying the standoff, no doubt, but I had no intention of allowing her to defeat us. I let out a deep sigh and regained my composure.

"All right," I calmly addressed her. "How do we go about getting this *skilled* nurse?"

"Well, ah don't know where you'd get one at this late notice," she replied sarcastically. "You might try calling one of the local agencies," she offered.

But that was all the help we would get from her. That woman clearly did not like me, hadn't from the start, and she was determined to be a thorn in my side right up to the end. That thought no sooner formed in my mind when I decided right then and there that we would indeed take our leave, one way or another, Talia and her skilled nurse be damned. We would go over her, through her, or around her, but we were taking Pasquale out of there this time; there was no way I would see him disappointed again. We were leaving her little regime that day, come what may. Smirking at Talia's perceived authority, I glanced at Nicki, one of the aides who regularly attended Pasquale, as she leaned against the opposite wall watching the scene unfold.

"Hey, Nicki," I addressed her with a mischievous tone. "Want to go for a ride?"

"Sure," she responded readily. "Ah've never been to Pennsylvania!"

At that, Talia huffed, turned on her heels and marched down the corridor from whence she came. She was of no further use to us and Fern Donnelly had long since retreated to her own office. Finally, Ray broke the spell.

"Uh, ma'am," he began, turning to me. "He didn't have any feeding lines when we brought him here," Ray informed us with a shrug. Uncle Sal, Ben, my mother, and I exchanged startled glances as that revelation registered in our collective brains.

"And he wasn't nearly as stable, medically, as he is now," I observed aloud.

"Gosh darn it!" Uncle Sal cried out in anger. "This is a fine time to tell us he needs a nurse! They should have told us this last week, not today when we're ready to leave!"

My mother and Ben muttered similar sentiments then fell silent, looks of disgust on their faces. Uncle Sal began to pace; the ambulance attendants shifted nervously, awaiting a resolution, and Pasquale was getting restless as he lay in the hallway atop the motionless gurney. Finally, Pasquale lifted his head from the gurney and looked at me.

"Are we going?" he asked anxiously.

I studied the lines of concern etched into his forehead and knew there was no way I would allow anyone to disappoint him again.

"Yeah," I told him as I squeezed his hand warmly. "We're going, Uncle Pasquale."

I stepped away from the gurney, nodded to Ray and rendered my verdict.

"Heck with it. If he came down without it, he's going back without it," I told them determinedly. "We'll just have to trust the good God that brought him this far to preserve his health during the trip. We're out of here!"

Ray and his partner immediately took command of the gurney, striding purposefully as they pushed it toward the main entrance. Nurse Penny, God bless her, came to our rescue one last time as she suddenly fell in step alongside the ambulance attendants and quickly deposited a bag of liquid nutrition, feeding line, and pump syringe onto the gurney.

"Penny, you're an angel," I said as I stopped long enough to reach out and give her a quick hug.

Ray and his partner never broke stride as Ray acknowledged Penny's gift with a nod and told her that he was sure he could figure out how to use it if Pasquale needed it. Penny's final act of thoughtfulness touched my heart and sent a tear falling down my cheek. Pasquale, however, lay atop the gurney with his good arm folded casually behind his head, wearing a triumphant grin, obviously enjoying his ride to freedom. Ben, Sal, my mother, and I marched behind like a rear guard. No one attempted to stop us and I would have dared them to try!

Outside, Pasquale was loaded into the waiting ambulance. Uncle Sal stepped up onto the tailgate and climbed in after him, taking up a position on a bench that ran parallel to the gurney on which Pasquale lay. The bench, intended to hold a paramedic during the normally short trip to a medical facility, looked incredibly uncomfortable and we immediately questioned whether Uncle Sal would be able to sit there for the duration of the ride home. However, he insisted on staying there beside his brother, so the attendants closed the doors behind him then took their own places in the cab. Ben, my mother, and I followed behind the ambulance in Uncle Sal's car, with Ben taking the wheel for the first leg of the return journey.

Weary from the battle and glad to be heading for home at last, we rode in relative silence for the first hour. I leaned back against the headrest with mixed emotions, turning my head to watch through the window as buildings, trees, and people flew by. It was a landscape with which Ben and I had become all too familiar and we would both remember it for a long time to come.

It had been an exasperating, energy-sapping, often mind-numbing ordeal to gain Pasquale's freedom. Although I was glad to be leaving it all behind, what I did not foresee was the forging of new friendships in such a short time and the ache in my heart at the thought that I would probably never see any of them again.

"Please keep in touch and let me know how he's doing," Penny had said to Ben the day before our departure as she thrust a piece of paper into his hand on which she had written her address.

We would miss her warmth and perpetual smile. Yes, it was hard to leave behind those who had staunchly taken up Pasquale's cause and helped us gain his release.

During our first refueling stop in northern Virginia, Uncle Sal disembarked from the back of the ambulance to stretch his legs. Like the changing of the guard, I climbed in, slid across the slippery vinyl-coated bench and protectively took Uncle Sal's place for a few moments next to Pasquale.

"What's going on?" Pasquale asked quizzically as I climbed in beside him.

I told him we had just stopped for fuel and food and would be on the road again shortly.

"Want a milkshake?" I asked, remembering his fondness for ice cream.

He said he did not need anything and that he felt "pretty good." Thankfully, the feelings of anxiousness that engulfed him that morning had receded. As he lay there inside the ambulance, he wore the nonchalant expression of a tourist on holiday without a care in the world. He was the most relaxed he had been in months and happy to finally be on his way home.

I relieved Ben at the wheel of Uncle Sal's car for the next leg of the journey. Ray and his partner also traded places and it seemed that the pace of the ambulance picked up considerably once we were on the open highway again. As I learned during another stop later that day, Ray's traveling companion was a young man recently discharged from the Army who saw active combat on the European continent. As a medic there, he tended to wounded soldiers on the battlefield then sped away with them in an ambulance to the relative safety of a field hospital, often under enemy fire. That knowledge served to explain why the ambulance proceeded at a maddeningly accelerated pace while he was at the wheel!

It was not so difficult to keep up with him as long as we remained on the highways. However, soon after we had exited the last four-lane highway in Pennsylvania and began to follow a route that wound along the mountains, his driving style quickly became cause for alarm. Not only for me as I struggled to keep pace with him, but also for Uncle Sal, who was perched precariously on the edge of the slippery bench next to Uncle Pasquale. The speed with which I had driven to Virginia just over two weeks before was nothing compared to the race that afternoon. Occasionally, when we were near enough to the ambulance tailgate, we were able to see Uncle Sal through the rear window, jostled about, as he clung to the edge of the bench in an attempt to remain upright.

"He's going to be sore when this ride is over," Ben observed, shaking his head.

Shortly after 9 p.m., when the ambulance finally arrived at the nursing care facility in Smithton, Pennsylvania, Uncle Sal disembarked with one hand gripping the small of his back and the other holding on to the rear door of the ambulance for balance. He looked like a man who had just endured a wild ride on a bucking bronco.

Ray and his partner quickly unloaded Pasquale and wheeled him into the facility. When he finally reached his new quarters, eight more family members—Pasquale's other siblings and their children—swelled our ranks to greet him, hugging Pasquale and splashing their tears all over him.

For Pasquale, however, that joy was short-lived. A spate of turbulent emotions overcame him moments after the nurses settled him into his bed.

"I hope they never find me!" he cried as he recalled his horrible ordeal.

He had been through a bad time, no doubt. Still, the fear he expressed at the prospect of Julie finding him was alarming so I flew to the nurse's station for help.

A male orderly stood behind the desk talking on a telephone while a middle-aged nurse sat next to him writing furiously. I stood in front of her quietly, arms resting atop the chest-high counter, waiting politely for her to finish her task and take notice of me. She was a thick-set woman with short razor-cut brown hair wearing what my brothers and I used to call Coke-bottle glasses when we were kids. Finally, the pen in her hand was still and she looked up at me.

"Yes? Can I help you?"

A tone of annoyance in her voice made me hesitate. I wasn't certain I wanted her help after all. Quickly glancing around and realizing she was pretty much the only offering, I pressed on.

※ ※ ※

I introduced myself and quickly told her that my uncle, newly arrived, was a little anxious due to somewhat strained relations with his stepdaughter. To my surprise, she already knew all about it. In fact, she was one of the nurses who had tended Pasquale before he was whisked away to Virginia. She was well-versed about his situation and had actually tangled with Julie herself.

"I have no use for that woman," she informed me.

I felt the tension in my muscles relax as I breathed a sigh of relief. This nurse was a tough character all right, just like the one we encountered at the nursing home in Virginia. But this time it would be to Pasquale's benefit, not Julie's.

"Don't you worry," she assured me. "We won't put up with any nonsense here."

She readily agreed to talk to Pasquale in the hope that he would remember her and find a measure of security in a familiar face.

I followed her back to Pasquale's room as she marched before me with arms swinging in cadence like a drill sergeant. She waded through the relatives gathered around Pasquale's bed, then leaned over him as she wiped away his tears.

"Mr. DiAngeli!" she addressed Pasquale in a loud firm voice to get his attention. "Do you remember me? You're back in Smithton now and I'm taking care of you. No one is going to hurt you here. You're safe. Do you understand?"

It was then that we learned from the nurse that Julie had telephoned ahead, just a few hours before our arrival, to tell Laura Johnson, the director of the nursing home, that she had changed her mind and did not want Pasquale admitted there after all. We were flabbergasted. Would she never give up?

※※※

During our return drive to Pennsylvania, we decided to put the past in the past, bury the hatchet and remember Nora and Julie's folly no more. Pasquale was safe again and we would see to his recovery. In the meantime, we felt we could rise above the maliciousness Julie and her mother had shown toward Pasquale. If we refused to stoop to their level, we felt, perhaps they would eventually rise to ours. For Pasquale's sake as well as Nora's, we felt that we should not stand in the way if Julie decided to bring her mother to visit Pasquale. In fact, we had planned to welcome both of them back into the family with open arms in the hope that Julie would turn over a new leaf and learn to behave herself.

But this new information left us shaking our heads. What was Julie thinking?

Laura had denied Julie's request, telling her that the paperwork had already been processed and they had no choice but to accept him. If Laura had not taken that stand, would Julie have directed the ambulance to take Uncle Pasquale to some undisclosed location so that we would not be able to find him again? I had no doubt that she would.

Was she having second thoughts about Pasquale's release? Did it finally occur to her that by releasing him, she would lose command over his assets as well? Or, maybe she thought it would be a good joke to have Pasquale turned away like a man without a country so that, with nowhere else to go, he'd have no choice but to go back to her. In spite of the fact that Pasquale was physically out of her grasp, she was still his legal attorney-in-fact by virtue of the power of attorney document that Pasquale had yet to revoke. Though her motive eluded us, her action served to impress a renewed sense of urgency upon us. We suddenly realized that we could not relax our guard. Not yet.

***

Julie's fresh attack, coupled with Pasquale's obvious fear of her, caused us to accelerate our plans. Before leaving Virginia, I had phoned Tom Cavanaugh, the attorney who initially put me in touch with Jonas Maxwell. I brought Tom up to speed, telling him we had secured Pasquale's release and would be bringing him home. Tom already knew that Julie had a power of attorney for Pasquale. However, Tom claimed that her power to act on his behalf was automatically void at the point when Pasquale was able to express his own desires about his affairs. Since that milestone had arrived and considering that Pasquale was once again on home turf where we could keep a watchful eye on his recovery, Tom felt no urgent need to take the legal steps required to revoke Julie's power officially.

As a result, I had initially arranged for Tom to visit Uncle Pasquale at the nursing home only after Pasquale had at least a week to settle in and aggressive therapeutic care had begun. However, Julie's fresh assault made it necessary for me to accelerate that timeline. She obviously thought she was still in control and could threaten Pasquale as long as she held that piece of paper in her hands. I needed to do something about that. Fast!

By eight o'clock the following morning, I had Tom on the telephone.

"Looks like we're going to have to step up the pace," I told him. "Julie has made it clear that she will continue to thwart our efforts to see to Pasquale's recovery as long as she believes she has the power to do so. We can't have that. Pasquale needs to be assured that Julie no longer has any power over him."

After hearing about Julie's latest antic, Tom agreed that a legal revocation of her power of attorney should be drawn up immediately. However, he had appointments in court all week and was unable to break free even for a few hours. Instead, he arranged for one of his junior partners to meet with Pasquale at the nursing home that very afternoon. I could only hope that Julie would give us all a break and recede into the proverbial woodwork until that time.

The revocation of Julie's power of attorney plus the new power of attorney document not only had to be signed by Pasquale, but both documents then had to be recorded at the local courthouse. After recording, the revocation could then be delivered to Julie to ensure she took no further action as Pasquale's legal agent. Pasquale had been freed from his Virginia prison, but in his mind and on paper, he was still a captive. I meant to see to that last detail and free Pasquale from his stepdaughter once and for all.

CHAPTER TWELVE

The Price of Freedom

TUESDAY, APRIL 20

"A belief in a supernatural source of evil is not necessary; men alone are quite capable of every wickedness."

–JOSEPH CONRAD

Pasquale was finally back in Pennsylvania, but our efforts on his behalf had not yet ended. In the days immediately following his return, clues to the financial carnage Julie left behind had barely begun to surface. However, we could not tend to those matters yet. In light of persistent threats posed by Julie to regain control of Pasquale's destiny, the first order of business was to revoke her power of attorney and put a more responsible person in charge of Pasquale's affairs.

To accomplish that, Tom Cavanaugh arranged for a junior partner from his law firm to draw up a revocation then meet with Pasquale at the nursing home at three o'clock that afternoon. There was no longer any question as to whether or not Pasquale was of sound mind, but during my conversation with Tom, I wondered aloud if Pasquale would be able to provide the requisite signature. Pasquale's right side was still partially paralyzed as a result of the stroke he suffered months before, and he was not yet able to use his right hand.

"He only needs to make an X on the signature line," Tom assured me. "I'll send a notary along. She'll affix her seal testifying that your uncle made the mark himself."

With that matter momentarily laid to rest, I eyed the clock. I had more than three hours to kill before Pasquale's appointment, so I decided to use the time to learn what I could about the status of Pasquale's house. The week before Ben and I traveled to Virginia, I found the real estate advertisement on the internet and telephoned the agent who had contracted with Julie and Nora to list the property for sale.

I explained Pasquale's situation to him and attempted to appeal to the compassionate side of his nature, urging him to withdraw the home from the market. I assured him that Pasquale had no intention of selling and in fact, intended to take up residence there again as soon as he recovered. The man flatly refused. Certainly he would listen to the voice of reason, I thought, so I tried appealing to good business sense, one real estate agent to another, telling him that he would wind up on the wrong end of a lawsuit if he allowed a sale to take place under present circumstances. That tactic failed to sway him.

I have heard it said that like attracts like and the longer I talked to him, the more convinced I became that the man was clearly a charter member of the same Greed Club to which Julie belonged. Citing the same power of attorney document that had been a thorn in our sides in Virginia, the real estate agent felt he had a valid listing contract and intended to fulfill it. Translate that: *I have a commission coming and by golly, I'm going to get it!* My argument that Julie was using her power of attorney under false pretenses, that is, she was not acting in the spirit of the law by abiding with Pasquale's wishes, failed to move him. Neither did he appear to be concerned when I advised him that Nora suffered from dementia and was therefore not legally able to contract.

"She seemed all right to me," he defended. "We had a nice conversation and turns out we know some of the same people."

"You should have asked her what she had for breakfast that morning. She would've been hard-pressed to tell you. Dementia wreaks havoc with short-term memory. By the time she walked from your office to the parking lot, I'll bet she didn't even remember why she was there except to visit with you. Believe me when I tell you there will be consequences if you proceed."

■■■

I'm not sure who hung up on whom, but I walked away shaking my head. Every profession that is commission-driven has its slimy underbelly. Ambulance-chasing attorneys, fast-talking used car salesmen, and the real estate business is no different. Inevitably, you will find those who operate seemingly without a conscience; those who will take full advantage of every opportunity to get some green in their hands. At whose expense the money rolls their way is of no consequence to such people, and this man clearly had no problem tossing an elderly man out on the street to earn a few bucks. The man truly turned my stomach.

At the time I'd had that conversation with him, Pasquale's house was not yet under agreement of sale. However, Uncle Pasquale was still helplessly under house arrest in Virginia and Julie held all the cards. Though we were racing against time, I held out hope that we would get Pasquale back home in time to stop a sale.

On that Tuesday morning, as I sat at my parent's breakfast table remembering the conversation, I knew it would be useless to try and tangle with that real estate agent again. Instead, I looked up an old friend in the local telephone book and gave him a call. I had known David Scott more than fifteen years before, when he was a real estate appraiser and I was a loan officer for a mortgage lender in Smithton.

David handled all of the appraisal work for that mortgage company and I remembered him as a competent professional. When David put his name on a valuation, you could take it to the bank. David was the type of trustworthy individual I needed. However, I was not certain exactly how he would be able to help, or if he would even remember me. At the very least, I thought he would be able to research the local multi-list service and tell me if Pasquale's home had been listed at a fair price in the event I was too late to stop a sale.

"I would have known you anywhere!" David exclaimed, taking my hand and greeting me enthusiastically after I walked through the doorway of his office.

To my surprise, not only did David remember me, even better, he had added Real Estate Broker to his list of credentials. I was ecstatic!

We engaged in small talk, catching up on years that melted away in minutes, and then I got down to business. David was astounded at the tale I told, shaking his head in disbelief as I recounted the details of my uncle's circumstances since his stroke and his stepdaughter's subsequent attempts to see to his demise. David efficiently tapped out Pasquale's address on his computer keyboard, calling up the online records from the local Realtor association. I moved around to his side of the desk and stood next to him watching as he scrolled through the list of homes for sale in Pasquale's neighborhood. Finally, 1455 Maple Grove Avenue appeared on the screen. My heart sank when I saw the word, "Pending." In Realtor lingo, that meant it was under agreement of sale but had not yet gone to settlement. Pasquale would be crushed.

"Now," David said as he manipulated the mouse to click on the address and fully open the record. "Let's see who sold it and when."

❏❏❏

The data that appeared on the screen caused both of us to pause then stare at each other in open-mouthed amazement. An agent from David's own brokerage firm had represented the buyer for my uncle's home!

"What are the chances of *that* happening?" David exclaimed.

"Oh, about one in a gazillion," I countered, grinning.

"I'll be right back," he said as he rose from the chair and jogged down the hallway outside his office. Minutes later, David returned with a legal sized manila file folder in his hand.

"You didn't see this," he cautioned, "but this is your lucky day!"

"I don't think luck had anything to do with it," I assured him. "It's called ask and you shall receive!"

What we learned was that an agreement of sale had been signed on April 15, the day before Julie relented and agreed to release Pasquale from the nursing home in Virginia. That bit of knowledge gave me some insight into her timing. Undoubtedly, Julie thought she was home free and would be able to cash in on the sale without interference. The fact that she thought she was sending Pasquale home with no home to go to wasn't lost on me either, and I intended to see that her plans went awry in a big way.

The contract contained a stipulation that the seller (Nora) had to find a suitable home within thirty days of the date of the contract or it would be null and void. The contract was signed by Julie on behalf of Pasquale. I looked at my watch then looked at David.

"I've got news for all of them," I told him. "In a few more hours, that contract will be null and void because a certain power of attorney will have been revoked and neither Julie nor her mother will be able to execute a deed to consummate the sale."

"Wow!" David exclaimed. "Let me know as soon as that happens so I can tell my agent to call the buyers. I'm sure they won't be happy."

"I'm sure you're right," I echoed sympathetically. "I feel bad about inconveniencing them, I really do. But there isn't anything unique about my uncle's home that would allow a buyer to force the issue. It's just a basic raised ranch with more sentimental value for my uncle than for anyone else. I'm sure your agent can find at least a half dozen other houses like it for the buyers to choose from."

"You know, they could sue your uncle for specific performance under the terms of the contract," David warned.

"Let them try," I told him. "I sincerely doubt there's a judge in the land who would force an old man to give up his home under these circumstances. That house has been my uncle's home for over thirty years. He built it for his first wife. And it's gonna remain his home until the day he dies if I have anything to say about it!"

After leaving David's office, I drove to my sister's house to use her computer. I had to send an e-mail message to Jonas Maxwell directing him to close his file, take his fee from the retainer he held, then forward the difference to Tom Cavanaugh's law firm. I knew there would not be much money left, but it would be enough to allow Tom to open a case for Pasquale and begin to work on his behalf. In his reply to my e-mail, Max asked me to keep in touch, writing that he would be interested in learning how it all turned out for Pasquale.

"I promise not to bill you for reading your e-mail," he quipped light-heartedly.

After finishing that task, I drove out to Good Shepherd Nursing Home in the suburbs to check on Pasquale. It was 1:30 p.m. and he was sleeping soundly. I decided not to wake him. After what he had been through, I thought he deserved the extra rest. Instead, I said a prayer over him asking that he have clarity of thought and speech for his meeting with the attorney. It was imperative that nothing go wrong when the attorney met with Pasquale; we simply had to have Julie's power revoked before the raiding of Pasquale's assets was complete.

While I drove, I thought back to the previous weeks and the resistance we encountered from the nursing home administration in Virginia. I knew that Betty Crocker and crew were only trying to cover their legal behinds, but I felt they had made the entire process more difficult than it had to be. It just seemed to me that they had worked overtime in preventing Pasquale from exercising his right to name a new attorney-in-fact or call his own shots and I wondered what their legal liability would be in the event Pasquale suffered irretrievable losses. I hoped I didn't need to go down that road. At that point, I just wanted to see an end to the legal wrangling, financial carnage, and the physical and emotional toll it had taken on Pasquale.

By contrast, the nursing home in Pennsylvania was familiar with Julie's tactics.

We even learned that they had threatened to have her escorted out at one point during Pasquale's previous time there because Julie refused to refrain from using her cell phone as their visitor policy dictates. They had no desire to deal with her again now, so they were more than happy to stand aside and allow us to do whatever we felt was legally necessary to protect Pasquale by moving Julie out of the picture.

Shortly after 2:30 p.m., my parents and I arrived at the nursing home, where we were joined by Uncle Sal and his wife plus a longtime family friend who would serve as a witness. Pasquale was still in a deep sleep and we had difficulty rousing him.

Once again, an all too familiar scene played out as I flew into action, placing cold, damp towels against Pasquale's face and neck in an effort to revive him. Pasquale frowned when the wet cloth touched his skin, but his eyes remained tightly shut as if he were simply responding to an irritating dream.

"He doesn't look so good," Uncle Sal observed direly from the foot of Pasquale's bed.

The others expressed similar sentiments: too much medication, too hot in the room, no air circulation, while we counted down the minutes until the attorney's arrival.

"He'll be all right," I optimistically told them while I swabbed his face.

Uncle Sal moved to the side of the bed and nudged his brother's shoulder in an attempt to wake him.

"Hey, Pasquale!" he practically shouted. "Are you going to wake up?"

No response from the figure lying in the bed. Uncle Sal looked to me.

"Are you sure he's going to be able to do this?" he asked apprehensively.

"The only thing I know for sure is that God didn't bring him this far for nothing. I'm going for help," I announced. "Keep talking to him."

As I hurried out of the room, I caught Uncle Sal's shrug as he said to the others, "Well, she's been right so far. I hope she's right again."

I smiled inwardly at the innocence of that remark as I jogged to the nurse's station.

It was not a matter of being right; it was a matter of belief, faith, and determination. Today there is an entire movement centered on that principle. It's called the law of attraction. The law of attraction dictates that when the mind is acutely focused on a specific result and steps, however small, are taken toward it, then the desired end result must manifest. There can be no other outcome.

If you are of a religious nature, then you probably know of the story in the Bible where Jesus tells his apostles that if they had a measure of faith even as small as a mustard seed, and that's pretty tiny, they could move mountains. The hard part is removing all traces of doubt from our minds so those mountains *can* be moved. It is the doubt that clouds our adult minds, preventing us from confidently moving forward and accomplishing great things. For me, on that particular afternoon, I no longer had any lingering doubts. The events in Virginia only served to bolster my confidence that all future efforts on Pasquale's behalf would be successful.

Minutes after running to the nurse's station, I returned to Pasquale's room with two nurses in tow. They raised the head of Pasquale's bed and helped him into a sitting position. Unfortunately, there were no individual air conditioning units in the rooms at that facility. The temperature in Pasquale's room was the temperature that had been set for the entire building. However, one of the nurses did reduce the temperature on the hallway thermostat to try and achieve a slight cooling effect. The minutes ticked by. Finally, Pasquale came around, peered out from beneath half-closed eyelids, and began to speak. The words were still a little thick on his tongue and his body tended to slump sideways, but a few well-placed pillows aided his posture.

No sooner had the nurses finished their handiwork than the attorney and his notary walked into the room and introduced themselves. I, in turn, introduced them to Uncle Pasquale and the others. To the family's astonishment, Pasquale seemed to come alive just then. He was suddenly alert and articulate, concentrating on what the attorney had to say. At one point, he even held up his hand in a signal for those near his bed to hush as the low-level murmuring was distracting him and he did not want to miss a word.

Throughout Pasquale's ordeal I had consciously made a practice of thinking positive thoughts to feed into the outlook that all would be well, but what I witnessed that afternoon far surpassed my own optimistic expectations. Pasquale carefully and clearly articulated each word as he conversed with the attorney, telling him that he thought he looked familiar and perhaps he had used his services at some time in the past. That part of Pasquale's performance was amazing enough, but the best was yet to come.

When the attorney produced the documents that would revoke Julie's legal authority once and for all, showing Pasquale where he was required to sign, Pasquale said to him in an attitude of humility and concern, "I just want to do what's right."

"That's why we're all here," the attorney assured him.

Pasquale insisted on reading the document in its entirety before signing, a move that stunned us all into silence. Since he still had the use of only one hand, I held the documents for him and turned the pages when he nodded for me to do so. That level of participation was completely unexpected considering the semi-comatose state Pasquale had wavered in and out of for days on end. In fact, so much medication was still being poured into him that more often than not, he fought to remain awake long enough to say hello, let alone sustain an intelligent conversation.

With that in mind, Sal put a pen into Pasquale's right hand and showed him where to make an X. Sal was completely prepared to assist him by steadying Pasquale's hand with his own since, in the preceding days, Pasquale had managed only minimal movement of his swollen fingers. Just the day before, Pasquale was still unable to flex his fingers completely. The muscles in his hand were so weak that he couldn't grasp even lightweight objects. More often than not, the hand simply lay limp at his side. There was no earthly reason to believe that he could manage to scrawl anything that remotely resembled his former signature.

We stood there at his side, a small, silent audience watching intently, fully expecting that Pasquale would only mark the signature line with an X as the attorney instructed and leave it at that. However, Pasquale took the pen in his right hand and with pride and firmness, he began slowly and deliberately moving the pen above the signature line at the bottom of the pages—first, signing the revocation then the new power of attorney document naming me, his brother Sal, and his sister Natalie as his new attorneys-in-fact. In eloquent, albeit lop-sided, strokes above those signature lines, Pasquale made swirls and flourishes reminiscent of the manner in which he had been accustomed to penning his signature, proving that he knew exactly what he was doing.

The finished result was not his normal, neat penmanship, but then, I have seen less legible writing on a prescription. We stood there in awe, watching as he carefully manipulated the pen. The room was so quiet we could have heard a mouse sneeze. In fact, I don't believe any one of us exhaled until Pasquale had laid the pen aside and the precious documents had been handed over to the notary for her seal and signature.

Within minutes of the attorney's departure, Pasquale again lapsed into a deep sleep. As he lay back against the pillows, eyelids slammed shut, he addressed us in a grumpy voice.

"Now go away and let me get some sleep, for crying out loud!"

Sal grinned broadly as he reached out to muss the gray hairs on Pasquale's head.

"You did good!" he told him.

But Pasquale did not appear to hear. He was already snoring!

In any event, we had what we needed; Julie would bother Pasquale no more.

While the attorney waited, I took the originals of both the revocation and the new power of attorney and made photocopies in the nursing administrator's office. I handed the originals back to the attorney for recording at the county courthouse, kept one set of copies for myself, and gave one each to Uncle Sal and my mother. We had been appointed as Pasquale's new agents and we had much to do.

While his brother, sisters, and I scrambled to do financial damage control in the days that followed, Pasquale languished in the nursing home in a largely incoherent state, leaving no doubt in our minds that we had witnessed a miracle that afternoon. My mother and Uncle Sal took on the task of dealing with doctors and nursing home staff to plan a course of therapy, which included modification of Pasquale's medication, speech and physical therapy regimens, plus his gradual reintroduction to solid foods and weaning from the stomach tube. Pasquale had lost valuable recovery time at Julie's hands and we meant to see that he regained as much as possible.

We discovered that Julie had placed a forwarding order at the Smithton Post Office so that she would receive all of Pasquale and Nora's mail at her own home in Virginia. She even had Pasquale's pension and social security checks rerouted to her own bank via direct deposit order. Uncle Sal immediately opened a mailbox for Pasquale at the post office closest to him and promptly diverted all of Pasquale's mail from Julie's hands. My mother opened a new bank account in Pasquale's name alone so he would have benefit of his own income again with no challenge from Nora. It was my task to visit the local Social Security Office to fill out the proper forms to redirect Pasquale's monthly benefits into his new bank account.

While my mother and Uncle Sal tended to their own details, I also took my copy of the legal documents and made the rounds of local banks where Pasquale had been known to keep accounts. What we eventually learned was that Julie's raiding of his assets was almost complete. Over a quarter of a million dollars, a substantial chunk of his life's savings, had been withdrawn from his accounts, then parked in a trust account in another city. Shortly afterward, the bulk of the money promptly disappeared. By the time we found the trail, little more than fifty thousand dollars remained. Pasquale's attorney immediately ordered a freeze on those funds, then requested a full accounting from Pasquale's stepdaughter through the attorney she had since hired.

With those tasks completed, I turned my attention back to the pending sale of Pasquale's house. I faxed a copy of the legal documents bearing Pasquale's signature along with my letter notifying the listing agent that the sale would not be consummated, as neither Pasquale nor his new agents would consent to sign the deed. After dispensing with that detail, I phoned David again and arranged for him to meet me at Pasquale's house so he could perform an appraisal. David had already determined, during my first meeting with him, that Pasquale's property had been sold at a fire-sale price, well under its true market value. Surely the buyers were aware of the bargain price and I wanted to be ready with that ammunition to counter any attempt on their part to force a sale.

The next afternoon, my parents decided to accompany me to meet David at Pasquale's home on Maple Grove Avenue. My mother had a key Pasquale had given her some months before to be used in the event of an emergency, and she wanted to be able to take inventory so she could reassure her brother that his possessions were intact. Uncle Sal, who had taken enough of Julie's bullying in preceding weeks, was in a mood to fight back, so he followed behind us in his car. However, when our little procession turned onto the avenue and Pasquale's property came into view, we spotted two cars already parked in the driveway. One we recognized as belonging to Nora. Nora herself stood in the driveway, one hand on her hip, the other wielding a garden hose as she doused the shrubbery. They had followed us back to Pennsylvania! My father slowed the car mid-way down the block.

"What do you want to do?" he asked, glancing at me in the rearview mirror.

Legally, we could have tossed Julie out of the house since her name was not on the deed and her status as Pasquale's attorney-in-fact had been revoked. Nora was another matter. Her name was on the deed and she had every right to be there, but could not stay there alone. We made a fast decision to turn back, avoiding what would surely have been a nasty confrontation. I quickly dialed David's cell phone number from my own and aborted the mission. We did not know if Pasquale's wife and stepdaughter had returned to monitor his recovery or simply intended to gather the remainder of Nora's possessions. We hoped for the latter and that they would soon be gone. Unfortunately, that was not the case. We didn't have to wait long to find out what they were up to.

Their appearance, coming as it did on the heels of Pasquale's escape, was disconcerting to say the least. In light of the attempts, documented by the Virginia nursing home, to interrupt Pasquale's life-sustaining fluid intake, Uncle Sal immediately returned to the nursing home and gave strict orders to the staff that neither Nora nor any member of her immediate family was to have access to Pasquale. If they were found in his room, they were to be ushered out by the home's security guards. Sal also alerted the rest of Pasquale's siblings, who flew into action, taking up shifts at his bedside as they had months before, from early in the morning until the nursing home closed their doors for the night.

While those protective measures were put into place, I called Pasquale's new attorney and requested that he immediately send an official letter to Nora and her daughter advising them that their authority over Pasquale had been revoked and that they were to refrain from visiting him for at least thirty days. While I regretted having to take such action against fragile Nora, we all felt that thirty days was not only an appropriate, but a necessary time frame for uninterrupted therapy and for Pasquale to gather physical strength. We had also hoped that the time of quiet, free of the turbulence that always followed in the wake of Julie's and Nora's visits, would allow Pasquale to begin healing from the emotional trauma as well. After a month's reprieve, we decided, Pasquale himself would determine if he wanted to see either Julie or Nora again. It would be his decision, his alone, and one that we would abide by no matter what he chose.

That evening, Pasquale's sister, Eleanor, received a disturbing telephone call from a friend who was one of Pasquale's neighbors on Maple Grove Avenue. She told Eleanor that a number of garbage bags and open boxes had been set at the curb in front of Pasquale's house in the pouring rain to await the regularly scheduled trash pickup the next morning. Several passers-by had stopped to rummage through the boxes earlier in the evening only to be chased away by Julie. Eleanor asked her friend to wander across the street after dark to see what those boxes contained, but by the time she did so, several had already been scavenged. What remained of Pasquale's clothing, shoes, and personal possessions lay scattered in the yard near the street. The news was devastating.

Would those people stop at nothing? Why did they feel the need to destroy his life so completely? Was it simply because he refused to die for them? How would we ever tell him that his loving wife and stepdaughter had taken the ultimate step in obliterating his existence? We could not, would not bring ourselves to utter the words. In Pasquale's still precarious state of health it could well have been the final nail in his coffin; the blow that would cause his heart to seize and his body to wither and die.

As far as Pasquale's siblings were concerned, it was definitely the last straw. If Pasquale was dead to Nora and Julie, then the two of them were dead to our family as well. There would be no forgiveness, they vowed, no reconciliation. In fact, there would be no contact between them, Pasquale, and members of our family whatsoever outside a court of law. They would see that Nora and Julie paid dearly for what they had done. The price Pasquale paid for his freedom was incomprehensible.

CHAPTER THIRTEEN

Millstones and Milestones

TUESDAY, JUNE 29

It had been four months since the hemorrhage of his brain had so completely incapacitated Pasquale and two full months since his return to Pennsylvania. He remained at the Good Shepherd Nursing Home and during that time, a full complement of doctors and therapists rallied around him to aid in his recovery. He still suffered with occasional bouts of depression, so deep were the emotional scars inflicted by Julie's callousness. However, those spells gradually diminished as his family kept up a steady presence at his bedside and Pasquale began to take more of an interest in his own physical rehabilitation progress.

During his first two weeks at Good Shepherd, my mother reported to me that Pasquale still refused to eat solid foods even though the staff brought a tray to him three times a day. As a result, he continued to receive forced feedings through his stomach tube at regular intervals throughout the day.

When members of his family were present during meal times, they tried to coax him into eating, but Pasquale's unenthusiastic response was always the same, "I'm not hungry. I'll eat tomorrow."

I drove across the state to visit with him one weekend in May. Arriving early in the morning, I was sitting on the edge of his bed engaged in conversation when a nurse's aide entered with his breakfast tray. Having greeted Pasquale, she deposited the tray on the portable bedside table then exited just as quickly as she arrived. Minutes later, another nurse breezed in and approached Pasquale's bed. Knowing that he still did not have full use of his right hand, I naturally assumed that the reason for the second nurse's arrival was to assist Pasquale with his meal. When I saw that she was preparing to inject a thick milky substance into his stomach tube instead, I held up a hand to stop her.

"Wait!" I practically commanded her. "Aren't you going to give him a chance to eat breakfast on his own before you pump that slush into him?"

"Doctor's orders," she snapped. "If he doesn't eat the food brought to him, I've got to pump it into him."

"But," I protested, "he needs help eating and the food was just brought in two minutes ago! Doesn't anyone come in here to help him eat?"

She said she did not know (nor did she appear to care). She stated that she was the medication nurse and she only followed the directives in his chart, but she would find someone else to assist with his meal.

That was the first inkling that Pasquale's care was more maintenance routine than progressive therapy and I was furious. When I followed the nurse out into the hallway and pressed the matter with her, I learned that she administered those feedings into Pasquale's stomach tube four times per day beginning at 4 a.m. The cumulative daily ration equated to fifteen hundred calories, the amount required to sustain an *active* man of his size per medically accepted standards. With fifteen hundred calories pumped daily into the stomach of an inert individual, it made perfect sense to me that he would not be hungry enough to bother with solid food. Why couldn't they see that?

"4 a.m.?" I echoed incredulously, hands on my hips, as I stood in the hallway watching her sort pills from a wheeled cart. My challenge did not faze her and she continued with her routine while I protested. "Does it not strike you as coincidental that he is not hungry when the eight o'clock breakfast tray arrives? You people are supposed to be weaning him *off* the forced feedings. How is that supposed to happen if no one helps him eat and you just keep pumping that ... that *stuff* ... into him?!" When the nurse told me she saw nothing in Pasquale's charts to that effect, I saw red and immediately turned on my heels and strode down the hall toward the nursing director's office.

"Laura, we've got a problem," I informed her from the doorway of her office.

After I reiterated my conversation with the nurse, Laura followed me back down the hall toward Pasquale's room. The nurse was still standing there in the hallway behind her pushcart, busily plopping colorful pills into little paper cups as she consulted the charts hanging on a clipboard. A tense conversation ensued between the two of them, ending with the nurse angrily declaring that if someone would update the charts she might know what she is supposed to be doing. Before returning to Pasquale's room, I extracted a promise from Laura that the 4 a.m. feedings would be withheld from Pasquale for a few days to see if it would help to increase his morning appetite. Laura had to clear the request with Pasquale's attending physician, but she didn't think he would object.

When I related that incident to my mother that evening at supper, I told her that she and Uncle Sal had to be more mindful of the fact that Pasquale was doing his recovery time in a nursing home. While we fully expected him to walk out of there one day, the vast majority of their patients were there for the rest of their lives. It had to be up to Pasquale's siblings to keep the staff on their toes and remind them, periodically, that we expected them to be working toward his recovery and eventual release.

Several days later, after I had returned to my own home on the other side of the state, my mother happily reported to me that the early morning tube feedings had ceased and Pasquale actually began to nibble at the foods on his breakfast tray. That was great news! The only problem was that Pasquale complained that the food didn't taste right or that he still felt too full to eat. Both sensations were normal enough, as he had not eaten solid food in more than two months. His taste buds undoubtedly suffered and we also knew that certain medications might have such an effect. Once again, his siblings put their heads together and came up with a plan: they would take turns "visiting" at meal times to make sure Pasquale ate something from every tray that was set before him.

When Pasquale began to complain about the quality of the food, homemade goodies like Aunt Eleanor's meatballs and my mother's soft-breaded chicken were smuggled in to him. Those occasional surprise treats served to keep him interested in food long enough to ensure the eventual discontinuation of the noontime tube feeding as well as the discontinued 4 a.m. feeding. As it happened, that event coincided with a summer picnic the staff had planned on the hospital's grounds. My mother and Uncle Sal attended with Pasquale, who wore a new baseball hat and munched a hamburger, held with his left hand, while reluctantly mingling with other residents. They were thrilled at his progress! My mother kept me informed from across the state and reported roughly two weeks later that Pasquale was finally consuming an adequate amount of solid food throughout the day that he required only one supplemental feeding.

Not long afterward, I again drove across the state to Smithton to check on Pasquale myself. While my mother and I were visiting with Pasquale in his room that day, a speech therapist entered and introduced herself to us. She then asked me if I would retrieve a few personal items from Pasquale's home that she might use in her therapy sessions with him. She also requested that some of his own clothing be brought to him. The reason for her request, she said, was that Pasquale seemed to be losing interest in his speech and physical therapy sessions telling the therapist at one point that he had nothing left to live for.

Pasquale also complained that he was wearing someone else's clothes. Unbeknownst to Pasquale's siblings, the nursing home staff had taken to dressing Pasquale in used clothing donated by the Salvation Army before wheeling him out of his room to his therapy sessions. At first, Pasquale complied but as he progressed to the point where he was wearing street clothes more often than pajamas, he began to protest. He wanted his own clothes. We knew that moment would arrive eventually, the time when we would have no choice but to tell Pasquale how thoroughly Julie had dismantled his former life, and we all dreaded inflicting a fresh bout of depression and anger that was sure to follow such a revelation.

I rose from my chair and motioned for the therapist to follow me out into the hallway while my mother remained in the room with Pasquale.

"He has nothing left," I told her when we were out of earshot. "His wife and stepdaughter took all material items of value, drained his bank accounts, then threw away all of his clothing and personal possessions. If there was a scrap of paper or a thread of clothing left, I would bring it to him, but his house is empty. It looks as if he never lived there at all."

It was true that Uncle Sal and I had attempted to recover the items in Pasquale's safe deposit box, but Julie had been there one day ahead of us and cleaned that out as well. None of us knew what that safe deposit box contained. Pasquale was either unable to form the words or simply could not remember what he had stored there, but it was still, at that point, an unresolved issue.

The therapist was at a loss for words. She told me she had a break in her rounds an hour later and asked if I would meet with her then. She wanted to hear the *whole* story, from the beginning, so she could help Pasquale work through the grief then move beyond it during their therapy sessions.

In the days that followed, we broke the news to Pasquale as gently as possible, telling him they were just material things, items that could be replaced, but even we knew that was a lie. The fact was many of his possessions were irreplaceable: his Army helmet from World War II, photos of him, fellow soldiers who served with him and the Pacific islanders they befriended, the Italian-made revolver he said he had purchased as a gift for his father while he was overseas, a brass pocket watch that came to this country in the pocket of his father, family photos, letters written by relatives living in Italy decades earlier, Pasquale's wood-working tools, and the many household objects he proudly created with those tools. All were lost through the senseless, vengeful actions of his stepdaughter. All that remained were his memories, and those were too painful for him to recall. What was important, we attempted to convince him, was that he was alive and getting stronger every day.

"Easy for you to say!" he cried out in anger. "You're not in this mess. I am!"

We did not give Pasquale all the sordid details, but in the days following Julie's and Nora's return to Pennsylvania, Pasquale's sister received another telephone call from the neighbor who kept her abreast of the happenings at Pasquale's home. She reported that moving vans had arrived under cover of darkness to carry off the furniture and appliances. In addition, we learned that a tearful Nora had knocked on another neighbor's door to say good-bye. According to that neighbor, Nora stated that she did not intend for things to turn out the way they had and that she was only complying with the demands of her son-in-law, a man she was afraid to cross. That was the second time she had voiced such fears.

The neighbor's report of Nora's sad visit caused me to regret our aborted mission. Perhaps my family and I should have intervened after all on the day we saw Nora in the driveway. Perhaps she too needed rescuing.

We later learned that when yet another neighbor inquired at the house after Pasquale's health, Nora's son-in-law, Danny, told him, "Pasquale's finished. He's never coming back here."

That was wishful thinking on Danny's part. The Pasquale I knew was far from finished.

As the weeks went by, Pasquale continued to make half-hearted attempts to engage in physical therapy, complaining that the exercises were too hard and the therapist too demanding. It would prove to be one of the most challenging aspects of his recovery, since he was required to use some muscles that he had not used in months and others that had been neglected for years. Drained from the physical effort and often feeling defeated, he occasionally lapsed into a state of careless lethargy, sleeping too much, eating too little, and easily moved to tears. His speech became garbled as a result of the stress and he lost patience with his brother and sisters when they failed to comprehend the words his mouth failed to form. Uncle Sal, who had maintained a daily schedule of early morning visits, reported that Pasquale frequently faded out just as he was about to convey a thought.

"Tomorrow I want you to ..." Pasquale told him one day just before nodding off again.

That was all Uncle Sal could understand and it frustrated him to no end that he was unable to determine what his brother wanted him to do.

The doctors and nurses who attended Pasquale assured his family that his symptoms were normal for a stroke victim. They claimed there was simply no way to predict just how long the effects would last. However, unknown to his brothers and sisters, and apparently to his doctors as well, Pasquale was actually in a downward spiral heading toward a medical crisis. On Tuesday evening, June 29, my mother received a telephone call from the nursing home. Pasquale had stopped breathing and paramedics had rushed him to a nearby hospital's emergency room.

I didn't receive the news about Pasquale's crisis until a few days after the episode had passed. As my mother told the story to me, Pasquale had been sitting in a wheelchair in the corridor outside his room. An orderly happened by and noticed that Pasquale had slumped forward in his chair. When the orderly moved closer to Pasquale and noticed the ashen pallor in his face and slight bluing of his lips, the orderly flew into action. While he worked to get oxygen flowing into Pasquale's lungs, a nurse called for an ambulance. Fifteen minutes later, Pasquale was in the ER.

Numerous medical tests were performed on Pasquale while he was in the hospital. The cause of his collapse, the ER doctor finally determined, was quite simply an abnormally high level of drugs that his system could not handle. I couldn't believe it! I had campaigned so hard to have Pasquale's medication reduced or withheld while he was still in Virginia. That end was finally achieved just before he returned home, but apparently, his new doctor in Pennsylvania failed to read down that far on the medical charts and he had Pasquale back in the chemical soup again. As if Julie's attempt at murder were not enough, Pasquale's own doctor nearly killed him with an overdose!

For some people, there comes a time when they feel that Western medical practices have failed them. I had just such an experience almost a decade before when two doctors made futile attempts to figure out what was triggering my steadily rising blood pressure. After pronouncing me *otherwise healthy*, they simply wrote a prescription for a drug they claimed would solve the problem. I was unimpressed and did not intend to ingest chemicals so some doctor could claim he cured me. That, I felt, was not true healing; it was nothing more than delivering a panacea to mask the symptoms.

Following a friend's advice, I made an appointment with a homeopathic practitioner who analyzed urine and saliva samples to determine what vital nutrients my body lacked. The regimen of nutritional supplements he prescribed had me feeling better in two weeks than I had felt in years. I was no longer lethargic, allergy symptoms disappeared, and I had the energy to begin an aerobic exercise routine that I kept up with for years afterward. Not only had my blood pressure returned to a normal range, but it was not necessary for me to seek the services of a general physician again for another six years.

Perhaps because of my own experience, I seemed to be more opposed than other family members were to the daily dumping of chemicals into Pasquale's body. Each time I visited him, I would quiz the nurses about their progress in weaning Pasquale from no less than eight different drugs that they administered on a daily basis. Each time, their response was the same: we had to consult Pasquale's doctor to affect a change in orders. However, Pasquale's doctor was never at the nursing home during my sporadic weekend visits and my mother and Uncle Sal seemed to be so overwhelmed with the handling of Pasquale's other affairs that quite often, they simply forgot.

Good fortune and an alert nursing home attendant saved Pasquale's life. The bonus was that the ER to which they transported him was in the hospital where his niece, Emily, was employed as a physican assistant. Emily not only kept a watchful eye on his charts, but she insisted that her father, Sal, appoint another physician to monitor Pasquale's care. According to Emily, the doctor who previously tended Pasquale had a reputation for over-medicating his patients. Hearing that, Sal followed his daughter's advice and Dr. Madison soon took charge of Pasquale's continuing recovery. He proved to be a marvelous physician who took care to administer only the medications he felt Pasquale absolutely required, and then only in the minimum doses to achieve the desired healing effect. Pasquale's condition improved dramatically under his care.

Pasquale remained in the hospital for several days while his new doctor weaned him from the pharmaceutical overload. The result was nothing less than remarkable. On Sunday, July 4, Pasquale returned to the nursing home a new man. His siblings gathered in his room, teary-eyed, for a homecoming of sorts and witnessed the miracle of his restoration. According to my mother, it was as if he had simply awakened, totally refreshed, from a very long nap.

That Sunday afternoon, his siblings were able to engage in rich conversation with Pasquale on a level they had not experienced since before his stroke. They shared memories and good humor and were so overwhelmed with joy at having their brother restored to them, memory and speech intact, that several of them left his room in tears.

In homeopathic medicine, there is a phenomenon known as a healing crisis during which the patient's physical condition during treatment suddenly hits rock bottom.

Just when the patient is seemingly near death, an equally dramatic rebound occurs after which the patient, oftentimes, experiences a complete cure. On rare occasions, I have heard of similar instances in Western medical practices. Did Pasquale experience a healing crisis that day? If it was, then that crisis marked the beginning of a new phase in Pasquale's recovery. He was more eager to participate in physical therapy sessions and his appetite for food, for life itself, increased dramatically. By the time I broke free from my own obligations long enough to make the drive across the state again, another two weeks had elapsed and Pasquale was indeed a changed man.

Gone was the perpetual ashen pallor, replaced by the radiant glow of health. Gone was the flimsy hospital gown; he was fully clothed in comfortable looking charcoal leisure slacks and a maroon polo sweater. Instead of lying flat on his back in bed, he sat in a padded lounge chair, holding court with his visitors.

When my parents and I arrived in his room, a lively Pasquale was already entertaining his siblings and several of my cousins with his quick wit. After I greeted everyone, Pasquale looked at me and proudly proclaimed, "Ho-ho, look what I can do!"

While I watched, he proceeded to do leg lifts in rapid succession from his seated position, kicking up first his right leg then the left.

"You could try out for the Radio City Rockettes!" I gleefully declared.

"I'm going to walk out of here," he firmly asserted. "You just watch and see!"

And I believed him. Pasquale was back in the driver's seat, taking charge of his own life. I could not have been happier for him.

He asked his sister to bring his financial records the next time she visited so he could begin to assess the damage Julie had done to his resources. Instead of caving in to the pain and suffering, willing himself to roll over and die, Pasquale had begun to pick up the pieces and move forward. While he talked about preliminary plans for his future, more immediate concerns suddenly came to his mind. Complaining once again "I have no pants!" he ordered Sal to go shopping for him.

"And bring me a decent pair of shoes, too!" he added.

A good-natured sparring match bubbled between the two of them, ending with both erupting into laughter.

Twenty-two days after he crashed, Pasquale had reached a new plateau in his recovery, earning a transfer out of the nursing home and into a rehabilitation center in a nearby town. The rehab center had a reputation for taking on difficult injury cases and successfully bringing about life-changing results. We heard many stories about stroke and accident victims whose own doctors predicted that they would never walk or talk again, and those patients beat the odds under the care of the rehab center's qualified staff. The pace was intense; therefore, the center accepted only patients they deemed physically and emotionally ready to accept the challenge.

For Pasquale, however, it was another bittersweet victory. During his residency at Good Shepherd, he became attached to several nurses, aides, and therapists who had cared for him. He had lost one family in Nora and Julie and had no sooner developed a surrogate family when he had to say good-bye to them as well.

As they entered his room, preparing for his departure, Pasquale tearfully embraced each one in turn and they congratulated him and wished him well. Afterward they lined the hallway, everyone clapping and cheering while an orderly maneuvered a wheelchair bearing Pasquale out of his room and down the corridor to the awaiting transport. It had been a rocky road at times, but the staff at that nursing home rose to the challenge and took my uncle to a crucial point on the road to recovery. He did not walk out of there as he had planned; nevertheless, it was an incredibly proud moment for all of them.

Prior to his arrival at the rehab center, the administrator had outlined an intense plan of daily activities for Pasquale that swept him up in their momentum almost as soon as he was wheeled through the door. With the exception of a scheduled nap after lunch to gather strength for the afternoon therapy sessions, Pasquale was busy throughout the day with a full complement of therapeutic specialists at his side. One therapist worked to restore muscular strength and coordination so he could walk again. Another taught him to hold eating utensils and writing implements with his left hand, since it appeared the motor skills in his right hand might be irreparably damaged. Yet another therapist concentrated on clarity of speech and thought processes.

After his first full day of therapy, Pasquale wondered aloud to Sal and Natalie whether he would be able to maintain such an arduous pace. However, as they had done from the beginning of his ordeal, his siblings kept up a routine of daily visits, encouraging him every step of the way and never allowing him to falter. I received regular reports from my mother and as I caught the excitement in her voice each time Pasquale regained yet another formerly lost motor skill, I longed to be there to see the transformation myself.

Five days after Pasquale entered the program, I managed to get away from my business long enough to pay a visit. Shortly after twelve o'clock one afternoon, I walked into the rehab center flanked by my parents. After we passed the main entrance, my mother led us to Pasquale's room, but he wasn't there. We retraced our steps and stood near the front desk waiting for a staff member to appear so we could inquire as to his whereabouts.

While we stood there, the sound of clattering utensils accompanied by a low murmur of voices caught my attention. It came from a room just to the left of the reception desk so I took a few tentative steps in that direction, just far enough to peer through the slightly open door without being seen. There was Pasquale, seated at a small round table along with three other residents, eating his lunch completely unassisted. He didn't see me, but that didn't keep me from grinning over his accomplishment. When I told my parents what I saw, we decided to wait in the lobby until the lunch hour had ended. We didn't want to disturb that triumphant moment.

Afterward, we caught up with Pasquale in his room. He immediately took advantage of our visit, requesting that my mother and I clean out his clothes closet. In a few short months, Pasquale had gone from being the man with no pants to a man with such a jumble of new and passed-down clothing in his tiny bedside closet that he needed someone to sort it all out.

The rehab center held their residents to tough standards, not permitting them to wear pajamas or hospital gowns during the day. Dress for success was their philosophy, and that meant that Pasquale had to wear street clothes during waking hours. To comply with the dress code, Sal had made small purchases for Pasquale: a few shirts, sweatpants, and undergarments. However, Pasquale did not yet possess a full wardrobe of his own design. Some of the clothes that made the transition with him from the nursing home were the ill-fitting donations acquired through the Salvation Army, and Pasquale was not satisfied. He wanted everything gone that did not belong to him. He wanted to begin afresh with his own possessions, purchased with his own money. So while Pasquale supervised, my mother and I filled a trash bag with rejected clothing. Afterward, Pasquale dictated a list of items he wanted us to purchase for him.

While we finished the task, Pasquale yawned loudly, complaining that he could barely keep his eyes open. As if on cue, a nurse sailed into his room just then, announcing that it was time for Pasquale's afternoon nap. She smiled graciously as Pasquale went on about his grueling physical schedule while she turned down the covers and helped him out of his wheelchair and onto the bed. No sooner had his head hit the pillow than his eyelids slammed shut.

As we prepared to make our exit, collecting the trash bag full of rejected clothing and our own sweaters and purses, I told a shut-eyed Pasquale that we were going shopping to fulfill his list and would see him later in the evening.

"Is there anything else you want us to buy for you while we're out?" I asked.

With his eyes still closed, he replied wearily from his prone position, "Buy me a casket!"

It was typical Pasquale humor and we roared with laughter. Without missing a beat, my father asked him, "What color do you want?"

"Gold," was his quick reply.

"And I'll bring the roses," I interjected, good-naturedly. "But right now you need to rest. We'll see you later."

We were still chuckling, shaking our heads in disbelief as we walked out to the parking lot on our way to fulfilling Pasquale's shopping list.

In the weeks that followed, Pasquale gained physical strength and stamina. He became more tolerant of his daily routine, and it appeared that he made some new friends as well. One afternoon while his sister visited, a familiar face appeared in the doorway to Pasquale's room. Duane, a therapist who had worked with Pasquale at the Good Shepherd Nursing Home, crossed the room to hug Pasquale and plant a kiss on his forehead.

"This old man is as dear to me as my own uncle," Duane told my mother.

As it turned out, Duane worked part-time at both the nursing home where Pasquale had previously resided and the rehab center, so he would continue to see Pasquale on a somewhat regular basis. That continuity helped Pasquale adjust to his residency at the new facility and he certainly seemed grateful.

However, after Duane left, Pasquale turned to his sister and said, "He embarrasses me. Every time he sees me, he has to kiss me!"

My mother laughed and that made Pasquale grin.

"I'm bad, huh?" he said.

In the following weeks, Pasquale dished out his fair share of hugs and kisses as well. He was growing more pleased with his progress and wore a happier countenance as a result. He told his siblings that he actually looked forward to his therapy sessions and jokingly referred to his therapists as "the teachers." Not surprisingly then, the head of physical therapy became "the principal." Pasquale's siblings always heard about Pasquale's "tests" and how well he had done that week.

As a matter of standard procedure, the rehabilitation center administration required that a nurse or orderly steer Pasquale down the corridors from his room to his therapy sessions while he sat like robed royalty in his wheelchair. It was not long, however, before that rule went right out Pasquale's bedroom window and he began sneaking down the corridors unaided, wheeling himself on exploratory expeditions. When the staff caught on to Pasquale's independent nature, they admonished him with a stern warning that he was not permitted to wheel himself out of his room until they told him he was ready to do so, and under no circumstances was he to attempt to arise from the chair unassisted. Pasquale dutifully obeyed those orders for a few days, until he himself decided he had reached the point where he was physically capable of disobeying.

One afternoon, while his sister walked down the corridor toward Pasquale's room, she was stopped in her tracks, gaping in disbelief at the sight of Pasquale, alone and grinning, as he zipped down the hall toward her in his wheelchair. Coming to an almost screeching halt in front of her, he looked up sheepishly and defended himself to her open-mouthed stare.

"I don't know why I have to wait for *them*," he explained. "I can do it myself. They don't know how much I can do already!"

On July 26, Pasquale traded in his wheelchair for a lightweight aluminum walker with two wheels. It was the first time since his stroke that he was ambulatory, albeit closely supervised by his therapist, but up on his legs nevertheless. A few weeks after that, Pasquale was walking by himself, aided only with a four-legged cane. He was making rapid progress. Exactly six weeks after he entered the program at the rehab center, he walked triumphantly up and down short flights of stairs, proudly practiced his neat, left-handed penmanship (unfortunately, his right hand had remained uncooperative), and he looked forward to going home.

"Where is Gina?" he kept asking my mother one day. "When is she coming home?"

That was my cue. I had promised Pasquale while he was still in Virginia that I would break camp in eastern Pennsylvania and join him when he was ready to return to his own home in Smithton, and it appeared that moment had finally arrived. It was time for me to wrap up my business affairs in preparation for moving day. Meanwhile, Pasquale's life had taken on the aspect of a new adventure, and he greeted each victorious milestone with the determination to do even better.

During the long months of his recovery, Pasquale had no contact with Nora. She did call Good Shepherd Nursing Home once, approximately two weeks after Pasquale's return to Pennsylvania. Even though we did not object to the nurses keeping Nora abreast of Pasquale's progress by phone, they informed us that legally they could not do so. As it turned out, the same power of attorney laws that got Pasquale into such a mess in the first place had a negative impact on Nora as well.

The tables were turned and although it was unintended, she and her daughter were suddenly the odd ones out. The nurses told Nora she would have to obtain her information directly from Pasquale's new attorneys-in-fact: my Uncle Sal, my mother, or me. Sadly, Nora never phoned any of us and we knew it would be futile to attempt to contact her since she resided with Julie, who had come to hate us all. On rare occasions, Pasquale mentioned his former family, but only in the context of conversations regarding his financial affairs and his emphatic vow to *settle accounts with them* upon his release from rehab. Toward that end, Pasquale fired the junior attorney who drafted the revocation of Julie's power of attorney as he felt the man was dragging his feet. The attorney had made no progress in bringing Julie to account for the raiding of Pasquale's assets. His efforts amounted to a half-hearted letter-writing campaign that produced no results, even though laws governing attorneys-in-fact require that they make full disclosure of all expenditures from their principal's funds.

Pasquale replaced the man with an attorney of his own choosing, one who had served him well in the past, a man with an excellent reputation for getting things done. With that accomplished, Pasquale rested a little easier, turning his thoughts once again to his future.

His days at the rehab center marked the return of a Pasquale that everyone in the family knew and loved. Pasquale, in return, deeply appreciated his siblings and everything they were doing for him. Through their efforts to research and recover Pasquale's finances, his siblings, Sal and Natalie, managed to locate a small investment account that Julie had attempted to grab for herself but failed to secure in time. Sal saw to it that the money returned to Pasquale's control, though Pasquale still lamented the loss of the rest of his life's savings and all of his personal possessions.

One evening, while his brother and sisters visited with him, they marveled at how far Pasquale had come down the long road to recovery. Their conversation caused Pasquale to reflect on past events and he asked them why he could not remember traveling to Virginia. In fact, he told them, he did not remember much at all about being there. Sal attempted to fill in the void, explaining that Julie had ordered him sedated for the journey and that sedation continued until Ben and I arrived and began the fight for his freedom.

"It isn't that your memory is bad," Sal assured him. "You just slept away the time."

After he heard the story of our two-week battle for his release, Pasquale quietly reflected, then told them, "I have my family now; that's all I need."

Even though Pasquale was emerging the victor, it was a victory fraught with pain and emotional torment. As the time for Pasquale's release from the rehab center drew near, he again lapsed into a tearful state of depression over his circumstances and regretted his parting with Nora. Shortly after her final visit to Pennsylvania in April, we learned that Nora's daughter placed her in a nursing home in Virginia. How typical of Julie, we could not help thinking. Her own mother was just as expendable as Pasquale had been. Granted, Nora was easily confused in the fog of dementia and definitely would not be able to live alone, but she certainly did not appear to be in need of that level of full-time care. Julie's live-in, intentionally unemployed, twenty-year-old daughter was also at hand to look after Nora during the day if Julie was now employed full-time. Apparently, neither of them wanted to be bothered. That was the thanks Nora received after funding their existence for years!

Pasquale shook his head in sadness when he heard of it. He told his sister that he wanted to write to Nora as soon as his penmanship was a little better and even talked about flying back down to Virginia to retrieve her. On Nora's birthday, Pasquale insisted that Natalie wire a bouquet of flowers to her with a note from Pasquale. He had hoped that the fragrance of his wife's favorite flowers and a card bearing his name would open the lines of communication, but no reply came. Natalie called the nursing home to find out whether or not Nora had received Pasquale's gift. The helpful attendant who answered the telephone confirmed that Nora did receive the flowers; however, her daughter had forbidden Nora contact with anyone in Pennsylvania. The nursing home staff had orders that Nora was not allowed to use the telephone and the residence staff was not permitted to put Pasquale's calls through to her.

It was not difficult for us to guess the reason that such a wall of silence had been erected around Nora. Julie knew that Nora would return to Pasquale in a heartbeat if she knew the extent of his recovery. Julie did not intend to let that happen. Some days Pasquale willfully expressed a desire to phone his wife anyway, stepdaughter be damned. At other times, his eyes welled up with the pain of emotional turmoil as he vowed he would have nothing more to do with any of them. At times, he voiced a desire to return to his own home on Maple Grove Avenue and the next moment he would cry out in bitterness saying that he never wanted to see that house again. Pasquale was on a rollercoaster ride of emotions during that period, even stating at one point that we should have just left him in Virginia to die, a thought that saddened us all after what we had come through with him.

His brother and sisters continued to rally protectively around Pasquale, providing much needed reassurance, emotional support, and help with his financial and medical affairs. Finally, the day arrived when Pasquale seemed to settle into a mode of acceptance and gratitude for what he did have.

During one Sunday afternoon, as his family gathered around him in lighthearted conversation, he conceded, "I probably have a few good years left."

Then, as he cast his eyes over his family and considered the measure of love represented among them, he added, reflectively, "I guess I'm a pretty rich man after all."

❏❏❏

On August 29, Pasquale's family celebrated his release from the rehab center by gathering for a banquet dinner at the local Italian restaurant where we had celebrated numerous family birthdays and anniversaries over the years. Pasquale proudly walked into the dining room under his own power, aided only by the four-footed cane, amidst cheers and applause from the thirty-two members of his family who had gathered in his honor. I made the drive across the state for the occasion, arriving shortly after everyone was seated. After dinner, I walked across the dining room to sit down beside my uncle.

"They won't let me pay for dinner," he complained good-naturedly.

"It isn't your turn," I lightly scolded him, laughing.

He looked at me quizzically until I reminded him that he paid for a similar family dinner years before in honor of my parents' anniversary. He grinned at the memory and it served to satisfy him that he had done his part after all.

That afternoon, Pasquale and I talked about moving into his former home together. After I stopped the sale, the real estate agent who had marketed the property sent an invoice to Pasquale for a sixty-five hundred dollar commission, claiming that because he had located a ready, willing, and able buyer, he had fulfilled his part of the contract and should be paid. Using the appropriate legalese, Pasquale's new attorney basically told the man to go pound sand. I also heard from my friend, David, the real estate broker whose agency had represented the buyer. He told me that the listing agent called him, asking that David join him in a lawsuit against my uncle. David, naturally, declined, telling the man that isn't the way he treats clients and anyway, such a move would only generate bad publicity and that is not the way David conducts his business.

The last we had heard of the greedy little man, he had sent his invoice directly to Julie, determined that someone was going to pay his fee. The prospective buyer, through yet another attorney, threatened to sue Pasquale for breach of contract in an attempt to gain possession of the home, but a few weeks went by without another word so we assumed they thought better of that course of action.

Approximately two months later, we read in the real estate section of the Smithton Times newspaper that the buyer had purchased another home in the same neighborhood. With that threat apparently removed, Pasquale was free to take up residence again at his home on Maple Grove Avenue and he remembered my promise to him. While we sat together at the restaurant that Sunday afternoon, he asked me when I planned to move back there to be with him. I told him I had hoped to wrap up my affairs by November, in time to celebrate the Thanksgiving holiday with him.

"I'll clean, you cook!" I teased playfully.

He grinned at the suggestion and we reminisced about the fun we had together decades before when I played housekeeper for him before he married Nora.

Then, he took on a more somber expression and in all seriousness he said, "You know, I haven't cooked in six months."

"You'll get the hang of it again," I laughingly assured him.

Several days after the dinner party, I sent a digital photo of a smiling Pasquale, sitting center-front at the restaurant, surrounded by his family, via e-mail to Jonas Maxwell.

"If a picture says a thousand words," I wrote, "then this one says it all! Thank you again, for all you did for Pasquale."

In his reply, Max wrote that he shed tears of his own when he saw Pasquale's grinning face gazing out from the photo where he sat, taking his rightful place among his family.

As I mulled over his words, a vision of Nora came to my mind and I saw her, once again, seated in the visitor's lounge at the nursing home in Virginia, with her hands folded in her lap and her head bent in sorrow over the prospect of Pasquale's return to Pennsylvania. As that memory flashed through my mind, I could not help wondering if Nora was in her rightful place. Who was the prisoner now?

CHAPTER FOURTEEN

Homeward Bound

By November, Pasquale had settled into a regular if somewhat uncomfortable routine at the assisted living facility where he had taken up temporary quarters upon his release from the rehab center. I was still attempting to get the last few of my real estate clients to the settlement table so I could close up shop and move west. With only a few weeks remaining before Thanksgiving, it appeared that I would not be able to celebrate that holiday with Pasquale after all. Regretfully, I adjusted my timeline and vowed that I would be there by Christmas. In the meantime, Pasquale's siblings, nieces, and nephews visited with him regularly. Rarely did a day pass without a family member stopping in with food or just to keep him company, and the residence staff made every effort to help him adjust and feel welcome.

While I worked to wrap up business affairs and pack up my house, Pasquale battled on through periodic fits of depression amidst the difficulty of adjusting, for the fourth time in eight months, to a new setting and new faces. The approaching holiday season only served to remind him that he had lost all contact with Nora and since it did not serve Julie's purposes to alter that course, it began to appear as though he would never learn Nora's fate. Did she miss him as much as he missed her? Was she well cared for in the nursing home where Julie had planted her? Would there ever be an opportunity for Pasquale to visit with her in person again? These were the questions that plagued Pasquale. During the course of his marriage with Nora, Pasquale had come to look upon Julie as family. He treated her like the daughter he never had. Not in his wildest dreams did he think Julie would turn on him and seek to destroy his life so completely as she had done.

Pasquale's moods continued to fluctuate between self-pity and anger with only sporadic respites, courtesy of Sal's cajoling. Throughout his life, Pasquale had cultivated many friendships. He was known as a hard-working, jovial, and genuinely likable individual who never hesitated to offer help, financial or otherwise, to those in need. He and his first wife, Angie, enjoyed a vibrant social life, rarely declining invitations to weddings, anniversary parties, bowling team banquets, and other events sponsored by Pasquale's employer or the many local clubs and organizations to which he claimed membership. But Nora was more of an introvert than Angie. During the latter few years of their marriage, Pasquale and Nora rarely left home and ceased entertaining in their own home altogether when various physical maladies began to plague their aging bodies.

Partly as a result of that sedentary lifestyle and partly because Pasquale viewed his current quarters as temporary, it was difficult for him to emotionally engage and interact with the other residents. He refused to join any of the weekly activities such as bowling, card playing, and social hours, and he politely declined any attempts by others to draw him into their social network.

"You go ahead," he told the lady who occupied the room across the hall. "Don't worry about me; I'm content. Anyway, my niece will be here soon."

Continuing in that vein, he was largely uncommunicative with the staff as well. Pasquale was gracious and grateful as the staff tended to his daily needs, helping him to shower, shave, and making certain he was able to safely get in and out of bed. But he absolutely refused to allow anyone to make a fuss over him. If he was not happy with the food or some other aspect of the services provided, he complained to members of our family but never to the staff. Pasquale somehow felt that it would have been unkind to do so. Sal and my mother regularly reprimanded him, telling him that he should speak up for himself and ask for whatever it was that he needed. After all, he was paying to live there; it was not the Salvation Army shelter.

"I don't want to bother anybody," was the excuse Pasquale gave them. He had been proudly self-sufficient his entire life and now it was difficult for Pasquale to admit that he was the one who needed help.

Fortunately, Janice, one of the younger female residents who had no such qualms about making her needs known, took a liking to Pasquale and took it upon herself to watch over him. When Pasquale learned that Janice's sister was a good friend of his own sister, Eleanor, that put Janice in good stead with Pasquale and he eventually opened up to her.

Permanently assigned places at the dining room table ensured that Janice always sat across from Pasquale at meal times. That practice maintained a sense of order for the residents with failing memories, but it also aided the kitchen staff in delivering meals to those with special dietary concerns or residents who required assistance in getting their food from plate to fork to mouth.

One afternoon Janice observed Pasquale listlessly pushing vegetables across his plate with a fork. He had barely touched the gravy-coated meatloaf.

"What's wrong, Pasquale? Don't you care for the food?" she asked with concern.

Pasquale grimaced, shook his head and set the fork down on the table. "They'll bring you something else," Janice assured him, simultaneously waving to one of the servers.

"Nah!" Pasquale angrily waved her away. "I don't want to be treated any different than anyone else!" he declared.

"The rest of us don't always like the food either, and they bring us something else when we ask for it. It doesn't mean we're more special than anyone else; it's just a matter of personal preference."

But Pasquale would not be persuaded. If the menu did not appeal to him or if the consistency of the meal was such that he could not pierce it with a fork, he simply nibbled what little he could, then sat in silence until it was time to return to his room.

When Janice reported these incidents to Pasquale's sister, she and Sal ordered an apartment-sized refrigerator for Pasquale's room. Thereafter, Pasquale had fresh fruits, raw vegetables, and a variety of other finger foods and beverages at hand, which he frequently invited Janice to share. His siblings were careful not to provide too much food, however, as they knew it would only encourage Pasquale to remain in seclusion in his room, depriving him of a hot meal and the opportunity for socializing during his otherwise self-imposed solitude.

At times, his complaints about the taste or quality of the food were only a cover for another difficulty that caused Pasquale more than a small measure of discomfort. Because full function never returned to his right hand, he could not use a knife and fork simultaneously to cut his food and he was too embarrassed to ask for help. When Natalie learned of it, again tipped off by Janice, she approached the dietary staff, who readily agreed to cut Pasquale's meat into bite-sized pieces before setting the plate before him. That measure served to ensure that he enjoyed a more successful dining experience. His physical therapist still worked with him twice per week, but the therapist was of the opinion that Pasquale's right hand was left untreated too long. As the therapist shared with me one afternoon after his session with Pasquale, "It's too bad his stepdaughter prevented physical therapy in the weeks immediately following his stroke. That's the best time to begin treatment to restore muscle movement and try to remediate nerve damage."

Pasquale kept at it, however, and eventually recovered the use of the fingers on his right hand. Unfortunately, his right arm muscles would go into uncontrollable and unpredictable spasms at the worst possible moment, so he eventually learned that in order to avoid accidental spills, he needed to reach for a beverage with his left hand and use the right hand solely for wielding a fork or pen.

Pasquale was thoroughly delighted with the acquisition of his new refrigerator and frequently thereafter used his own stores as an excuse not to participate in group dining. It was such a small matter but one that raised his spirits tremendously.

As the family watched over him and attempted to assess his needs, one theme kept ringing loud and clear: independence. Pasquale had lost control over his life as he previously knew it and had been thrust, quite suddenly, into an environment where he was forced to rely on others for his every need. That did not sit well with him; he was accustomed to doing for himself. Moreover, *he* was always the one who helped *others*, as he frequently reminded his family, not the reverse. When a neighbor needed to borrow tools, they came to Pasquale. When he worked in the steel mill and discovered that an employee was short of cash before payday, Pasquale lent him the money he needed. It had been a recurrent theme in his life; he was the helper, not the one who required help, and he simply could not swallow his pride long enough to ask.

Indeed, he was so inept at even making the attempt that we usually discovered what Pasquale wanted only by way of a more generalized conversation that waltzed around the issue before bringing it center floor. For example, during one of my visits, I commented approvingly on the cozy feel of his new quarters and asked him if he was getting what he needed from the staff.

"You take the good with the bad in these places," he replied. "But I'm all right."

He did, however, complain about the poor lighting in his room. A sixteen-inch table lamp with a dark green shade and matching canister style base stood on his nightstand; a replica, in miniature, occupied the desk in front of the window. Both were standard issue, provided by the facility, but neither lamp provided much in the way of practical or cheerful illumination.

Instead of coming right out and asking if I would bring a better lamp for him, Pasquale exclaimed, "I'm tired of living like a hermit!"

"What makes you feel like a hermit?" I inquired curiously.

"There's not enough light in here," he responded. "When I get out of here I want to go shopping and get a decent lamp!"

"We can get another lamp for you. What type of lamp do you want?"

"A floor lamp; something I can put beside my chair so I can read."

"I'll get one for you," I offered.

"But I want to pay for it!" he emphasized, poking a finger at his own chest.

"That's fine, Uncle Pasquale. Whatever you want, we'll do."

"Good," he replied and quickly crossed the room to retrieve his wallet from the nightstand. "How much do you need?" he asked, turning toward me with his wallet open.

"Depends on what you want to spend," I replied. "You can buy a cheap lamp for about twenty-five dollars or you can spend a hundred. It's up to you."

"Twenty-five dollars!" he cried. "That's too much!"

Uncle Sal walked into the room during our exchange and chuckled at Pasquale's naive rebuke.

"How much do you think a lamp costs these days?" Sal asked him.

"No more than ten or fifteen dollars," Pasquale replied, matter-of-factly.

"Maybe thirty years ago," said Sal, "but not today. When was the last time you bought a lamp?"

"I don't know, maybe ten or fifteen years ago," Pasquale replied thoughtfully.

"I'll tell you what, Uncle Pasquale," I ventured. "I have a floor lamp that I'm not using. I'll bring it to you and if you like it you keep it. If not, we'll go shopping and you can pick out your own, okay?"

"Okay," he replied hesitantly. "But I'll pay you for it just the same!"

"All right, all right," I assured him. "You can pay."

The next day I delivered an old but still serviceable floor lamp with an oak base and built in oak table, a 3-way light bulb so Pasquale could control the level of brightness in his room, and two lamp shades, a maroon colored shade and an ivory shade. Pasquale absolutely beamed. The little round table built into the lamp's column was exactly what he wanted to hold a beverage, book, or the TV remote control within reach while he relaxed in his recliner. Not surprisingly, he chose the ivory colored lamp shade.

"This one provides better light," he decided.

Gradually, Pasquale opened up about other things he felt he needed, and as long as we disguised the item as a gift or allowed him to "reimburse" the expenditure for a modest sum such as five or ten dollars, he was a happy man. Eventually, his quarters took on a more home-like ambience and Pasquale finally seemed to relax more and settle in. He even found that he had a few friends among the other residents after all, one of whom had been employed at the same steel mill where Pasquale made his career and another who grew up in the same small village where Pasquale was born.

In the weeks preceding the holiday, my parents made plans to fetch Pasquale and take him to their home for Thanksgiving dinner. I was getting closer to wrapping up business affairs in eastern Pennsylvania, but I simply could not break away to join them since I had a property settlement to attend the Friday morning after Thanksgiving. Though I felt awful having to disappoint him, at least I knew that Pasquale would be spending the holiday amidst his close-knit family and that was all that mattered to me.

Meanwhile, in his zeal to speed his independence, Pasquale attempted to take on more and more of his own physical care. He steadily gained strength in his legs as physical therapy sessions progressed, but he still relied heavily on his four-footed cane as his right foot still issued forth with a slight drag. His physical therapist cautioned the staff that he should have assistance getting to and from the bathroom whether Pasquale felt he needed their assistance or not. In fact, the therapist instructed him to press the call button near his bed if he had to use the bathroom during the night instead of attempting to get there on his own. However, Pasquale, proud and stubborn as always, failed to heed that warning. Impatient with infirmity and insisting, "I can do it myself," he would not stoop to pressing that call button.

Five days before Thanksgiving, Pasquale's brother, Sal, was rudely awakened by the ringing of his telephone at two o'clock in the morning. One of the night attendants at Pasquale's residence answered Sal's sleepy hello, and communicated that Pasquale had attempted to get to the bathroom alone and had taken a nasty fall. Pasquale was en route to the hospital by ambulance as they spoke. Apologetically, the attendant told Sal that she feared Pasquale had broken his hip.

Sal immediately roused his sister, Natalie, and in the ominous silence of a cold, damp, pre-dawn darkness, they began the twenty-minute drive to the hospital praying for the best, but fearing the worst. By the time they walked into the emergency room, Pasquale had already been taken for x-rays. As feared, his hip was indeed broken, and in three places! Sal and my mother hung their heads in sorrow, tears welling in their eyes. Pasquale had come such a long way down the road to recovery, was almost home, in fact, but now his dreams of independence had been dashed in an instant.

Pasquale remained in the hospital for two weeks. A broken hip can have dire consequences for the elderly as other complications can develop due to the lack of mobility. Many die a short time after such an accident. Not so for Pasquale, whose ironclad constitution and remarkable resiliency amazed us once more and had him back on the road to recovery in no time at all.

Upon his release from the hospital, Pasquale checked in once again at the rehab center where he had learned to walk, eat, and write just a few months before.

Two weeks of therapy was the prescribed course of treatment this time before he could return to his rooms at the assisted living residence.

When he was finally discharged from the rehab center for the second time in six months, the nursing director stood over Pasquale in his wheelchair, hands on her hips in mock exasperation.

"We enjoyed having you with us again," she told him. "But we really don't want to see you back here!"

"And I don't *want* to come back," Pasquale replied emphatically.

They both grinned, Pasquale thanked her profusely for the wonderful care he received, and then he was on his way once more, back to his temporary quarters while he waited for me to complete my own relocation.

By the time my moving van pulled into the driveway at Pasquale's home on Maple Grove Avenue two days before Christmas, he was just getting resettled at the assisted living facility. He was happy that I had come home but sad that he would not be able to move back into the house with me just yet. He simply would not be able to navigate the stairs until his hip had completely healed.

"It's okay," I assured him. "I'm back for good. When you're ready to come home, I'll be there for you."

"Is the place clean?" That was all he wanted to know.

Even in the midst of a fresh assault on his aging body, Pasquale was concerned not for himself, but for me. He knew that Nora's frail condition resulted in less than perfect housekeeping and he hated to see anyone else clean up after them.

"The house is fine," I lied. "I just want you to worry about getting better."

The truth was that Julie's smash-and-grab modus operandi had resulted in scraped walls and nicked molding in several places. Immediately after I moved in, I began systematically removing and cleaning light fixtures, wiping down the walls, cleaning dirty fingerprints from light switch plates, polishing the kitchen cabinets and brass hardware, cleaning window blinds and washing curtains. The fireplace in the family room had not been swept out since the previous winter, when Nora and Pasquale had sat warming themselves in their favorite chairs. Julie hadn't even cleaned the carpeting before placing the home on the market. It was no wonder her effort to sell the place had produced such a low offer.

In a strange twist of fate, the moving company I had hired to carry my belongings from the eastern side of the state had sent the same driver who had delivered several items of Nora's furniture from the house on Maple Grove Avenue to her new quarters in Virginia. The driver recognized the house immediately.

"I was just here a few months ago," he told me.

When I acknowledged that I knew the woman and that the house belonged to her and my uncle, the driver shared a disconcerting detail about that particular moving job.

When he saw Nora in Pennsylvania just days before the move as he walked through the house jotting notes to provide an estimate, she appeared to be in reasonably good health physically, though somewhat distraught. However, when he saw her in Virginia just a week later, her nose was swollen and both eyes were blackened! Nora's daughter told the driver that Nora had tripped on a sidewalk, fell and had broken her nose in the process. Given the neighbor's previous report of a frightened, sobbing Nora hiding in the woods in a feeble attempt to avoid being taken away on the day the movers arrived, my imagination went wild. Did she truly trip and fall while trying to get away from them? Or did they manhandle her to gain her cooperation? Either way, it was a pitifully sad affair. Once upon a time, she had longed to be in Virginia with her daughter, and my heart ached knowing how badly it had all turned out for her.

Meanwhile, back in Pennsylvania, Julie made good on another of her threats and used her status as her mother's attorney-in-fact to file a suit for divorce on Nora's behalf. The first attorney Julie contacted, we learned later, refused to take on the case after hearing the details, but Julie managed to locate another pond-skimmer who happily swallowed her tale of woe and went after Pasquale with both barrels loaded.

If it had not been such a sordid state of affairs, the fifteen-page legal complaint would have been laughable. In it, Nora, or rather, Julie on behalf of Nora, depending on how one viewed the matter, claimed that Pasquale had abandoned her and left her destitute so that she was barely able to afford the apartment she lived in. Never mind the fact that Julie was named as administrator of the trust that had been created with Pasquale and Nora's money. Never mind the fact that it was Pasquale who had been torn from his home, whisked across state lines, then left with nothing. Never mind the fact that Nora had her own pension and Social Security and had arrived in Virginia with all of her own possessions intact, while Pasquale's possessions were scattered in the rain and left for the garbage collectors. The icing on the cake was that they insisted that Pasquale sell his house so that Nora could receive her share of the equity.

Pasquale shook his head in disgust over the entire business and voiced regret over adding Nora's name to the deed. When he married Nora, she sold her own home and moved into Pasquale's. When she asked Pasquale how she should handle the proceeds from that sale, he insisted that she divide the money between her son and daughter.

"I didn't need it," Pasquale explained to me as he recalled the beginning of his and Nora's lives together. "And I didn't want there to be any hard feelings right out of the gate, so she gave the money to them. Now they want my house too. They already got everything else, why can't they leave my house alone?" he cried.

As if it were not enough that Pasquale was grounded, once again confined to a wheelchair, the issue of a divorce sent him into an emotional tailspin all over again.

He cried for days, ate sparingly, and rued the day that he returned to Pennsylvania.

"You should have let me die down there," he complained to his sister and me one afternoon, tears welling up in his eyes. "Those bastards took everything I had; they should have just killed me!"

"Don't you talk like that!" his sister admonished, standing over him with her hands on her hips. "If you give up now," she continued, "Julie *will* get everything! Is that what you want? Are you going to let her suck the life right out of you?"

Pasquale shook his head.

"What am I going to do?" he cried.

"Fight back, that's what!" she snapped. "You have a good attorney now; let him do his job. He'll deal with Julie."

"Okay, okay," he conceded. "It just makes me so mad! Why did they have to do this to me? I never hurt Julie and I never hurt her mother. And Nora never did anything to me. We had a good life together. Why couldn't they just leave us alone?"

As I listened to this exchange, I recalled my visit to one of Pasquale's former neighbors, who told me that Nora had sat sobbing at their kitchen table while her daughter and son-in-law cleared her home of all earthly possessions next door. That neighbor, too, asked Nora why she didn't simply put her foot down and tell her kids to clear out and leave her alone. But Nora claimed she feared them, especially her son-in-law, Danny. Nora could not bring herself to stand up to him.

The following day, when that same neighbor knocked at Nora's door to say good-bye, Julie told her that Nora was not seeing anyone. Julie said the ordeal had taken its toll and Nora needed to rest. However, it was more likely that Julie and company had taken *their* toll on Nora. When another neighbor asked to see Nora later that day, she too was turned away. Why? Why had Nora suddenly been sequestered by her own family? Had Nora's bruises already been inflicted by that time? Were Nora's daughter and son-in-law afraid someone might actually come to Nora's aid and ruin their plans? The sad fact is that even if Nora had called out for help, her daughter would have been able to latch onto the dementia defense and neatly shoo away any potential rescuers. As Pasquale had lamented, why couldn't Nora's children leave them alone? We had no other answers for Pasquale, only conjecture. We could only let him know that we would be there for him every step of the way until the awful mess was sorted out.

A week later, Pasquale finally rose above the emotional eddy that had sucked him under. He broke through the surface prepared to fight for his life. And Nora's.

"To hell with all of them," he declared. "I'm not giving her a divorce! There's no reason for it and it's against my religion. Unless I see her standing in front of me telling me herself that's what she wants, I'm not signing anything!"

And that is where the matter lay for four months. Pasquale kept up with daily physical therapy sessions and for a time, weekly communications with his attorney, who determined they would simply treat the divorce action as a fraud until they heard from Nora herself.

When Pasquale saw the handwriting on the interrogatory that came from the opposing attorney, he said, "Who are they trying to kid? That isn't my wife's handwriting!"

If birds of a feather flock together, then Julie's attorney must have been of the vulture variety. The fact of the matter was that Julie had already schemed her way through two nursing homes, gunning for Pasquale, without showing any signs of slowing her charge. Now, her new attorney was right there beside her, attacking Pasquale's integrity with renewed gusto. It was beginning to look as though he would be in for a long contest.

In the meantime, having left home and career to take up residence with Pasquale and get him through the legal battles, I was suddenly without a job and my own savings account was dwindling. I decided not to resume my career in real estate. The whole business left a sour taste in my mouth, especially after the aborted sale of Pasquale's own house, and I no longer had the spirit to be one of the industry crusaders who attempt to make a positive difference. I would scrub floors, I resolved, before I would dust off my real estate license again!

While I searched for a salaried position in and around Smithton, I made it a point to visit with Pasquale at least three times per week. Some days I arrived in time to be his cheerleader during sessions with his physical therapist, other times I took food to share while we chatted in his room. In spite of the fact that his stepdaughter remained a constant thorn in his side, Pasquale rallied once more, taking pride in even the smallest physical achievement, such as being able to put his socks and shoes on by himself. Rising from the wheelchair and taking three steps to seat himself in his new reclining chair was cause for celebration!

When he first entered the physical therapy program at his new residence, two therapists were assigned to work with him. While one concentrated on strengthening his legs and restoring mobility, another worked to restore the motor skills in his right hand. It was the second time since his stroke that a therapist specifically targeted that limb, determining that it might yet be possible to coax some life into it.

The prospect of actually using that hand again excited Pasquale, and he worked diligently on coordination and dexterity exercises in an attempt to regain control. It was an uphill battle since the arm attached to the hand did not always obey his brain. Often, the arm flailed about spasmodically as he aimed his grasping fingers toward their target. But gradually he felt the life and strength returning. The simple act of being able to pick up a napkin and wipe his mouth was a major triumph. Every time I visited with him, he eagerly displayed his progress, either flexing his fingers or showing me how high he could kick his legs from a seated position.

Aside from the limited use of his right hand, the only other telltale evidence of the massive stroke he had suffered was in the occasional slip of his tongue. Pasquale's brain was able to summon the correct words, but sometimes his tongue delivered the letters in a slightly different order, or he voiced a similar sounding word instead. The resulting faux pas was often hilarious, although it frustrated him to distraction.

"Tell your mother I need some clean horses," he said to me one afternoon. Then, seeing the puzzled look on my face, he attempted to correct himself. "Horshes, you know," he tugged at his pants.

"Oh! You mean shorts!"

"Yeah, yeah, shorts. See if your mom washed them yet."

During one of my mother's visits, while she and Pasquale engaged in light-hearted conversation, he suddenly switched from English to Italian. As the youngest of the siblings, born and raised on everything American, Natalie was not as fluent in the Italian language as Pasquale, although she understood some of what he was saying and did not protest. Then, just as suddenly as Pasquale's language switch had flipped, he stopped and looked at his sister with his head cocked in question.

"Why am I speaking in Italian?" he asked her. He then continued the conversation in English without missing another beat.

Finally, during the first week of April the following year, Pasquale visited the hip surgeon to hear whether he would be able to put the wheelchair aside and walk with his cane again. As the doctor viewed the x-rays, he whistled appreciatively.

"I can barely tell where it was broken," he told Pasquale. "Your hip has healed as solid as a rock!"

Pasquale beamed with pride at the welcome news. At last, he would be able to walk again. That meant he could practice going up and down steps and that, in turn, opened up a world of possibilities. Not the least of which would be getting out of the assisted living residence a few times per week! Pasquale wasted no time enlisting the services of his brother as chauffeur and Sal willingly complied. They were a sight, the two of them, as they ambled down city sidewalks together arm in arm with matching bow-legged gaits, on their way to breakfast, to a doctor appointment, to lunch, to the hearing aid shop, to the mall. Pasquale was having fun again—life was good! At that time in his life, his former antagonists were but a distant memory. *Julie who?* I couldn't wait for the day that I would drive him home and watch him proudly walk up the steps to his own front door. Yes, life was good!

CHAPTER FIFTEEN

Adventures with Wine (Part Two)

On April 14, almost a year after Pasquale had returned to Pennsylvania, a preliminary hearing was held before a domestic relations master in Smithton. Pasquale's attorney warned him that Nora might not be there and, in fact, was not required to appear since it was only a preliminary hearing. Pasquale hung his head in disappointment.

"Julie won't bring her mother," he said. "She knows that as soon as Nora sees me, she'll run to me."

"It's okay, Uncle Pasquale," I consoled him. "There are other ways to do this. Don't back down," I advised him. "If Julie refuses to bring Nora to the hearing, then you must insist that her attorney get her on the telephone so you can at least talk to her."

And that is exactly what happened, but with disastrous results. It was not clear whether or not Nora knew that Pasquale would be listening when her voice came through the telephone's speaker. She may have thought that only the attorneys and the hearing master were present. In any event, after her attorney asked if she truly wanted a divorce, Nora said she did. When asked why, Nora began her response slowly and deliberately, almost as if she were reading from a script.

"Because he dragged me out into the driveway and beat me," she replied.

Nora's response drew gasps from Pasquale and his siblings; they knew she was lying. "I'm not going back there," Nora continued, "because I don't want any more beatings."

That was more than Pasquale could bear.

"That's a lie!" he cried out. "I never laid a hand on you!"

If Nora did not know Pasquale was present before, she knew it then. At the sound of Pasquale's voice, she began to sob.

"Do you want to come home?" Pasquale asked her. "You can stay with me."

Nora claimed she could not leave. She too, had suffered a stroke and it rendered her unable to walk.

"I can't even leave the building," she cried.

Nora was unable to go on and within minutes the call was terminated. We did not know if Julie was sitting beside Nora while she spoke, but we were willing to bet on it. The lengths to which Julie was willing to go in her quest for what Max had termed "found money" left us stunned. Pasquale's only fault was that he refused to die and Julie meant to see that he paid dearly for that. As for Nora, she was just a pawn in the game, moved at Julie's command.

Pasquale's attorney said he believed that he had never laid a hand on Nora. The attorney even went so far as to state that he felt Nora's attorney knew it as well; however, there was no proof either way and it would be pointless to challenge her statement. Natalie was livid.

"No proof?" she cried. "Believe me, if he had ever hit her this family would have known it!"

The attorney cut her short and that irritated me to no end. The ordeal was difficult enough for everyone involved. No one needed a rude attorney.

"We could sit here and argue all day," he said, insolently. "It won't change anything. The best thing to do is agree to the divorce, settle with her, and move on."

"I'm not signing anything!" Pasquale maintained. "They can all go to hell!"

❈❈❈

With the attitude Pasquale's attorney had shown toward his client that afternoon, I thought he might do well to join Julie on that particular trip. There is nothing I detest more than having to remind a lawyer for whom he is working. I would have my chance later when I dealt with him over the mishandled sale of Pasquale's real estate, but for now we needed to pick the pieces of Pasquale up off the floor.

As I was quickly learning, Jonas Maxwell was indeed a rarity among attorneys. His clients had his complete, undivided attention, and the professional, compassionate manner with which he tackled every issue left no doubt that he took his cases very seriously and had his client's best interest at heart. By comparison, the attorneys that had, so far, worked for Pasquale in Pennsylvania were maddeningly mundane and almost lackadaisical in their approach to his dilemma. There were many occasions when I found myself wanting to drive back down to Virginia for the sole purpose of bringing Max back to Pennsylvania to show the locals what genuine legal counsel looked like.

Later, after we had returned Pasquale to his residence, we reflected on Nora's words at the hearing. Was Nora coerced by Julie—handed a script to read from—or, somewhere in her addled mind, did she really believe that Pasquale had struck her?

Looking back on that incident, I thought of a third explanation. Nora never actually said that *Pasquale* had beaten her. She simply said *"He* dragged me out into the driveway and beat me." Was that her way of trying to tell Pasquale that her son-in-law, Danny, had beaten her into submission? Did we completely misread that statement and fail to act on Nora's plea for help? It made me sick to think that may have been the case, because that meant that we had failed her miserably!

"Remember what their neighbors told me?" I said to my mother and Pasquale. "Nora walked into the woods behind Uncle Pasquale's home to hide from them the day they planned to take her to Virginia for good. Do you think maybe Danny roughed her up to get her into the car?"

"At this point, I think I'd believe just about anything," she replied wryly.

If Nora really believed Pasquale hit her, she probably would have fought back when he called her a liar. It was more telling, I thought, that she simply burst into tears after she heard his voice.

As Pasquale's attorney had said, we could have speculated 'til doomsday but it would not have made an iota of difference. On that account, at least, he was right. The only action that would change the course of events would be if Nora herself withdrew the suit for divorce and that did not appear likely. Up to that point, we had managed to obtain some measure of justice for Pasquale, but where was justice for Nora? How I prayed she would somehow be set free from her daughter's clutches!

Our family had been strained to the breaking point with the events of the preceding year. We were exhausted from our efforts, particularly my mother and Uncle Sal, who bore the greater burden in tending to their brother's physical, medical, emotional, and financial needs. As much as everyone would have liked to throw in the towel, I knew we could not. We had to soldier on for Pasquale's sake.

When I saw Pasquale again the week after the hearing, he was, surprisingly, in good spirits. Having stopped at a little convenience store on my way, I entered his room with a paper bag in my hand and a newspaper for him tucked under my arm.

"What did you bring?" he asked with a child's curiosity, indicating the bag.

When I opened it and pulled out two ice-cream sandwiches, one for him and one for me, his face lit up. It was a popular treat when I was a child, creamy vanilla ice cream sandwiched between two wafer-thin, soft chocolate cookies. A little piece of heaven! I peeled off the paper wrapper and handed one to him.

"Boy, I haven't had one of these for a long time," he sighed appreciatively after taking a bite.

We ate our treats in companionable silence. Afterward, Pasquale became reflective.

"I'm going to go ahead and give them what they want," he told me matter-of-factly as he wiped a drop of ice cream from his lips. "If they want a divorce, they can have it so long as they go away and leave me in peace."

I rested my hand consolingly on his arm, not quite believing what I was hearing.

"If that's what you truly want to do," I told him. "I'm with you, you know that. And if you want to fire that useless, self-serving lawyer and find someone who will actually fight for you, I'll stand behind you on that count too!"

"I know," he acknowledged. "Heck with it. The good Lord is going to take me to heaven soon anyway."

"How do you know that?" I frowned at the suggestion. "Your mother lived past ninety and your father was older than you when he died."

"Then I'll go pretty soon," he decided. "A couple more years to enjoy some peace after what those bastards put me through then *whoosh*, I'll be gone!"

"You'll go when the Lord is ready for you," I chided, "and not before! Until then, we can still buy a small house, one story so you don't have to worry about stairs, then we'll get you out of here. You can teach me how to make wine."

"We'll see," he said. "Maybe I'll buy *this* place," he mused, his entrepreneurial wheels turning as he glanced around. Then a mischievous grin lit his face. "First thing I'd do is fire the cook!" he announced.

We laughed at the thought of Pasquale running the very retirement home where he was living. No doubt, he would have been up to the task and would have enjoyed every minute of it. He had, years before, invested in a small convenience store and gas station with Sal. It was a profitable venture for decades, until they decided they no longer wanted the day-to-day hassle of running a business and so they sold it.

In any event, Pasquale had made up his mind about one thing: he was through fighting. He chose peace in the face of Julie's persistent persecution. The victory of life and peace were suddenly more important to him than vengeance. Pasquale had always been a wise man and there was no doubt in my mind that his wisdom would carry him placidly through the months and years to come.

"Let's go," he said. "I'd like to get out to K-Mart and pick up a few things."

"Should we make a list?"

"I already did." He retrieved the list from the little desk under the window and handed it to me. "Oh," he said as I scanned the list. "I almost forgot. Write down *masher*."

"*Masher?*" I repeated.

Pasquale's brain still occasionally took a word and rearranged the letters. The scary part was that my own brain was getting rather adept at processing those words and coming up with the correct translation so that our conversations sometimes took on the characteristics of a comedy routine. But this word, *masher*, had stumped me.

"Like a potato masher?" I asked, though I couldn't imagine what he would want with one of those.

"No," he said as he attempted to correct himself. "Not masher, *smasher!*"

Dumbfounded, I shook my head.

"I'm sorry, Uncle Pasquale. I just don't know what that means."

"It's okay," he grinned. "I'll know it when I see it. C'mon, let's get out of here."

He stood with the help of his cane as I plopped his cap on his head. "Grab that chicken, will ya?" he said, pointing to a chair cushion as he headed for the door. Pasquale liked to have a little extra padding handy in case his hip became sore. Grinning at the faux pas and without missing a beat, I snatched up the extra cushion from his easy chair and off we went for what was becoming our ritual Saturday morning shopping excursion.

Months later, with legal battles still looming over him, Pasquale decided to go ahead and sell his house, declaring, "They ruined it for me. I don't even want to go back there now."

His final decision meant that I had to find a competent real estate agent to list his home for sale. It also necessitated my move out of Pasquale's house and into a rented Victorian I found across town. On weekends I packed boxes—once again—and carried them in the back of my SUV to my new residence. Fortunately, with able-bodied siblings and cousins nearby, it wasn't necessary for me to hire a moving company this time. For the price of a few pizzas and beverages, the male members of my clan managed the moving of furniture and other heavy items within a few hours on a Sunday afternoon.

Pasquale and I both settled into our own routines during this period. Weekdays would find me taking time off from my job when it was necessary to handle attorneys, interview real estate agents, or take Pasquale to a doctor appointment.

Pasquale busied himself making lists. He resigned himself to taking up permanent residence right where he was and determined to make it as comfortable a home as possible. On Saturdays, we shopped. Sometimes we took the walker and other days, when Pasquale's legs were feeling a little weak, we took the wheelchair. I always deposited him just inside the front entrance to the department store, telling him to wait for me there while I parked the car. And it never failed, Pasquale was never where I left him and I found myself briskly walking the aisles trying to find him.

During one of those Saturday expeditions, I finally spotted Pasquale in the hardware aisle. He was grinning and proudly holding a fly-swatter aloft when he saw me making my way toward him.

"Smasher!" he proclaimed.

"Ah, a *swatter*, so that's what you meant!" I replied.

Pasquale bought kitchen utensils, a small toolbox, and an assortment of everyday tools such as screw drivers, a small hammer, and a wrench. To those items, he added a large clock to hang on the wall opposite the foot of his bed so he could see "how much longer I have to sleep" as he put it, should he find himself awake during the night. Shopping expeditions with Pasquale were always an adventure. I never knew what else he would come up with to add to his list. Those Saturday mornings with Pasquale were the highlight of my week—and his too.

One Saturday morning, I arrived to pick up Pasquale and saw "typewriter"on his list. Since Pasquale still had difficulty writing, he decided he could solve that problem by typing his shopping lists, typing letters to relatives, birthday greetings, etc., but I had my doubts that in the age of PCs we would find such an antiquated device. It was difficult to find even a used typewriter since laptops and PCs with keyboards had taken over. Eventually, one of the nurse's aides at his residence learned what Pasquale was looking for and she generously loaned him her own typewriter. It was a Selectric from a by-gone era, but it served Pasquale's purposes beautifully.

❏❏❏

"It was just sitting in my attic collecting dust," she told Pasquale. "You're welcome to it."

Before long, Pasquale had mastered a two-fingered approach to his new writing tool. Visitors to his room would frequently find him punching those keys at lightning speed as he typed out his shopping lists, addressed envelopes for birthday and anniversary cards, and wrote to former neighbors in Smithton. Thereafter, paper, typewriter ribbons, white-out, and stationery were frequently added to his Saturday shopping lists.

Pasquale and I made the rounds of dollar stores, grocery stores, department stores, all of the places where Pasquale and Nora used to shop. Occasionally, we would run into someone from his old neighborhood and that always pleased him. One of those encounters must have prodded a memory as he turned to me in the aisle of a store one day with a thoughtful expression on his face.

"You know what I miss?" he said. "I miss making my own wine."

I told him that wine-making kits were easy enough to find if that's what he wanted.

"No, if you're going to do it that way, it has to be done right. With the right equipment. And I don't have the space for that."

What he and my grandfather used to do when they weren't making their own wine from scratch with local grapes, he explained, was to buy two different kinds of wine at the liquor store and create their own blend. That afternoon Pasquale purchased a bottle of Paisano Red and selected a rosé from a different vineyard. During the following week, Pasquale called around to his brother and sisters to see who might have a two-gallon glass jug and a stainless steel funnel they could lend to him.

The following Saturday, acquired supplies in hand, Pasquale and I made wine. Making wine in Pasquale's living quarters meant using the tiny bathroom sink as our work area. There was no bathroom vanity and precious little work space, so that pouring the contents of each of the two smaller bottles of wine into the larger glass jug while I balanced the jug in a sloped sink was quite a feat. I was not certain if the facility's management allowed alcohol in their residents' rooms, and when I posed the question to Pasquale, he simply shrugged.

I thought about that for a minute then said to him, "How much trouble can we possibly get into? The worst they can do is take it away."

We decided we would simply keep our activities to ourselves and see what happened. Pasquale acted as look-out while I worked behind the closed bathroom door. Occasionally, Pasquale would poke his head in to see how I was managing and both of us would giggle like naughty children.

On one such afternoon while I was covertly blending wine in the bathroom, I heard the door to Pasquale's room open and a nurse's aide asking if he wanted an afternoon snack. I held my breath as I heard her walk past the closed bathroom door while she chatted to my uncle. This particular aide had taken a liking to Pasquale and often sat and visited with him for a few minutes during her rounds. Determined not to allow her to get comfortable, Pasquale politely declined the offer of a snack and ushered her back out the door, claiming he was busy and needed to get some work done on his typewriter. No sooner had I heard the outer door close than the bathroom door opened and Pasquale stuck his head in.

"She's gone," he announced. "You finished yet?"

"Just about," I replied with a grin after pouring the last of the rosé into the two-gallon jug. "I just need to pour this back into the smaller bottles, but I'll need your help."

Pasquale stepped into the bathroom beside me, plopped the funnel into one of the smaller wine bottles and held it over the sink while I filled it from the blended contents of the larger and heavier glass jug. When we finished our little production, Pasquale had four bottles of blended wine and enough left over to fill an old-fashioned pony-sized soda bottle that I found in my parent's basement. Pasquale would keep that little bottle in his refrigerator for his after-dinner *digestif* and he would enlist the help of various family members to refill it when they went to visit him.

It was a few weeks later, while hanging Pasquale's freshly laundered clothing, that an aide found the wine bottles, loosely wrapped in paper bags, where we had stashed them in the bottom corner of Pasquale's bedroom closet. She dutifully alerted the residence manager and the two of them returned to confront Pasquale. He got a kick out of being found out and subsequently admonished for his illicit activity, but the manager only required a note from his doctor to let him keep his stash "for medicinal purposes," which I promptly procured.

Now that Pasquale's wine-making was "legal," playing mixologist in his bathroom became a regular pastime for us and it wasn't long before he noted "extra glasses" on his shopping list. Soon, he was hosting wine-tasting parties with anyone who went to visit. When Pasquale offered his nephew, Ben, a glass of his home-mixed wine one Sunday afternoon, Ben reflected appreciatively after tasting the wine.

"That's pretty good!" Ben declared. "What did you mix together? Write that down for me."

Pasquale was thrilled. For all the times his visitors arrived bearing gifts for him, Pasquale finally had something to offer them in return and it pleased him immensely.

That was the beginning of a new era for Pasquale. His previous personae of the displaced elderly man down on his luck had melted away. From that point forward, his outlook was more that of a well-adjusted bachelor in an active retirement home. He ventured out of his room more often to converse with the other residents in the recreation room. He made friends there and was beginning to feel more useful. On warmer summer days when the double doors at the rear of the recreation room were left open to allow a breeze to flow through—and, inevitably, a few stray flies—Pasquale would venture out of his room, *masher* in hand, and take up a position as self-appointed exterminator. He happily chased down those flies and swatted them so they would not annoy the other residents.

He also became president of the bowling league, something I thought I would never see. This turn of events I learned from one of the nurse's aides, not from Pasquale himself. As was typical, Pasquale never bragged about any of the accomplishments in his life. He accepted the appointment as bowling league president with the same humility, grace, and gratitude with which he accepted promotions during his lengthy career at the local steel mill.

Soon after his appointment as bowling league president, with a newly-found self-confidence and regained sense of self-worth, Pasquale began watching over some of the more frail fellow residents just as Janice had watched over him when he first arrived. Quickly making his way to the nurse's station by wheelchair one evening, Pasquale reported that Robert, the resident alcoholic, had escaped out the back door again to visit the local tavern. He then watched, satisfied, at the large windows overlooking the parking lot as an aide raced down the lane to retrieve Robert. While making his rounds at the rooms of his friends one day, Pasquale found one of them lying in pain in their bed and unable to reach the call button. He summoned help for that resident as well.

Throughout that period, the fun-loving side of Pasquale emerged in full measure as he joked with the staff and the other residents. He even taught one particular aide how to swear in Italian so her manager would not know what she was saying. That delighted both of them to no end. Pasquale was now a fully-engaged, socially active resident and having a wonderful time. Life was good for him once more. When I walked away after visiting with him, I was no longer weighed down by sadness and fear for his future. Pasquale was free of the anguish and turmoil that had weighed down his spirit during the preceding years. He had truly come home.

CHAPTER SIXTEEN

Independence Day

As the fourth anniversary of Pasquale's stroke passed, the lawsuits were finally settled. It had been quite a time-consuming, emotionally draining, tangled mess. The final lawsuit came from the buyers who had contracted with Julie to purchase Pasquale's home. When Julie's power of attorney was revoked and the buyers learned that Pasquale's new agents had no intention of executing a deed of sale, the buyers filed suit against Pasquale, Julie, Nora, and me. Julie, in turn, sued me and Pasquale for interfering with a contract. I wondered when someone would get around to that, but I still held to the opinion that I had shared with my real estate broker friend, David, whose agent represented the buyers. I still believed that nothing would come of it when the presiding judge heard the circumstances of that sale.

As it turned out, we never had to appear before a judge. The case never went to trial. Pasquale and I were required to appear at a single deposition meeting with Pasquale's attorney, the attorney representing the buyers, a court-appointed referee, and a court transcriber in attendance. Pasquale and I took turns telling his story and in the end, the buyers decided to drop our names from the suit and go after Julie, and only Julie, to recover the $6,000 or so they claimed to have lost as a result of the failed sale. According to Pasquale's attorney, Julie eventually paid up, settling the matter out of court, after which she dropped the suit against me and Pasquale on advisement from her own legal counsel, probably the first intelligent advice given to her by that attorney.

After that matter was finally put to rest, only one hurdle remained, but Pasquale had changed his mind once again and refused to participate in the divorce caper that Julie had concocted. In the State of Pennsylvania, a divorce can be automatic after three years if the opposing party makes no legal challenge. Pasquale did not care about that part. He was quite simply adamant that he would not sign his name on any document that would indicate he consented to the offensive deed.

❊❊❊

Seasons came and went as yet another two years unfolded, putting additional emotional distance between trying circumstances and Pasquale's eventual rise up and out of it all. Christmas, as always, was difficult for Pasquale and we rallied around him, decorating his small efficiency apartment, helping him to send greeting cards, taking him shopping for small gifts for the residence staff, all in an effort to keep him engaged in the festivities.

Summer's milder weather brought the annual lakeside family reunion, which meant more outings in general and more visitors for Pasquale. He eventually did sell his home, determining that he could no longer live there and it made no sense to keep it. When I wasn't at work or visiting with Pasquale, I continued to immerse myself in the room-by-room restoration of the old Victorian I called home. It was balm for my own wounds as I took stock of where I was geographically and career-wise and what I had left behind.

Taking up Pasquale's cause meant the end to a real estate career that I loved. The small town in which I had grown up, the town that pulled me back for Pasquale's sake, had been economically depressed for decades, just another sad remnant of the country's once-thriving steel industry. Not only was it not practical to think I could support myself in a real estate career with the meager commissions earned from the sale of houses worth an average of $100,000, but I could not allow such an all-consuming venture to take up so much of my time during the period when Pasquale's care and legal entanglements demanded so much of me.

Instead, I settled for a job as someone's executive secretary making travel arrangements, handling international correspondence, and doing all the things that secretaries do. It was a small company, an offshoot of an out-of-state business and I could not, for the life of me, understand why they chose tiny Smithton for a satellite branch office, but the job provided me with a steady income and free evenings and weekends for almost four years. At the end of that period, almost five years after the company's branch had opened, I suppose the owners finally asked themselves the same question I had asked as they closed the office and moved operations to New Jersey. Once again, I found myself among the ranks of the unemployed in a town with few prospects.

With Uncle Pasquale out of the woods and comfortably ensconced in the retirement residence, I knew it was time for me to make the return trip east and try to reestablish myself there. At that juncture, my mother, in her mid-seventies by that time and growing accustomed to having her daughter close at hand, did not take the news nearly as well as Pasquale did.

"You have to have a life too," Pasquale calmly advised me when I visited with him. "I'll miss you and I appreciate all you have done for me, but you go and don't worry about me. You just be careful out there, okay?"

I hugged him and cried, knowing that I would miss him as well. Pasquale's well-being had been my focus for years. It would be hard to step aside from that and focus, once again, on my own life.

Within two weeks of breaking the news to Pasquale, I had landed a position in Philadelphia handling foreclosed bank-owned properties with a nationwide real estate firm. I rented a tiny apartment until I could get my bearings again and save up enough for a down payment on a house. Meanwhile, I commuted forty minutes one-way from suburbia to my new job in the city. Though Pasquale was always at the back of my mind, I was in my element once again and overjoyed that I had finally come home.

◘ ◘ ◘

I managed to make the four-hour drive back to Smithton to visit my parents and Pasquale frequently during the months that followed my relocation. However, as the national foreclosure rate rose to unprecedented proportions during the 2008-2009 mortgage meltdown, my job demanded more and more of my time. During the final six months of Pasquale's life, I saw him only sporadically, but each time I visited we picked up right where we had left off with shopping trips and mixing wine at his bathroom sink. Pasquale had a good final run and was in a good place physically and emotionally.

We also thought his health had reached a point of comfortable stability until his doctor discovered the cancer. It was one of those sneaky types of cancer, the doctor told us, with no pain and no major symptoms.

"He'll stop eating one day and the cancer will simply take him away in his sleep," the doctor predicted.

We should all be so lucky as to die peacefully in our sleep, I thought when I heard the news.

❁ ❁ ❁

The last time I saw him, Pasquale said to me, "You know I'm not going to be around much longer."

"I know," I quietly replied as I held his hand.

The call came from my mother at dusk on the Fourth of July. I answered the phone while I stood on the little balcony attached to my apartment waiting for the fireworks to begin lighting up the sky from a nearby field. Tears spilled over my cheeks as she delivered the sad news that Pasquale was gone. Shortly after I hung up the phone, as if on cue, the fireworks lit up the sky above the tree line surrounding the apartment complex. How fitting that Pasquale should go out with the fireworks, I thought as I stood there. He was so full of life, the spark that ignited laughter wherever he went. Besides, it was Independence Day and Pasquale had been fully and completely liberated. He was finally free from the toils and cares of this life.

Afterword

In spite of the physical and emotional punishment Pasquale had endured, he thrived for almost seven years after the massive stroke that marked the beginning of the destructive campaign launched by his stepdaughter. Pasquale's folly was that he had signed two common legal documents, the format and wording of which, he had been told, was *standard* and therefore should serve his purposes without alteration. Had Pasquale followed his own instincts instead of the advice of an attorney, he might have executed a more limited, specific power of attorney document and/or a less liberal living will that would have prevented the designated attorney-in-fact, his stepdaughter, Julie, from taking such complete advantage of the circumstances that almost cost him his life.

If he'd had a more competent general family physician, one who was cautious enough to wait for the outcome instead of caving in to a family who demanded that he do nothing less than declare Pasquale dead while he still breathed, the quality of his remaining life might have been much better. Overall, things might have turned out differently for him.

At the time that Pasquale was experiencing the trials and tribulations resulting from the execution of those two documents, I believed the laws governing agents operating under a power of attorney should be revised to limit the extent to which the designated agent can liquidate the principal's assets for anyone's benefit but the principal. In fact, I made my feelings known in a letter to a local state representative, but with no result at that time.

For example, the Pennsylvania statute governing the terms of a durable power of attorney quite liberally allowed an agent acting under that power to divest a principal of funds for the purpose of bestowing "gifts" upon themselves, other family members, or whomever they chose, supposedly under the guise of avoiding inheritance taxes if the principal named in those documents was near death. When I read that section of the law, I could not help but wonder why it even existed as it only encouraged theft.

There is plenty of time after someone dies to bestow gifts in their memory. Why would someone simply give away another person's life savings while that person was actually *recovering* in a hospital?

The law also dictates that an agent must keep full account of all expenditures while acting for the principal under a durable power of attorney. However, if the verbal information I have obtained from several attorneys is accurate, lawsuits are rarely filed against the named agent and if they are, rarely is the stolen money recovered. Indeed, several people I came across in nursing homes and hospitals during my journey with Pasquale told me they had suffered similar financial and material losses at the hands of family members, losses tallying from tens of thousands to hundreds of thousands of dollars. One of those encounters occurred in a nursing home's family room while I waited for Pasquale to return from physical therapy. The middle-aged couple I met there shared with me that they were waiting to visit an aunt who was also recovering from a stroke.

"She was in such bad shape," the man told me, "we didn't think she'd ever leave the hospital. So, we emptied out her apartment, sold her furniture, and canceled the lease. Now that it looks like she can actually go home, she doesn't have a home to go to. We feel terrible about that." And they *should* feel terrible, I thought to myself as I listened to their tale.

Why aren't people willing to wait for the outcome? According to the doctors who tended to Pasquale immediately following his stroke, a patient will either show signs of recovery or decline in the two weeks immediately following a medical crisis. Thirty days is the next milestone at which recovery is measured, and sixty days, in most cases, is an adequate period to predict the extent of recovery. Of course, there are exceptions such as a patient in the UK who woke up after several *years* in a coma, but those are the extremes.

For the average victim of head or brain trauma, under current statutes, if that person lives and they put their signatures to the same legal documents my uncle signed, they could indeed experience a rude awakening. Imagine coming out of a coma, and making it through speech and physical therapy only to be told you have no home to return to—no possessions, and that your bank account has been wiped out. One woman I met told me that it was her nephew who raided her savings account while she languished in the hospital. Because he was her only relative and because he had already purchased a new car with her money, she did not prosecute him. How sad that she had to do without simply because a family member decided his need of a new car was paramount to his aunt's well-being.

In today's upside-down economy with so many people out of work and losing their homes to foreclosure, you can bet this drama is being played out every day in every state in the union. As attorney Jonas Maxwell said to me, "There is no more powerful motivator than the prospect of found money; not even sex." Sadly, I believe he is absolutely correct.

So, what can you do to protect yourself? First, you need to make certain the person you name as your attorney-in-fact on a power of attorney document is someone you truly feel can be trusted to carry on your affairs in a competent and respectful manner on your behalf. If you have no blood relations who fit the bill, then a long-time trusted friend may be your best bet. In either case, you should know enough about that person's own history to make an intelligent decision as to whether or not they are capable of handling your financial affairs to your satisfaction and with *your* benefit in mind, not their own.

If the person you are considering as your agent has a history of being mired in debt or frequently changing jobs, or has otherwise demonstrated financial incompetence in their own affairs, look to someone else to designate as your attorney-in-fact.

The penalties prescribed for abuse of a power of attorney currently seem to amount to nothing more than a slap on the wrist. Why are there no stiffer penalties? Surely a minimum mandatory fine should be enforced along with the return of the principal's assets.

In an attempt to obtain answers to the questions that arose during my fight for Pasquale's rights, I challenged one of Pennsylvania's state representatives to be the catalyst for change. I wrote a lengthy letter to him outlining Pasquale's predicament and citing what I viewed as the failure of the current statutes. I will give the man credit for listening and actually sending a request to the Pennsylvania state legislature to review the items I specifically referred to within the statute; however, nothing was gained—at least, not at that time. The official reply I received, on Pennsylvania state letterhead, was that the legislature felt the law was adequate the way it stood and to remove the item that gives an attorney-in-fact the authority to "gift" funds may prohibit someone from being able to tap into their Principal's bank accounts for legitimate reasons. And that, dear readers, is pure political hogwash. The standard durable power of attorney document gives the attorney-in-fact the routine ability to withdraw funds from the principal's bank accounts as needed so they can maintain housing expenses, medical expenses, etc. The separate provision that allows for gifts up to $15,000 is completely superfluous.

Ironically, while Pasquale battled for his life in Pennsylvania, a similar drama played out in the courts and in the media in Pinellas Park, Florida, where the plight of Terri Schiavo, a name that had been in and out of the news for a decade, had suddenly come to a head. Some experts who reviewed her case claimed that she was brain dead and unable to comprehend what was happening to her while others staunchly adhered to the opposite opinion. Sadly, we will never know. While Terri Schiavo's physical incapacity and non-verbal state clearly made her incapable of acting for herself and making her own wishes known, Pasquale, on the other hand, was not only aware of what had happened to him but was also able to hear, comprehend, and eventually voice his own objections. While his mind was held captive for thirty days in a body that refused to move, with a mouth that refused to obey his command to speak, he absorbed and stored away the conversations outlining the malicious designs of his stepfamily, feigning sleep while they plotted against him at his bedside. The terror he must have felt is unimaginable.

As President Bush said, in the midst of the political and legal wrangling surrounding Schiavo's case, "The essence of civilization is that the strong have a duty to protect the weak. In cases where there are serious doubts and questions, the presumption should be in the favor of life."

I would add to that statement by saying our medical community should be charged with waiting for the outcome, even when—and perhaps *especially* when—the victim has put their signature on a living will.

Oftentimes, a coma is nothing more than the body's own normal, protective measure to allow healing to take place. That is a known medical fact. It boggles my mind to think that in this century, with the advances in modern medicine and the fact we are living longer than in decades past, there are still physicians in practice who believe a coma is a death knell and they practically encourage the victim's family to begin making funeral arrangements.

As I shared details of Pasquale's misadventure with others, I heard many similar heartbreaking stories. I was amazed at the number of people I encountered, just at the local level, who lost their homes and possessions while lying in a hospital bed because someone in their immediate family was in a position, by virtue of a durable power of attorney, to make choices for them with selfish ulterior motives.

One solution seems rather obvious to me: a living will should not be permitted to be exercised, nor should someone's agent under a durable power of attorney have the power, to stop all life-sustaining medical therapy and liquidate the principal's assets until at least sixty days after the onset of the illness or accident. Have we become such a callous, greedy society that we cannot bear to wait that long for the outcome?

Were it not for the tireless few who loved my uncle and the prayerful many who believed in the intervention of a higher power, Pasquale would have been cold in his grave seven years before his time. While Pasquale's stepfamily rushed toward his demise, carelessly raiding his assets, his true family fought for the right to wait for the outcome—and we are glad we did. Pasquale was grateful that we intervened on his behalf and the memories of those last years with him are memories we will always cherish.

If the media accounts are accurate, millions of Americans rushed to obtain living wills for themselves after Terri Schiavo's story made headlines. But what if … what if your brain is really alive, but you are unable to tell anyone? What if you are only temporarily incapacitated and the agent you appointed to act on your behalf orders your execution? Were you disturbed or angered as you read Pasquale's story? Are you horrified at the possibility that a similar incident could one day happen to you? You should be. What happened to Pasquale could happen to anyone.

If, prior to 2016, you already executed a durable power of attorney document that contains broad provisions for your named agent to access and dispose of your assets, you should have a new document drawn up and recorded today. Newly introduced legislation has resulted in changes to the language within the standard document that is accepted across the

United States. In addition, a few states have spelled out more specific amendments that are in effect now or will be in the very near future. For example, Pennsylvania has implemented additional changes that took effect in 2017. Those changes finally address medical decisions made by the named agent on behalf of the principal, more limited specifications for "gifting" funds from the principal's financial reserves, and a warning notice to the principal that by signing the durable power of attorney document (vs. having a specific power of attorney drafted), they are giving their named attorney-in-fact "broad powers" that include the ability to dispose of real estate owned by the principal. If you live in Pennsylvania and want to read about all of the changes made to these statutes, go to the Pennsylvania Bar Institutes website at: www.PBI.org

Although the durable power of attorney is a document meant to be standardized across all states, take heed of the warning on the American Bar Association's website, "the rules and requirements differ from state to state." For answers to very general questions about a durable power of attorney and its implications for an individual, you can visit the American Bar Association's website at: www.americanbar.org.

To find out about power of attorney statutes, and recent changes to those statues, if any, for your particular state simply type the name of your state and the words *power of attorney* in the search field of the American Bar Association's website. For example, if you live in Nebraska, you would type into the ABA search bar: *Nebraska power of attorney*.

If you are moved by Pasquale's story, then I urge you to take action to protect yourself by reviewing any existing power of attorney you may have already signed and making appropriate amendments. It's too late to make changes after you are already in the thick of a medical crisis, putting the wheels in motion for your designated attorney-in-fact to begin making decisions for you. Your state legislator will not help you; doctors may not take up your cause. Unless a trusted friend or family ally suspects that your agent is not acting in your best interest and that person steps in to assist, you may die prematurely or find you have recovered from a medical event only to have lost your home, your savings, and all of your personal possessions.

It may cost an additional few hundred dollars now to have an attorney prepare a specific power of attorney document, but the extra expense up front can mean the difference between your financial security and destitution or ultimately, your life or death. Take steps today to protect yourself. No one else can state your desires as well as you can. While you're at it, be a voice for change in your own state. If, after reading your state statutes governing powers of attorney, you believe amendments are in order, contact your local state representative and be someone who speaks for those who cannot.